Volume 1 Topics 1-8

Authors

Randall I. Charles
Professor Emeritus
Department of Mathematics
San Jose State University
San Jose, California

Jennifer Bay-Williams
Professor of Mathematics Education
College of Education and Human
Development
University of Louisville
Louisville, Kentucky

Robert Q. Berry, III
Associate Professor of
Mathematics Education
Department of Curriculum,
Instruction and Special Education
University of Virginia
Charlottesville, Virginia

Janet H. Caldwell
Professor of Mathematics
Rowan University
Glassboro, New Jersey

Zachary Champagne
Assistant in Research
Florida Center for Research in Science,
Technology, Engineering, and
Mathematics (FCR-STEM)
Jacksonville, Florida

Juanita Copley
Professor Emerita, College of Education
University of Houston
Houston, Texas

Warren Crown
Professor Emeritus of Mathematics
Education
Graduate School of Education
Rutgers University
New Brunswick, New Jersey

Francis (Skip) Fennell
L. Stanley Bowlsbey Professor
of Education and Graduate and
Professional Studies
McDaniel College
Westminster, Maryland

Karen Karp
Professor of Mathematics Education
Department of Early Childhood and
Elementary Education
University of Louisville
Louisville, Kentucky

Stuart J. Murphy
Visual Learning Specialist
Boston, Massachusetts

Jane F. Schielack
Professor of Mathematics
Associate Dean for Assessment and
Pre K-12 Education, College of Science
Texas A&M University
College Station, Texas

Jennifer M. Suh
Associate Professor for
Mathematics Education
George Mason University
Fairfax, Virginia

Jonathan A. Wray
Mathematics Instructional Facilitator
Howard County Public Schools
Ellicott City, Maryland

PEARSON

Glenview, Illinois   Boston, Massachusetts   Chandler, Arizona   Hoboken, New Jersey

Mathematicians

Roger Howe
Professor of Mathematics
Yale University
New Haven, Connecticut

Gary Lippman
Professor of Mathematics and
Computer Science
California State University, East Bay
Hayward, California

ELL Consultants

Janice R. Corona
Independent Education Consultant
Dallas, Texas

Jim Cummins
Professor
The University of Toronto
Toronto, Canada

ISBN-13: 978-0-328-89107-8
ISBN-10: 0-328-89107-X

5 18

You'll be using these digital resources throughout the year!

Digital Resources

Go to PearsonRealize.com

 MP
Math Processes **Animations** to play anytime

 Solve
Solve & Share problems plus math tools

 Learn
Visual Learning Animation Plus with animation, interaction, and math tools

 Glossary
Animated Glossary in English and Spanish

 Tools
Math Tools to help you understand

 Assessment
Quick Check for each lesson

 Help
Another Look Homework Video for extra help

 Games
Math Games to help you learn

 eText
Student Edition online

 ACTIVe-book
Student Edition online for showing your work

PEARSON realize™ Everything you need for math anytime, anywhere

Contents

Digital Resources at PearsonRealize.com

And remember your eText is available at PearsonRealize.com!

TOPICS

1. Fluently Add and Subtract Within 20

2. Work with Equal Groups

3. Add Within 100 Using Strategies

4. Fluently Add Within 100

5. Subtract Within 100 Using Strategies

6. Fluently Subtract Within 100

7. More Solving Problems Involving Addition and Subtraction

8. Work with Time and Money

9. Numbers to 1,000

10. Add Within 1,000 Using Models and Strategies

11. Subtract Within 1,000 Using Models and Strategies

12. Measuring Length

13. More Addition, Subtraction, and Length

14. Graphs and Data

15. Shapes and Their Attributes

PearsonRealize.com

TOPIC 1
Fluently Add and Subtract Within 20

Math and Science Project. 1
Review What You Know. 2
Vocabulary Cards. 3

1-1 **Addition Fact Strategies**. 5
2.CA.1, PS.2, PS.4, PS.7, PS.8

1-2 **Doubles and Near Doubles**. 11
2.CA.1, PS.4, PS.6, PS.7, PS.8

1-3 **Make a 10 to Add** 17
2.CA.1, PS.1, PS.2, PS.3, PS.5, PS.7

1-4 **Addition Fact Patterns**. 23
2.CA.1, PS.2, PS.5, PS.6, PS.7, PS.8

1-5 **Count On and Count Back to Subtract**. 29
2.CA.1, PS.1, PS.2, PS.4, PS.5

1-6 **Think Addition to Subtract** 35
2.CA.1, PS.2, PS.7, PS.8

1-7 **Make a 10 to Subtract** 41
2.CA.1, PS.3, PS.4, PS.5, PS.7, PS.8

1-8 **Practice Addition and Subtraction Facts** 47
2.CA.1, PS.2, PS.3, PS.4, PS.8

1-9 **Solve Addition and Subtraction Word Problems**. 53
2.CA.2, 2.CA.1, PS.1, PS.2, PS.6

1-10 **PROBLEM SOLVING: Construct Arguments** 59
PS.3 Also PS.1, PS.2, PS.4, 2.CA.2, 2.CA.1

Fluency Practice Activity. 65
Vocabulary Review. 66
Reteaching 67
Topic Assessment 71
Topic Performance Assessment. 75

This shows how you can use ten-frames to make a 10.

Contents

TOPIC 2
Work with Equal Groups

Math and Science Project 77
Review What You Know 78
Vocabulary Cards 79

2-1 **Even and Odd Numbers** 81
2.NS.5, 2.CA.1, PS.4, PS.5, PS.6, PS.7

2-2 **Continue Even and Odd Numbers** 87
2.NS.5, 2.CA.1, PS.2, PS.4, PS.6, PS.7, PS.8

2-3 **Use Arrays to Find Totals** 93
2.CA.5, 2.CA.1, PS.1, PS.3, PS.4, PS.7

2-4 **Make Arrays to Find Totals** 99
2.CA.5, 2.CA.1, PS.2, PS.4, PS.5, PS.8

2-5 **PROBLEM SOLVING: Model with Math** 105
PS.4 Also PS.1, PS.3, PS.5, PS.6, PS.7, PS.8, 2.CA.2, 2.CA.5

Fluency Practice Activity 111
Vocabulary Review 112
Reteaching 113
Topic Assessment 115
Topic Performance Assessment 117

This shows how you can use connecting cubes to show that a number is even or odd.

8 is even.

$4 + 4 = 8$

9 is odd.

$5 + 4 = 9$

TOPIC 3
Add Within 100 Using Strategies

Math and Science Project 119
Review What You Know 120
Vocabulary Cards 121

3-1 Add Tens and Ones on a Hundred Chart 123
2.CA.1, PS.1, PS.2, PS.3, PS.5

3-2 Add Tens on an Open Number Line 129
2.CA.1, PS.1, PS.3, PS.4, PS.5, PS.6

3-3 Add Tens and Ones on an Open Number Line 135
2.CA.1, PS.2, PS.3, PS.4, PS.5, PS.6

3-4 Break Apart Numbers to Add 141
2.CA.1, PS.2, PS.4, PS.5, PS.7, PS.8

3-5 Continue to Break Apart Numbers to Add 147
2.CA.1, PS.1, PS.4, PS.7

3-6 Add Using Compensation 153
2.CA.1, PS.2, PS.3, PS.8

3-7 Practice Adding Using Strategies 159
2.CA.1, 2.CA.6, PS.2, PS.4, PS.5

3-8 Solve One-Step and Two-Step Problems 165
2.CA.2, PS.1, PS.2, PS.4, PS.6

3-9 PROBLEM SOLVING: Use Appropriate Tools 171
PS.5 Also PS.1, PS.2, PS.3, 2.CA.2, 2.CA.1

Fluency Practice Activity 177
Vocabulary Review 178
Reteaching 179
Topic Assessment 183
Topic Performance Assessment 187

This shows how you can add two-digit numbers using a hundred chart.

$54 + 18 = 72$

51	52	53	54	55	56	57	58	59	60
61	62	63	64	65	66	67	68	69	70
71	72	73	74	75	76	77	78	79	80

TOPIC 4
Fluently Add Within 100

Math and Science Project. 189
Review What You Know. 190
Vocabulary Cards. 191

4-1   **Add with Partial Sums** 193
2.CA.1, PS.1, PS.4, PS.5, PS.6, PS.7

4-2   **Continue to Add with Partial Sums**. 199
2.CA.1, PS.1, PS.2, PS.3, PS.4, PS.6

4-3   **Models to Add 2-Digit Numbers** 205
2.CA.1, PS.2, PS.3, PS.4, PS.5, PS.6

4-4   **Add 2-Digit Numbers** 211
2.CA.1, PS.1, PS.2, PS.3, PS.4, PS.6

4-5   **Add More than Two 2-Digit Numbers** 217
2.CA.6, PS.2, PS.3, PS.4, PS.6, PS.8

4-6   **Practice Adding** 223
2.CA.1, 2.CA.6, PS.2, PS.3, PS.4, PS.6, PS.7

4-7   **Solve One-Step and Two-Step Problems** 229
2.CA.2, PS.1, PS.4, PS.5, PS.8

4-8   **PROBLEM SOLVING: Model with Math**. 235
PS.4 Also PS.1, PS.2, PS.3, 2.CA.2, 2.CA.1

IN 1   **Checking Addition to 100 with Estimation*** IN3
2.CA.2, PS.1, PS.2, PS.6, PS.8

Fluency Practice Activity. 241
Vocabulary Review. 242
Reteaching. 243
Topic Assessment 247
Topic Performance Assessment. 251

*Lesson exclusively for Indiana at the end of this volume

This shows one way to model a 2-digit addition problem.

TOPIC 5
Subtract Within 100 Using Strategies

Math and Science Project. 253
Review What You Know. 254

5-1 **Subtract Tens and Ones on a Hundred Chart** 255
2.CA.1, PS.1, PS.3, PS.5, PS.6, PS.7

5-2 **Count Back to Subtract on an Open Number Line** 261
2.CA.1, PS.2, PS.3, PS.5, PS.8

5-3 **Continue to Count Back to Subtract on an Open Number Line** 267
2.CA.1, PS.1, PS.4, PS.5

5-4 **Add Up to Subtract Using an Open Number Line** 273
2.CA.1, PS.1, PS.2, PS.5, PS.6

5-5 **Break Apart Numbers to Subtract** 279
2.CA.1, PS.3, PS.6, PS.7

5-6 **Continue to Break Apart Numbers to Subtract** 285
2.CA.1, PS.1, PS.3, PS.6, PS.7

5-7 **Subtract Using Compensation** 291
2.CA.1, PS.1, PS.4, PS.7, PS.8

5-8 **Solve One-Step and Two-Step Problems** 297
2.CA.2, PS.1, PS.2, PS.4, PS.5

5-9 **PROBLEM SOLVING: Critique Reasoning** 303
PS.3 Also PS.1, PS.4, PS.7, 2.CA.2, 2.CA.1

Fluency Practice Activity. 309
Vocabulary Review. 310
Reteaching 311
Topic Assessment 315
Topic Performance Assessment. 319

This shows how you can add up to subtract on an open number line to find 57 − 28.

+2 +10 +10 +7

28 30   40   50   57

Contents

TOPIC 6
Fluently Subtract Within 100

Math and Science Project. 321
Review What You Know. 322

6-1 Regroup I Ten for 10 Ones. 323
2.CA.1, PS.1, PS.3, PS.5, PS.8

6-2 Models to Subtract 2-Digit and I-Digit Numbers. 329
2.CA.1, PS.3, PS.4, PS.5

6-3 Subtract 2-Digit and I-Digit Numbers. 335
2.CA.1, PS.4, PS.5, PS.6, PS.8

6-4 Models to Subtract 2-Digit Numbers. 341
2.CA.1, PS.3, PS.4, PS.5, PS.7

6-5 Subtract 2-Digit Numbers. 347
2.CA.1, PS.2, PS.3, PS.4, PS.5, PS.6

6-6 Use Addition to Check Subtraction. 353
2.CA.1, PS.1, PS.2, PS.3, PS.4

6-7 Practice Subtracting 359
2.CA.1, PS.1, PS.2, PS.6, PS.7

6-8 Solve One-Step and Two-Step Problems 365
2.CA.2, PS.1, PS.2, PS.4, PS.7

6-9 PROBLEM SOLVING: Reasoning 371
PS.2 Also PS.1, PS.4, PS.5, PS.6, 2.CA.2

Fluency Practice Activity. 377
Vocabulary Review. 378
Reteaching 379
Topic Assessment 383
Topic Performance Assessment. 387

This shows how addition and subtraction are related. You can use addition to check subtraction.

$$
\begin{array}{r} {\scriptstyle 1\,14} \\ \cancel{24} \\ -\ 9 \\ \hline 15 \end{array}
\qquad
\begin{array}{r} {\scriptstyle 1} \\ 15 \\ +\ 9 \\ \hline 24 \end{array}
$$

24

| 9 | 15 |

TOPIC 7
More Solving Problems Involving Addition and Subtraction

Math and Science Project.. 389
Review What You Know.. 390

7-1 Represent Addition and Subtraction Problems.................. 391
2.CA.2, PS.2, PS.4, PS.5, PS.8

7-2 Mixed Practice: Solve Addition and Subtraction Problems......... 397
2.CA.2, PS.1, PS.2, PS.3, PS.4

7-3 Continue Practice with Addition and Subtraction Problems........ 403
2.CA.2, PS.1, PS.2, PS.4, PS.8

7-4 Solve Two-Step Problems 409
2.CA.2, PS.1, PS.2, PS.4, PS.6

7-5 Continue to Solve Two-Step Problems 415
2.CA.2, PS.1, PS.3, PS.4, PS.6

7-6 PROBLEM SOLVING: Reasoning 421
PS.2 Also PS.1, PS.3, PS.4, PS.7, 2.CA.2

Fluency Practice Activity... 427
Vocabulary Review... 428
Reteaching 429
Topic Assessment 431
Topic Performance Assessment....................................... 433

This shows how bar diagrams can be used to model and solve a two-step problem.

Mia sees 15 yellow birds and 16 red birds. Some birds fly away and now Mia sees 14 birds. How many birds flew away?

?
15	16

31
?	14

© Pearson Education, Inc. 2

Contents

TOPIC 8
Work with Time and Money

Math and Science Project. 435
Review What You Know. 436
Vocabulary Cards. 437

8-1   **Solve Problems with Coins**. 443
2.M.7, 2.NS.1, PS.1, PS.2, PS.3, PS.5

8-2   **Continue to Solve Problems with Coins** 449
2.M.7, 2.NS.1, PS.3, PS.4, PS.5, PS.6

8-3   **Solve Problems with Dollar Bills** 455
2.M.7, 2.NS.1, PS.2, PS.4, PS.6, PS.7

8-4   **Continue to Solve Problems with Dollar Bills** 461
2.M.7, 2.CA.2, PS.1, PS.2, PS.4, PS.6

8-5   **PROBLEM SOLVING: Reasoning** 467
PS.2 Also PS.1, PS.3, PS.4, PS.8, 2.M.7, 2.CA.2

8-6   **Tell Time to Five Minutes** 473
2.M.5, PS.2, PS.5, PS.6, PS.8

8-7   **Tell Time Before and After the Hour** 479
2.M.5, PS.3, PS.4, PS.6, PS.8

8-8   **A.M and P.M.**. 485
2.M.5, PS.2, PS.6, PS.8

IN 2   **Time Intervals***. IN11
2.M.5, PS.1, PS.5, PS.6, PS.7

IN 3   **Time Relatlonships***. IN17
2.M.6, PS.2, PS.3, PS.6, PS.8

Fluency Practice Activity. 491
Vocabulary Review. 492

*Lesson exclusively for Indiana at the end of this volume

Glossary G1

This shows how to count on to find the total value.

Micah has the coins shown below.
How many cents does Micah have?

50¢   75¢   85¢   90¢   91¢

Indiana Mathematics Standards

NUMBER SENSE

2.NS.1 Count by ones, twos, fives, tens, and hundreds up to at least 1,000 from any given number.

2.NS.2 Read and write whole numbers up to 1,000. Use words, models, standard form and expanded form to represent and show equivalent forms of whole numbers up to 1,000.

2.NS.3 Plot and compare whole numbers up to 1,000 on a number line.

2.NS.4 Match the ordinal numbers first, second, third, etc., with an ordered set up to 30 items.

2.NS.5 Determine whether a group of objects (up to 20) has an odd or even number of members (e.g., by placing that number of objects in two groups of the same size and recognizing that for even numbers no object will be left over and for odd numbers one object will be left over, or by pairing objects or counting them by 2s).

2.NS.6 Understand that the three digits of a three-digit number represent amounts of hundreds, tens, and ones (e.g., 706 equals 7 hundreds, 0 tens, and 6 ones). Understand that 100 can be thought of as a group of ten tens — called a "hundred." Understand that the numbers 100, 200, 300, 400, 500, 600, 700, 800, 900 refer to one, two, three, four, five, six, seven, eight, or nine hundreds (and 0 tens and 0 ones).

2.NS.7 Use place value understanding to compare two three-digit numbers based on meanings of the hundreds, tens, and ones digits, using >, =, and < symbols to record the results of comparisons.

Dear Families,

The standards on the following pages describe the math that students will learn this year.

Indiana Mathematics Standards

COMPUTATION AND ALGEBRAIC THINKING

2.CA.1 Add and subtract fluently within 100.

2.CA.2 Solve real-world problems involving addition and subtraction within 100 in situations of adding to, taking from, putting together, taking apart, and comparing, with unknowns in all parts of the addition or subtraction problem (e.g., by using drawings and equations with a symbol for the unknown number to represent the problem). Use estimation to decide whether answers are reasonable in addition problems.

2.CA.3 Solve real-world problems involving addition and subtraction within 100 in situations involving lengths that are given in the same units (e.g., by using drawings, such as drawings of rulers, and equations with a symbol for the unknown number to represent the problem).

2.CA.4 Add and subtract within 1000, using models or drawings and strategies based on place value, properties of operations, and/or the relationship between addition and subtraction; describe the strategy and explain the reasoning used. Understand that in adding or subtracting three-digit numbers, one adds or subtracts hundreds and hundreds, tens and tens, ones and ones, and that sometimes it is necessary to compose or decompose tens or hundreds.

2.CA.5 Use addition to find the total number of objects arranged in rectangular arrays with up to 5 rows and up to 5 columns; write an equation to express the total as a sum of equal groups.

2.CA.6 Show that the order in which two numbers are added (commutative property) and how the numbers are grouped in addition (associative property) will not change the sum. These properties can be used to show that numbers can be added in any order.

2.CA.7 Create, extend, and give an appropriate rule for number patterns using addition and subtraction within 1000.

GEOMETRY

2.G.1 Identify, describe, and classify two- and three-dimensional shapes (triangle, square, rectangle, cube, right rectangular prism) according to the number and shape of faces and the number of sides and/or vertices. Draw two-dimensional shapes.

2.G.2 Create squares, rectangles, triangles, cubes, and right rectangular prisms using appropriate materials.

2.G.3 Investigate and predict the result of composing and decomposing two- and three-dimensional shapes.

2.G.4 Partition a rectangle into rows and columns of same-size (unit) squares and count to find the total number of same-size squares.

2.G.5 Partition circles and rectangles into two, three, or four equal parts; describe the shares using the words halves, thirds, half of, a third of, etc.; and describe the whole as two halves, three thirds, four fourths. Recognize that equal parts of identical wholes need not have the same shape.

Indiana Mathematics Standards

MEASUREMENT

2.M.1 Describe the relationships among inch, foot, and yard. Describe the relationship between centimeter and meter.

2.M.2 Estimate and measure the length of an object by selecting and using appropriate tools, such as rulers, yardsticks, meter sticks, and measuring tapes to the nearest inch, foot, yard, centimeter and meter.

2.M.3 Understand that the length of an object does not change regardless of the units used. Measure the length of an object twice using length units of different lengths for the two measurements. Describe how the two measurements relate to the size of the unit chosen.

2.M.4 Estimate and measure volume (capacity) using cups and pints.

2.M.5 Tell and write time to the nearest five minutes from analog clocks, using a.m. and p.m. Solve real-world problems involving addition and subtraction of time intervals on the hour or half hour.

2.M.6 Describe relationships of time, including: seconds in a minute; minutes in an hour; hours in a day; days in a week; and days, weeks, and months in a year.

2.M.7 Find the value of a collection of pennies, nickels, dimes, quarters and dollars.

DATA ANALYSIS

2.DA.1 Draw a picture graph (with single-unit scale) and a bar graph (with single-unit scale) to represent a data set with up to four choices (What is your favorite color? red, blue, yellow, green). Solve simple put-together, take-apart, and compare problems using information presented in the graphs.

Process Standards for Mathematics

PS.1 Make sense of problems and persevere in solving them.

Mathematically proficient students start by explaining to themselves the meaning of a problem and looking for entry points to its solution. They analyze givens, constraints, relationships, and goals. They make conjectures about the form and meaning of the solution and plan a solution pathway, rather than simply jumping into a solution attempt. They consider analogous problems and try special cases and simpler forms of the original problem in order to gain insight into its solution. They monitor and evaluate their progress and change course if necessary. Mathematically proficient students check their answers to problems using a different method, and they continually ask themselves, "Does this make sense?" and "Is my answer reasonable?" They understand the approaches of others to solving complex problems and identify correspondences between different approaches. Mathematically proficient students understand how mathematical ideas interconnect and build on one another to produce a coherent whole.

PS.2 Reason abstractly and quantitatively.

Mathematically proficient students make sense of quantities and their relationships in problem situations. They bring two complementary abilities to bear on problems involving quantitative relationships: the ability to decontextualize—to abstract a given situation and represent it symbolically and manipulate the representing symbols as if they have a life of their own, without necessarily attending to their referents—and the ability to contextualize, to pause as needed during the manipulation process in order to probe into the referents for the symbols involved. Quantitative reasoning entails habits of creating a coherent representation of the problem at hand; considering the units involved; attending to the meaning of quantities, not just how to compute them; and knowing and flexibly using different properties of operations and objects.

PS.3 Construct viable arguments and critique the reasoning of others.

Mathematically proficient students understand and use stated assumptions, definitions, and previously established results in constructing arguments. They make conjectures and build a logical progression of statements to explore the truth of their conjectures. They analyze situations by breaking them into cases and recognize and use counterexamples. They organize their mathematical thinking, justify their conclusions and communicate them to others, and respond to the arguments of others. They reason inductively about data, making plausible arguments that take into account the context from which the data arose. Mathematically proficient students are also able to compare the effectiveness of two plausible arguments, distinguish correct logic or reasoning from that which is flawed, and—if there is a flaw in an argument—explain what it is. They justify whether a given statement is true always, sometimes, or never. Mathematically proficient students participate and collaborate in a mathematics community. They listen to or read the arguments of others, decide whether they make sense, and ask useful questions to clarify or improve the arguments.

PS.4 Model with mathematics.

Mathematically proficient students apply the mathematics they know to solve problems arising in everyday life, society, and the workplace using a variety of appropriate strategies. They create and use a variety of representations to solve problems and to organize and communicate mathematical ideas. Mathematically proficient students apply what they know and are comfortable making assumptions and approximations to simplify a complicated situation, realizing that these may need revision later. They are able to identify important quantities in a practical situation and map their relationships using such tools as diagrams, two-way tables, graphs, flowcharts and formulas. They analyze those relationships mathematically to draw conclusions. They routinely interpret their mathematical results in the context of the situation and reflect on whether the results make sense, possibly improving the model if it has not served its purpose.

Process Standards for Mathematics

PS.5 Use appropriate tools strategically.

Mathematically proficient students consider the available tools when solving a mathematical problem. These tools might include pencil and paper, models, a ruler, a protractor, a calculator, a spreadsheet, a computer algebra system, a statistical package, or dynamic geometry software. Mathematically proficient students are sufficiently familiar with tools appropriate for their grade or course to make sound decisions about when each of these tools might be helpful, recognizing both the insight to be gained and their limitations. Mathematically proficient students identify relevant external mathematical resources, such as digital content, and use them to pose or solve problems. They use technological tools to explore and deepen their understanding of concepts and to support the development of learning mathematics. They use technology to contribute to concept development, simulation, representation, reasoning, communication and problem solving.

PS.6 Attend to precision.

Mathematically proficient students communicate precisely to others. They use clear definitions, including correct mathematical language, in discussion with others and in their own reasoning. They state the meaning of the symbols they choose, including using the equal sign consistently and appropriately. They express solutions clearly and logically by using the appropriate mathematical terms and notation. They specify units of measure and label axes to clarify the correspondence with quantities in a problem. They calculate accurately and efficiently and check the validity of their results in the context of the problem. They express numerical answers with a degree of precision appropriate for the problem context.

PS.7 Look for and make use of structure.

Mathematically proficient students look closely to discern a pattern or structure. They step back for an overview and shift perspective. They recognize and use properties of operations and equality. They organize and classify geometric shapes based on their attributes. They see expressions, equations, and geometric figures as single objects or as being composed of several objects.

PS.8 Look for and express regularity in repeated reasoning.

Mathematically proficient students notice if calculations are repeated and look for general methods and shortcuts. They notice regularity in mathematical problems and their work to create a rule or formula. Mathematically proficient students maintain oversight of the process, while attending to the details as they solve a problem. They continually evaluate the reasonableness of their intermediate results.

Problem Solving Handbook

Math processes are ways we think about and do math.

Math processes will help you solve problems.

Math Processes

1. Make sense of problems and persevere in solving them.

2. Reason abstractly and quantitatively.

3. Construct viable arguments and critique the reasoning of others.

4. Model with mathematics.

5. Use appropriate tools strategically.

6. Attend to precision.

7. Look for and make use of structure.

8. Look for and express regularity in repeated reasoning.

There are good Thinking Habits for each of these math processes.

1 Make sense of problems and persevere in solving them.

Good math thinkers know what the problem is about. They have a plan to solve it. They keep trying if they get stuck.

My plan is to use counters as trucks. I can act out the problem.

A store has some toy trucks.
Mike buys 2 of the trucks.
Now the store has 3 trucks.
How many trucks did the store have at the start?

5 – 2 = 3
5 trucks

Thinking Habits

What do I need to find?

What do I know?

What's my plan for solving the problem?

What else can I try if I get stuck?

How can I check that my solution makes sense?

2 Reason abstractly and quantitatively.

I completed a part-part-whole model. It shows how things in the problem are related.

Good math thinkers know how to think about words and numbers to solve problems.

Tony has 10 apples. 6 are red. The rest are green. How many apples are green?

10 − 6 = 4

4 apples are green.

Thinking Habits

What do the numbers stand for?

How are the numbers in the problem related?

How can I show a word problem using pictures or numbers?

How can I use a word problem to show what an equation means?

Problem Solving Handbook

3 Construct viable arguments and critique the reasoning of others.

I can use place-value blocks to check Paula's thinking. My explanation is clear and complete.

Good math thinkers use math to explain why they are right. They talk about math that others do, too.

Paula added 34 + 5.
She says she had to regroup the ones.
Is she correct? Show how you know.

34 has 4 ones.

4 ones and 5 ones are 9 ones.

Paula is incorrect.

You do not need to regroup ones.

Tens	Ones
|||	:::::

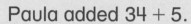

$34 + 5 = 39$

Thinking Habits

How can I use math to explain my work?

Am I using numbers and symbols correctly?

Is my explanation clear?

What questions can I ask to understand other people's thinking?

Are there mistakes in other people's thinking?

Can I improve other people's thinking?

4 Model with mathematics.

I can use ten-frames and counters to show the problem.

Good math thinkers use math they know to show and solve problems.

14 dogs are playing at a park.
9 dogs go home.
How many dogs are still at the park?

14 – 9 = 5

5 dogs

Thinking Habits

How can I use the math I know to help solve this problem?

Can I use a drawing, diagram, table, graph, or objects to show the problem?

Can I write an equation to show the problem?

5 Use appropriate tools strategically.

Good math thinkers know how to pick the right tools to solve math problems.

I chose connecting cubes to solve the problem.

Kai and Maddie each pick 6 apples.
Then Maddie picks 1 more apple.
How many apples do they pick in all?

6 + 7 = 13
13 apples

Thinking Habits

Which tools can I use?

Is there a different tool I could use?

Am I using the tool correctly?

6 Attend to precision.

Good math thinkers are careful about what they write and say, so their ideas about math are clear.

I can use the definition of a cube to help me describe what it looks like.

Circle each cube below.

Describe what a cube looks like.

A cube has 6 flat surfaces.

Each flat surface is the same size.

A cube has 12 edges.

Thinking Habits

Am I using numbers, units, and symbols correctly?

Am I using the correct definitions?

Is my answer clear?

Problem Solving Handbook

7 Look for and make use of structure.

MP

It is hard to add three numbers at once. I can add any two numbers first. I added 6 + 4 first to make the problem easier.

Good math thinkers look for patterns in math to help solve problems.

Jeff saw 6 brown frogs, 3 green frogs, and 4 spotted frogs.
How many frogs did Jeff see in all?

Show your work and explain your answer.

(6) + 3 + (4) = 13
        10

I made 10 then added 3 to make the problem easier.

Thinking Habits

Is there a pattern?

How can I describe the pattern?

Can I break the problem into simpler parts?

8 Look for and express regularity in repeated reasoning.

MP

I can compare the tens first. If the tens are the same, I can compare the ones.

Good math thinkers look for things that repeat in a problem. They use what they learn from one problem to help them solve other problems.

Compare each pair of numbers.
Write <, >, or =. Tell how you will
compare each pair of numbers.

57 < 75   49 < 52

36 > 34   61 = 61

Thinking Habits

Does something repeat in
the problem?

How can the solution
help me solve
another problem?

Problem Solving Guide

These questions can help you solve problems.

Make Sense of the Problem

Reason
- What do I need to find?
- What given information can I use?
- How are the quantities related?

Think About Similar Problems
- Have I solved problems like this before?

Persevere in Solving the Problem

Model with Math
- How can I use the math I know?
- How can I show the problem?
- Is there a pattern I can use?

Use Appropriate Tools
- What math tools could I use?
- How can I use those tools?

Check the Answer

Make Sense of the Answer
- Is my answer reasonable?

Check for Precision
- Did I check my work?
- Is my answer clear?
- Is my explanation clear?

Some Ways to Show Problems

- Draw a Picture
- Draw a Number Line
- Write an Equation

Some Math Tools

- Objects
- Rulers
- Technology
- Paper and Pencil

This sheet helps you organize your work.

Name Mary

Teaching Tool 1

Problem Solving Recording Sheet

Problem:
John bikes for 17 miles on Monday.
He bikes for 15 miles on Tuesday.
How many miles does John bike in all?

MAKE SENSE OF THE PROBLEM

Need to Find	Given
I need to find how many miles John bikes in all.	John bikes 17 miles on Monday and 15 miles on Tuesday.

PERSEVERE IN SOLVING THE PROBLEM

Some Ways to Represent Problems
☑ Draw a Picture
☐ Draw a Number Line
☑ Write an Equation

Some Math Tools
☐ Objects
☐ Rulers
☐ Technology
☑ Paper and Pencil

Solution and Answer

$17 + 15 = 32$

I made a 10.
John bikes 32 miles in all.

CHECK THE ANSWER

I checked my drawing of blocks.
They matched the problem and show 32 in all.

TT1

Digital Resources

Solve Learn Glossary

Tools Assessment Help Games

TOPIC 1 Fluently Add and Subtract Within 20

Essential Question: What are strategies for finding addition and subtraction facts?

Look at the different types of paper!

Different papers have different properties.

Wow! Let's do this project and learn more.

Math and Science Project: Material Math

Find Out Collect different types of paper. Talk about the uses of paper. Tell how strong each type of paper is. Tell how the paper feels. Tell if the paper can soak up water.

Journal: Make a Book Show what you find out in a book. In your book, also:

• Glue samples of paper and tell what you found.

• Choose a type of paper to make flash cards of addition and subtraction facts.

Name _____

Review What You Know

A-Z Vocabulary

1. Circle the symbol for **equals**.

$-$

$+$

$=$

2. Circle the symbol for **minus**.

$-$

$+$

$=$

3. Circle the number that is the **whole**.

$4 + 2 = 6$

Subtraction Stories

4. There are 7 birds on a fence. 2 fly away. How many birds are left?

_____ birds

Addition Stories

5. Write an equation to solve the problem.

Kate draws 4 big stars. Then she draws 2 small stars. How many stars does Kate draw in all?

_____ + _____ = _____

Making 10

6. Write the numbers that show a way to make 10.

_____ + _____ = _____

My Word Cards

Study the words on the front of the card.
Complete the activity on the back.

A-Z
Glossary

addend

$2 + 5 = 7$

↑ ↑
addends

sum

$3 + 4 = 7$

↑

$\begin{array}{r} 4 \\ + 3 \\ \hline 7 \end{array}$

sum → 7

equation

$3 + 4 = 7$

$14 - 6 = 8$

doubles

$4 + 4 = 8$

near doubles

$4 + 5 = 9$

difference

$14 - 6 = 8$

↑

$\begin{array}{r} 14 \\ - 6 \\ \hline 8 \end{array}$

difference → 8

My Word Cards

An _____

uses an equal sign (=) to show that the value on the left is the same as the value on the right.

The answer in an addition equation is called the

_____.

Numbers that are added are called

_____.

The answer in a subtraction equation is called the

_____.

Addition facts that have two addends that are close are called

_____.

Addition facts that have two addends that are the same are called

_____.

Name _____

Solve & Share

Use cubes to show $4 + 5$.

What will happen to the total number of cubes if you change the order of the numbers being added? Explain.

I can ...
count on to add and add in any order.

Content Standard 2.CA.1
Process Standards PS.2, PS.4, PS.7, PS.8

$4 + 5 = $ _____   _____ $+$ _____ $=$ _____

You can count on to find 6 + 3.

6   7   8   9

Or count on to find 3 + 6.

3   4   5   6   7   8   9

Counting on from the greater number is easier!

An **equation** uses an equal sign (=) to show that the value on the left is the same as the value on the right.

6 + 3 = 9

3 + 6 = 9

You can change the order of the **addends**.

6   +   3   =   9

3   +   6   =   9

addend addend **sum**

The sum is the same.

You can add numbers in any order, and the sum is the same.

So, 6 + 3 = 3 + 6.

You can write the facts this way, too.

6   3
+ 3   + 6
9   9

Do You Understand?

Show Me! Does 5 + 2 = 2 + 5? How do you know?

1.

   3 + 1 = 4

   1 + 3 = 4

2.   4
                          + 3
                          ☐

       ☐
                          +
                          ☐
                          ☐

Tools Assessment

Independent Practice

Count on to find the sum. Then change the order of the addends. Use cubes if needed.

3. $8 + 2 =$ ____

____ + ____ = ____

4. $8 + 5 =$ ____

____ + ____ = ____

5. $9 + 3 =$ ____

____ + ____ = ____

6. $8 + 4 =$ ____

____ + ____ = ____

7. $7 + 4 =$ ____

____ + ____ = ____

8. $7 + 3 =$ ____

____ + ____ = ____

9.
```
   7
 + 2
 ___
```

```
     □
   + □
   ___
     □
```

10.
```
   6
 + 2
 ___
```

```
     □
   + □
   ___
     □
```

11.
```
   5
 + 6
 ___
```

```
     □
   + □
   ___
     □
```

12. **Algebra** Write the missing numbers.

$6 +$ ____ $= 4 + 6$

$6 +$ ____ $= 5 + 6$

$9 + 3 = 3 +$ ____

$8 + 2 =$ ____ $+ 8$

____ $+ 7 = 7 + 4$

____ $+ 8 = 8 + 4$

13. **Model** Joy has 8 bean plants and 6 corn plants in her garden. How many plants does she have in all? Draw a picture. Then write facts for this story with the addends in a different order.

_____ + _____ = _____

_____ + _____ = _____

Your picture and your equation will show the problem.

14. **Higher Order Thinking** Find the objects in Box 1 and Box 2 that are the same. Write an equation to show how many of each object there are. Then change the order of the addends.

❤ _____ + _____ = _____ = _____ + _____

✿ _____ + _____ = _____ = _____ + _____

✾ _____ + _____ = _____ = _____ + _____

15. 🄳 **Assessment** Kate has 7 fish. Nick has 5 fish. How many fish do Kate and Nick have in all?

Which shows how to count on to solve the problem?

Ⓐ 7, 8, 9, 10, 11, 12

Ⓑ 1, 2, 3, 4, 5

Ⓒ 7 − 5

Ⓓ 7, 8, 9, 10, 11

Name _____

Another Look! You can count on to find a sum. Counting on from a greater number is easier.

 I can add numbers in any order and get the same sum.

5   6 7

2   3 4 5 6 7

$5 + 2 = \underline{7}$

$\underline{2} + \underline{5} = \underline{7}$

 Count on to find the sum. Then change the order of the addends.

1.

$3 + 4 = \underline{\quad}$

$\underline{\quad} + \underline{\quad} = \underline{\quad}$

2.

$\begin{array}{r} 5 \\ + \ 4 \\ \hline \square \end{array}$

$\begin{array}{r} \square \\ + \ \square \\ \hline \square \end{array}$

3.

$7 + 6 = \underline{\quad}$

$\underline{\quad} + \underline{\quad} = \underline{\quad}$

Write two addition facts for each story. Then solve.

4. **Reasoning** Danny collects toy train cars. He has 9 red train cars and 5 black train cars. How many train cars does he have in all?

_____ + _____ = _____

_____ + _____ = _____

_____ train cars

5. **Reasoning** Ana draws 3 red circles and 8 blue circles. How many circles does Ana draw?

_____ + _____ = _____

_____ + _____ = _____

_____ circles

6. **Higher Order Thinking** Draw a picture to solve. Then write two addition facts for the story.

15 cows live at a farm. Some of the cows are brown and some are white. How many of each color could be at the farm?

_____ + _____ = 15

_____ + _____ = 15

_____ brown cows

_____ white cows

7. **Assessment** Which shape belongs in the second equation?

 + ? =

Ⓐ   Ⓑ   Ⓒ   Ⓓ

© Pearson Education, Inc. 2

Solve & Share

You know that 2 + 2 = 4.
Tell how knowing that fact can help you find 2 + 3.

Solve

Lesson 1-2
Doubles and Near Doubles

I can ...
use doubles and near doubles to add quickly and accurately.

Content Standard 2.CA.1
Process Standards PS.4,
PS.6, PS.7, PS.8

$$2 + 2 = 4 \qquad\qquad 2 + 3 = \underline{\quad\quad}$$

Learn   Glossary

Find $7 + 8$ and find $7 + 9$.

You can use a doubles fact to help you add.

Doubles
$3 + 3$ $5 + 5$
$4 + 4$

You can use the doubles fact to help find a **near doubles** fact.

Doubles Fact: $7 + 7 = 14$

$7 + 8$ is 1 more than $7 + 7$.

$7 + 9$ is 2 more than $7 + 7$.

$7 + 8 = 15$ and $7 + 9 = 16$ These are near doubles facts.

Do You Understand?

Show Me! How could you use the doubles fact $7 + 7$ to find $7 + 9$?

☆ Guided Practice ☆

Complete the doubles facts.
Use the doubles facts to solve the near doubles.

1. $2 + 2 = \underline{4}$ $2 + 3 = \underline{}$

2. $\underline{} = 4 + 4$ $\underline{} = 4 + 5$

3. $\begin{array}{r} 3 \\ +3 \\ \hline \square \end{array}$ $\begin{array}{r} 3 \\ +4 \\ \hline \square \end{array}$

4. $\begin{array}{r} 5 \\ +5 \\ \hline \square \end{array}$ $\begin{array}{r} 5 \\ +7 \\ \hline \square \end{array}$

12 twelve

© Pearson Education, Inc. 2

Topic 1 | Lesson 2

Tools   Assessment

Independent Practice

Complete the doubles facts. Use the doubles facts to solve the near doubles.

5. 6 + 6 = ____   6 + 7 = ____   6. 5 + 5 = ____   5 + 6 = ____

7. 8 + 8 = ____   8 + 10 = ____   8. ____ = 1 + 1   ____ = 1 + 3

9.   2   2   10.   4   4   11.   8   8
   + 2   + 3   + 4   + 5   + 8   + 9
   ☐   ☐   ☐   ☐   ☐   ☐

12.   3   3   13.   5   5   14.   7   7
   + 3   + 5   + 5   + 7   + 7   + 9
   ☐   ☐   ☐   ☐   ☐   ☐

15. **Algebra** Complete the doubles and near doubles facts.

9 + ☐ = 18   ☐ + ☐ = 19

16. **Model** John drew 4 houses. Then he drew 5 more houses. How many houses did John draw in all?

Draw a picture and write an equation.

_____ + _____ = _____ houses

17. **Higher Order Thinking** Choose a doubles fact. Use that doubles fact to draw a picture that shows a near doubles story.

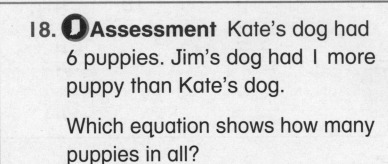

18. **Assessment** Kate's dog had 6 puppies. Jim's dog had 1 more puppy than Kate's dog.

Which equation shows how many puppies in all?

Ⓐ $6 + 1 = 7$

Ⓑ $6 + 6 = 12$

Ⓒ $6 + 7 = 13$

Ⓓ $7 + 7 = 14$

Topic 1 | Lesson 2

Name _____

Another Look! You can use a doubles fact to solve a near doubles fact.

To solve a near doubles fact, you can add 1 or 2 more to the doubles fact.

HOME ACTIVITY Have your child use common objects, such as pennies or buttons, to show doubles and near doubles. Then ask your child to write equations to show the facts.

$6 + 6 = \underline{12}$

Doubles Fact

$6 + 7 = \underline{13}$

Near Doubles Fact

Write and solve the doubles facts and the near doubles facts.

1.

___ + ___ = ___   ___ + ___ = ___

2.

___ + ___ = ___   ___ + ___ = ___

3. $7 + 7 = $ _____

$7 + 9 = $ _____

4. $8 + 8 = $ _____

$8 + 10 = $ _____

5. **Algebra** A number plus 6 equals 12.
What is the number?

_____ + _____ = _____

The number is _____.

6. **Algebra** 6 plus a number equals 13.
What is the number?

_____ + _____ = _____

The number is _____.

7. **A-Z Vocabulary** Which is a **near doubles** fact?
Circle the fact.

$4 + 4 = 8$ $4 + 5 = 9$

$2 + 7 = 9$ $0 + 5 = 5$

8. **Higher Order Thinking** Draw a picture to show the story.

Then write an equation for the story.

Jane has 5 books.
Fred has 2 more books than Jane.
How many books do Fred and
Jane have in all?

_____ + _____ = _____

_____ books

9. **Assessment** Terry's dollhouse has 7 windows on the first floor and 8 windows on the second floor.

Which shows how Terry found the number of windows in all?

Ⓐ $6 + 6$ and 1 more is 13.

Ⓑ $7 + 7$ and 1 more is 15.

Ⓒ $8 + 8$ and 1 more is 17.

Ⓓ $9 + 9$ and 1 more is 19.

Solve

Solve & Share

How can thinking about 10 help you find 9 + 3? Use the ten-frames and counters to show how.

I can …
make a 10 to help me add quickly and accurately.

Content Standard 2.CA.1
Process Standards PS.1, PS.2, PS.3, PS.5, PS.7

$$9 + 3$$

You can make a 10 to help you add.

$$\begin{array}{r} 8 \\ + 5 \\ \hline \boxed{?} \end{array}$$

Move 2 counters to make a 10.

Add with 10.

$$\begin{array}{r} 10 \\ + 3 \\ \hline 13 \end{array} \text{ so, } \begin{array}{r} 8 \\ + 5 \\ \hline 13 \end{array}$$

Do You Understand?

Show Me! Why do you move 2 counters to add 8 + 5?

✩ **Guided Practice** ✩ Make a 10 to add.
Use counters and ten-frames.

1. $$\begin{array}{r} 7 \\ + 4 \\ \hline \boxed{?} \end{array}$$

  →

$$\begin{array}{r} 10 \\ + \boxed{1} \\ \hline \boxed{11} \end{array} \text{ so, } \begin{array}{r} 7 \\ + \boxed{} \\ \hline \boxed{} \end{array}$$

© Pearson Education, Inc. 2

Tools Assessment

Independent Practice Make a 10 to add. Use counters and ten-frames.

2.   8
   + 4
   ▢

3.   3
   + 9
   ▢

4.   6
   + 7
   ▢

5.   5
   + 8
   ▢

6.   7
   + 5
   ▢

7. 5 + 9 = _____

8. 3 + 8 = _____

9. 4 + 9 = _____

10. 7 + 9 = _____

Algebra Which number is missing?

11. 8 + 5 = ▢ + 3

12. 6 + 9 = 10 + ▢

13. 8 + 9 = 10 + ▢

14. **Higher Order Thinking** Can you make a 10 to help you add 7 + 4 + 5? Explain.

_____

_____

_____

15. Tan's team scored 16 points in a game. During the first half, they scored 9 points. How many points did the team score in the second half of the game?

_____ points

16. Make Sense The school has a clothing drive for charity. Ana's class donates 8 coats. Nico's class donates 5 hats. Adam's class donates 8 coats. How many coats were donated in all?

_____ coats

17. Higher Order Thinking Draw a picture to show how you can make a 10 to help you add $3 + 5 + 9$.

18. Assessment Mary wrote an equation. Which number makes her equation true?

$$8 + 9 = 10 + \_\_\_\_$$

Ⓐ 5

Ⓑ 6

Ⓒ 7

Ⓓ 8

Think about making a 10. Find the missing addend!

© Pearson Education, Inc. 2

Name _____

Help   Tools   Games

Another Look! You can make a 10 to help you add.

This shows 8 + 4.

Show 10 + 2.
Move 2 counters to make a 10.

The sums are the same!

8 + 4   is the same as   10 + 2.

8 + 4 = 12

10 + 2 = 12

HOME ACTIVITY Have your child use buttons to make a group of 9 and a group of 5. Ask your child to show you how to make a group of 10 buttons to help find the sum.

Make a 10 to help you add.

1. Find 9 + 7.   Move 1 counter to make a 10.

9 + 7   is the same as   10 + ___.

9 + 7 = ___   ___ + ___ = ___

2. Find 7 + 5.

Move ____ counters to make a 10.

7 + 5 is the same as 10 + ___.

7 + 5 = ___   ___ + ___ = ___

Add. Then draw lines to match addition problems with the same sum.

3. 9 + 6 = ____   10 + 2 = ____

4. 7 + 5 = ____   10 + 3 = ____

5. 9 + 5 = ____   10 + 4 = ____

6. 5 + 8 = ____   10 + 5 = ____

7. **Explain** Blanca wants to add 5 + 8. Describe how she can make a 10 to solve.

5 + 8 = ____

_____

_____

_____

8. **Higher Order Thinking**
Jay has 14 blocks in all.
He has 6 yellow blocks.
The rest of the blocks are green.
How many green blocks does Jay have?
Make a 10 to solve.
Jay has ____ green blocks.

Explain how you solved the problem!

_____

_____

_____

9. **⬤Assessment** Beth has 8 fish and 7 snails. How can Beth make a 10 to find how many fish and snails she has in all?

10 + 9   10 + 8   10 + 7   10 + 5
   Ⓐ   Ⓑ   Ⓒ   Ⓓ

10. **⬤Assessment** Use the ten-frames. Show how to find 7 + 6 by making a 10.

© Pearson Education, Inc. 2

Topic 1 | Lesson 3

Name _____

Solve & Share

Look at the sums on an addition facts table for addends 0 to 5. Describe one of the patterns that you see.

Use words, colors, or addition facts to describe the patterns.

I can ...
use the patterns on an addition facts table to help me remember the addition facts.

Content Standard 2.CA.1
Process Standards PS.2, PS.5, PS.6, PS.7, PS.8

+	0	1	2	3	4	5
0	0	1	2	3	4	5
1	1	2	3	4	5	6
2	2	3	4	5	6	7
3	3	4	5	6	7	8
4	4	5	6	7	8	9
5	5	6	7	8	9	10

_____

_____

_____

_____

How can you describe a pattern for all the sums of six?

+	0	1	2	3	4	5	6	7	8	9	10
0	0	1	2	3	4	5	6	7	8	9	10
1	1	2	3	4	5	6	7	8	9	10	11
2	2	3	4	5	6	7	8	9	10	11	12
3	3	4	5	6	7	8	9	10	11	12	13
4	4	5	6	7	8	9	10	11	12	13	14
5	5	6	7	8	9	10	11	12	13	14	15
6	6	7	8	9	10	11	12	13	14	15	16
7	7	8	9	10	11	12	13	14	15	16	17
8	8	9	10	11	12	13	14	15	16	17	18
9	9	10	11	12	13	14	15	16	17	18	19
10	10	11	12	13	14	15	16	17	18	19	20

It makes a diagonal pattern.

You can write an addition equation.

$4 + 2 = 6$

4 and 2 are addends for the sum of 6.

+	0	1	2	3	4
0	0	1	2	3	4
1	1	2	3	4	5
2	2	3	4	5	6

Here are all the ways to make a sum of 6.

$6 + 0 = 6$
$5 + 1 = 6$
$4 + 2 = 6$
$3 + 3 = 6$
$2 + 4 = 6$
$1 + 5 = 6$
$0 + 6 = 6$

What pattern do you see?

Do You Understand?

Show Me! How can patterns on an addition facts table help you remember the addition facts?

☆ Guided Practice   Use fact patterns to complete each equation.

1. $10 + \underline{6} = 16$
   $9 + 7 = \underline{16}$
   $\underline{8} + 8 = 16$
   $7 + \underline{9} = 16$
   $6 + \underline{10} = 16$

2. $10 + \underline{} = 14$
   $\underline{} + 5 = 14$
   $8 + 6 = \underline{}$
   $7 + \underline{} = 14$
   $\underline{} + 6 = 14$
   $9 + \underline{} = 14$
   $\underline{} + 4 = 14$

3. $9 + \underline{} = 9$
   $\underline{} + 1 = 9$
   $7 + 2 = \underline{}$
   $6 + \underline{} = 9$
   $\underline{} + 4 = 9$
   $5 + \underline{} = 9$
   $3 + \underline{} = 9$
   $\underline{} + 2 = 9$
   $8 + 1 = \underline{}$
   $\underline{} + 0 = 9$

Topic 1 | Lesson 4

Tools   Assessment

Independent Practice ✫ Use fact patterns to complete each equation.

4. $10 + \_\_\_ = 12$

$\_\_\_ + 3 = 12$

$8 + 4 = \_\_\_$

$\_\_\_ + 7 = 12$

$6 + 6 = \_\_\_$

$7 + \_\_\_ = 12$

$\_\_\_ + 4 = 12$

$9 + \_\_\_ = 12$

5. $7 + \_\_\_ = 7$

$\_\_\_ + 1 = 7$

$5 + 2 = \_\_\_$

$\_\_\_ + 3 = 7$

$\_\_\_ + 4 = 7$

$\_\_\_ + 5 = 7$

$\_\_\_ + 6 = 7$

$0 + \_\_\_ = 7$

6. $10 + \_\_\_ = 15$

$\_\_\_ + 5 = 15$

$9 + 6 = \_\_\_$

$9 + \_\_\_ = 15$

$7 + \_\_\_ = 15$

$\_\_\_ + 7 = 15$

7. Number Sense Find the 8 in the top row of the addition facts table. Complete all of the equations using the 8-column on the table. What pattern do you see?

$8 + \_\_\_ = 8$

$8 + \_\_\_ = 9$

$8 + \_\_\_ = 10$

$8 + 3 = \_\_\_$

$8 + \_\_\_ = 12$

$8 + \_\_\_ = \_\_\_$

$8 + 6 = \_\_\_$

$8 + \_\_\_ = 15$

$8 + 8 = \_\_\_$

$8 + \_\_\_ = \_\_\_$

$8 + 10 = \_\_\_$

_____

_____

_____

_____

8. Reasoning Lucy is sorting items by their texture. She finds 6 items that are bumpy. Lucy finds 5 items that are smooth. How many items does Lucy find in all?

_____ items

9. A-Z Vocabulary Look at the **equation** below. Circle the **addends**. Draw a square around the **sum**.

$$9 \: + \: 5 \: = \: 14$$

10. Higher Order Thinking Write 8 addition facts that have a sum of 12. How can patterns help you?

_____

_____

_____

_____

11. ⓘAssessment Which have a sum of 17? Choose all that apply.

☐ $10 + 7 = ?$

☐ $7 + 6 = ?$

☐ $9 + 8 = ?$

☐ $8 + 8 = ?$

Think about fact patterns.

© Pearson Education, Inc. 2

Name _____

Help   Tools   Games

Homework & Practice 1-4

Addition Fact Patterns

Another Look! You can use your addition table to find the addition facts that have 7 as an addend.

Find the 7 in the top row of the table.
Write an equation for each sum in that column.

+	0	1	2	3	4	5	6	7	8	9	10
0	0	1	2	3	4	5	6	7	8	9	10
1	1	2	3	4	5	6	7	8	9	10	11
2	2	3	4	5	6	7	8	9	10	11	12
3	3	4	5	6	7	8	9	10	11	12	13
4	4	5	6	7	8	9	10	11	12	13	14
5	5	6	7	8	9	10	11	12	13	14	15
6	6	7	8	9	10	11	12	13	14	15	16
7	7	8	9	10	11	12	13	14	15	16	17
8	8	9	10	11	12	13	14	15	16	17	18
9	9	10	11	12	13	14	15	16	17	18	19
10	10	11	12	13	14	15	16	17	18	19	20

$0 + 7 = 7$ $5 + 7 = 12$

$1 + 7 = 8$ $6 + 7 = 13$

$2 + 7 = 9$ $7 + 7 = 14$

$3 + 7 = 10$ $8 + 7 = 15$

$4 + 7 = 11$ $9 + 7 = 16$

$10 + 7 = 17$

You can add in any order. So, complete the list by switching the order of the addends.

HOME ACTIVITY Have your child practice using an addition facts table by asking your child to write an equation for each sum that is 16.

Use fact patterns to complete each equation.

1. $9 + 6 =$ _____

_____ $+ 7 = 15$

$7 +$ _____ $= 15$

$6 +$ _____ $= 15$

2. $0 +$ _____ $= 4$

$1 + 3 =$ _____

_____ $+ 2 = 4$

$3 +$ _____ $= 4$

_____ $+ 4 = 4$

3. $5 +$ _____ $= 6$

$4 +$ _____ $= 6$

$3 + 3 =$ _____

_____ $+ 4 = 6$

_____ $+ 5 = 6$

Look for Patterns Use fact patterns to complete each equation.

4. $10 + \underline{\hspace{1cm}} = 11$ $5 + \underline{\hspace{1cm}} = 11$ 5. $9 + 9 = \underline{\hspace{1cm}}$ $\underline{\hspace{1cm}} + 4 = 13$

$\underline{\hspace{1cm}} + 2 = 11$ $4 + \underline{\hspace{1cm}} = 11$ $9 + \underline{\hspace{1cm}} = 17$ $9 + 3 = \underline{\hspace{1cm}}$

$8 + 3 = \underline{\hspace{1cm}}$ $3 + \underline{\hspace{1cm}} = 11$ $\underline{\hspace{1cm}} + 7 = 16$ $9 + \underline{\hspace{1cm}} = 11$

$7 + \underline{\hspace{1cm}} = 11$ $\underline{\hspace{1cm}} + 2 = 11$ $9 + 6 = \underline{\hspace{1cm}}$ $\underline{\hspace{1cm}} + 1 = 10$

$\underline{\hspace{1cm}} + 5 = 11$ $1 + 10 = \underline{\hspace{1cm}}$ $9 + \underline{\hspace{1cm}} = 14$ $9 + 0 = \underline{\hspace{1cm}}$

$0 + \underline{\hspace{1cm}} = 11$

6. **Higher Order Thinking** Write 8 equations with 2 addends that have a sum of 13. Use patterns to help you.

_____

_____

_____

7. ⬤**Assessment** Which have a sum of 19? Choose all that apply.

☐ $10 + 9 = ?$

☐ $8 + 8 = ?$

☐ $9 + 9 = ?$

☐ $9 + 10 = ?$

8. ⬤**Assessment** Which have a sum of 15? Choose all that apply.

☐ $7 + 8 = ?$

☐ $8 + 7 = ?$

☐ $9 + 6 = ?$

☐ $5 + 10 = ?$

Name _____

Solve & Share

How can counting help you find $12 - 4$?
Use the number line to show your work.

I can ...
count on and count back on a number line to subtract.

Content Standard 2.CA.1
Process Standards PS.1, PS.2, PS.4, PS.5

$$12 - 4 = \underline{\qquad}$$

Find 10 − 4.

Start with the lesser number.

Count on to 10 to find the **difference**.

4, _5_, _6_, _7_, _8_, _9_, _10_

It takes 6 moves to count on from 4 to 10.

So, 10 − 4 = 6.

You can also count back to subtract.

Start with the greater number.

Count back 4 moves.

10, _9_, _8_, _7_, _6_

You land on 6. So, 10 − 4 = 6.

Do You Understand?

Show Me! How can you count back on a number line to find 9 − 5?

☆ **Guided Practice** ☆ Count on or count back to subtract. Show your work on the number line.

1. 11 − 4 = [7]

2. 14 − 7 = [ ]

Tools Assessment

Independent Practice ☆ Count on or count back to subtract. Show your work on the number line.

3. $14 - 8 =$ ☐

4. $12 - 7 =$ ☐

5. $9 - 7 =$ ☐

6. $15 - 6 =$ ☐

7. **Higher Order Thinking** How can you count on to find $13 - 4$? Explain.

_____

_____

_____

8. Callie had 8 seeds.
She planted 2 of the seeds.
How many seeds does
Callie have now?

_____ seeds

9. Make Sense Peter has 16 grapes.
He eats some of the grapes. Peter has
10 grapes left. How many grapes did
Peter eat?

$$16 - \underline{\quad} = 10$$

_____ grapes

10. Higher Order Thinking Choose
2 numbers. Use the numbers to write
or draw a subtraction story. Write the
equation you used to solve your story.

_____ − _____ = _____

11. **Assessment** Jake is playing with
6 marbles. He gives 3 marbles to Sam.
How many marbles does Jake have now?

Use the numbers on the cards to show
how to count on to solve the problem.

| 6 | 3 | 5 | 4 |

Begin with ☐ . Then count on ☐ ,

☐ , ☐ .

Jake has _____ marbles now.

Name _____

Another Look! You can use a number line to count back to subtract.

Find 12 − 5.

Draw jumps on the number line as you count back!

0 1 2 3 4 5 6 7 8 9 10 11 12 13 14 15

Start at 12 on the line. Count back 5 moves.

11, 10, 9, 8, 7

So, 12 − 5 = __7__.

HOME ACTIVITY Draw a number line from 0 to 15. Have your child show you how to count back from 15 to find 15 − 6 on the line. Then have your child write an equation that includes 9 as the difference.

Count on or count back to subtract. Show your work on the number line.

1. 6 − 4 = ☐

0 1 2 3 4 5 6 7 8 9 10 11 12 13 14 15

2. 13 − 8 = ☐

0 1 2 3 4 5 6 7 8 9 10 11 12 13 14 15

3. **Model** Marta has 15 dinner plates.
   She uses 9 of them for a party.
   How many of Marta's plates are not used?
   Count on or count back to solve.

   _____ dinner plates

4. **Higher Order Thinking** Complete the squares so that the differences
   shown on the outside are correct.

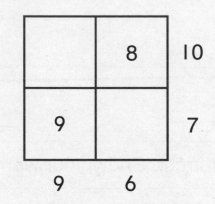

5. 🅓**Assessment** Pat has 12 flowers in his garden.
   4 flowers are pink and the rest are red.
   How many flowers are red?

   Use the numbers on the cards to show how to
   count back to solve the problem.

   | 10 | 12 | 8 | 9 |

   Begin with [   ]. Then count back 11, [   ], [   ], [   ].

   _____ flowers are red.

Name _____

Solve & Share

How can you use an addition fact to find 14 − 6? Use counters to help show how.

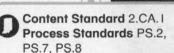

I can …
use addition to help me subtract quickly and accurately.

Content Standard 2.CA.1
Process Standards PS.2, PS.7, PS.8

_____ + _____ = _____

So, 14 − 6 = _____.

Find 15 − 7.

One way to subtract is to think about addition.

To find 15 − 7, you can think:

7 plus how many more is 15?
or
7 + ___ = 15

The missing number is the same in both equations.

7 + ___ = 15

15 − 7 = ___

You know the addition fact.

7 + _8_ = 15

You also know the subtraction fact.

15 − 7 = _8_

Do You Understand?

Show Me! How do you know which addition fact to use to complete the subtraction fact?

☆ Guided Practice   Think addition to help you subtract.

1. 6 − 4 = ?

    4 + _2_ = 6

    So, 6 − 4 = _2_.

2. 9 − 3 = ?

    3 + ___ = 9

    So, 9 − 3 = ___.

3. 14 − 5 = ?

    5 + ___ = 14

    So, 14 − 5 = ___.

4. 12 − 4 = ?

    4 + ___ = 12

    So, 12 − 4 = ___.

Tools   Assessment

Independent Practice ☆ Subtract. Write the addition fact that can help you.

5. 8 − 1 = _____

1 + _____ = 8

6. 10 − 2 = _____

2 + _____ = 10

7. 15 − 6 = _____

6 + _____ = 15

8. 17 − 7 = _____

7 + _____ = 17

9. 14 − 8 = _____

8 + _____ = 14

10. 9 − 5 = _____

5 + _____ = 9

11.

```
  18          8
− 8        + ☐
────       ────
 ☐          18
```

12.

```
  16          9
− 9        + ☐
────       ────
 ☐          16
```

13.

```
  19          9
− 9        + ☐
────       ────
 ☐          19
```

Higher Order Thinking Write a related addition fact to complete the subtraction fact.

14. 11 − _____ = 5

_____ + _____ = _____

15. 7 − _____ = 2

_____ + _____ = _____

16. 12 − _____ = 8

_____ + _____ = _____

17. Reasoning Kate had 6 pens.
She got 5 more pens from John.
How many pens does
Kate have in all?

_____ + _____ = _____

_____ pens

18. Reasoning John had 11 pens.
He gave 5 pens to Kate.
How many pens does
John have now?

_____ − _____ = _____

_____ pens

19. Higher Order Thinking Write a
subtraction story using the numbers
18 and 10. Then write an addition fact
that can help you solve the problem in
your story.

_____

_____

_____

_____

_____

_____ + _____ = _____

20. ⬤ **Assessment** Pam has 16 cherries.
She eats 7 cherries.
Which addition fact can help you
find how many cherries Pam has left?

$7 + 4 = 11$ $7 + 9 = 16$
        Ⓐ   Ⓒ

$7 + 6 = 13$ $9 + 9 = 18$
        Ⓑ   Ⓓ

Name _____

Another Look! Addition facts can help you subtract.
Use the pictures to find the missing numbers.

Addition Fact

Think $6 + \underline{8} = 14$.

Subtraction Fact

So, $14 - 6 = \underline{8}$.

HOME ACTIVITY Make up problems during daily activities such as, "If I have 12 eggs and I use 3 of them, how many eggs do I have left?" Have your child write and solve the subtraction sentence using addition facts.

Addition facts can help you subtract.
Use the pictures to find the missing numbers.

1.

Think $9 + \underline{} = 13$.

So, $13 - 9 = \underline{}$.

2.

Think $8 + \underline{} = 17$.

So, $17 - 8 = \underline{}$.

Higher Order Thinking Circle the addition fact that will help you subtract. Write an equation to solve each problem.

3. Lucy had 12 books. She gave 3 books to Michael. How many books does Lucy have now?

3 + 12

3 + 9

6 + 6

_____ − _____ = _____

_____ books

4. Pam has 20 marbles. She puts 10 marbles in a jar. How many marbles are **NOT** in the jar?

20 + 10

9 + 9

10 + 10

_____ − _____ = _____

_____ marbles

Think about the parts and the whole.

5. **Generalize** Subtract. Write the addition fact that can help you.

19 − 9 = _____

9 + _____ = 19

How do addition facts help you subtract?

_____

_____

_____

6. **Assessment** Maria has 11 rings. She loses 3 rings. Which addition fact can help you find how many rings Maria has left?

3 + 1 = 4
Ⓐ

3 + 8 = 11
Ⓑ

6 + 5 = 11
Ⓒ

2 + 9 = 11
Ⓓ

© Pearson Education, Inc. 2

Topic 1 | Lesson 6

Solve & Share

Name _____

14 ladybugs are on a leaf. 6 ladybugs fly away. How can thinking about 10 help you find how many ladybugs are left? Explain.

I can ...
make a 10 to help me subtract quickly and accurately.

Content Standard 2.CA.1
Process Standards PS.3, PS.4, PS.5, PS.7, PS.8

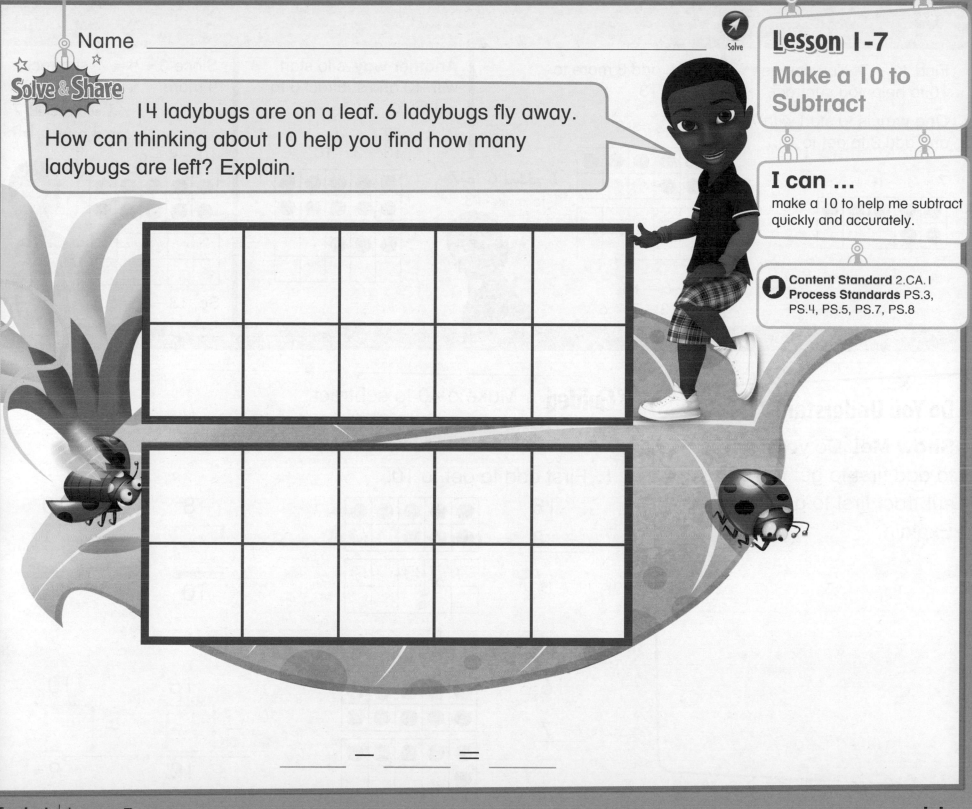

_____ − _____ = _____

Find 13 − 7. You can use 10 to help you subtract.

One way is to start with 7 and add 3 to get to 10.

$7 + 3 = 10$

Next, add 3 more to make 13.

$10 + 3 = 13$

$7 + 6 = 13$,
so $13 − 7 = 6$.

I added 6 to 7 to make 13.

Another way is to start with 13 and subtract 3 to get to 10.

$13 − 3 = 10$

Since $3 + 4 = 7$, subtract 4 more.

$10 − 4 = 6$

So, $13 − 7 = 6$.

I subtracted 7 and have 6 left.

Do You Understand?

Show Me! Do you prefer to add first to get to 10 or subtract first to get to 10? Explain.

☆ **Guided Practice** ☆ Make a 10 to subtract. Use counters and your workmat.

1. First add to get to 10.

$$\begin{array}{r} 15 \\ -8 \\ \hline 7 \end{array}$$

$$\begin{array}{r} 8 \\ +\boxed{2} \\ \hline 10 \end{array} \qquad \begin{array}{r} 10 \\ +\boxed{5} \\ \hline 15 \end{array}$$

2. First subtract to get to 10.

$$\begin{array}{r} 16 \\ -7 \end{array}$$

$$\begin{array}{r} 16 \\ -\boxed{} \\ \hline 10 \end{array} \qquad \begin{array}{r} 10 \\ -\boxed{} \\ \hline 9 \end{array}$$

Independent Practice ☆ Make a 10 to subtract. Use counters and your workmat.

3. 11
    − 4
    ____

4. 14
    − 8
    ____

5. 12
    − 7
    ____

6. 12
    − 4
    ____

> Think of the ways you know to make 10.

7. 18
    − 9
    ____

8. 17
    − 8
    ____

9. 16
    − 8
    ____

10. 13
     − 4
     ____

11. 15
     − 9
     ____

12. 14
     − 7
     ____

13. 12
     − 8
     ____

14. 16
     − 9
     ____

15. **Higher Order Thinking** Carol subtracts
    6 from 15. First, she adds to get to 10.
    Then she adds again to find her answer.
    Her answer is 10. Is Carol correct?
    Explain.

    _____

    _____

    _____

    _____

16. **Use Tools** Chen had 12 animal stickers. He gave 5 of the stickers away. How many animal stickers does Chen have now?

_____ animal stickers

17. **Use Tools** Angie bought 13 strawberries. She ate 8 of the strawberries. How many strawberries does Angie have now?

_____ strawberries

18. **Higher Order Thinking** Show how you can make a 10 to find 17 − 9.

19. **Assessment** Use the ten-frames. Show how to make a 10 to find 15 − 9. Start by subtracting to get to 10. Then complete the equations.

15 − _____ = 10

10 − _____ = _____

© Pearson Education, Inc. 2

Name _____

Another Look! You can make a 10 to help you subtract. Find 13 − 5.

One way

Subtract 13 − 3 to make a 10.
Subtract 2 more to subtract 5 in all.

$10 - 2 = 8$

You have 8 left. So, 13 − 5 = 8.

Another way

Add 5 + 5 to make a 10.
Add 3 more to make 13.

$10 + 3 = 13$

You added 5 + 8 = 13. So, 13 − 5 = 8.

HOME ACTIVITY Have your child use 12 small objects to explain how to find 12 − 8 by first subtracting to get 10.

Use the ten-frames to subtract. Think about the parts and the whole.

1. $11 - 7 = $ _____

2. $14 - 6 = $ _____

3. $12 - 5 = $ _____

Higher Order Thinking For each problem, pick a bin from each row. Subtract to find how many more bottles are in the bin from the top row than the bin from the bottom row.

4. Bin _____ has _____ more bottles than Bin _____.

5. Bin _____ has _____ more bottles than Bin _____.

6. Bin _____ has _____ more bottles than Bin _____.

7. Bin _____ has _____ more bottles than Bin _____.

8. **Model** Write two subtraction equations to show how to find $15 - 7$.

_____ $-$ _____ $=$ _____

_____ $-$ _____ $=$ _____

9. **⬤ Assessment** Which equations show you how to find $16 - 9$?

Ⓐ $9 + 1 = 10$, $10 + 5 = 15$

Ⓑ $9 + 1 = 10$, $10 + 6 = 16$

Ⓒ $9 + 2 = 11$, $11 + 6 = 17$

Ⓓ $9 + 1 = 10$, $10 + 9 = 19$

Solve & Share

Write four related facts that use both the numbers 7 and 9 as quickly as you can. Hold up your hand when you are done. Then, tell how you found each fact.

Solve

Lesson 1-8
Practice Addition and Subtraction Facts

I can ...

add and subtract quickly and accurately using mental math strategies.

Content Standard 2.CA.1
Process Standards PS.2, PS.3, PS.4, PS.8

___ + ___ = ___ | ___ − ___ = ___

___ + ___ = ___ | ___ − ___ = ___

Practice your basic facts to recall them quickly.

Find $7 - 4$.

Think of strategies to help you practice the facts.

One way to subtract is to think about addition.

$$4 + \boxed{3} = 7$$

So, $7 - 4 = \boxed{3}$.

Knowing doubles facts can help, too! Find $4 + 5$.

$4 + 4$ and 1.

$$4 + 5 = \boxed{9}$$

Practicing my basic facts will help me remember the facts quickly. Then my math problems will be easier.

Do You Understand?

Show Me! How can thinking about 10 help you find $14 - 8$?

⭐ Guided Practice   Add or subtract. Use any strategy.

1. $\begin{array}{r} 14 \\ -\ 9 \\ \hline 5 \end{array}$

2. $\begin{array}{r} 17 \\ -\ 9 \\ \hline \end{array}$

3. $\begin{array}{r} 5 \\ +\ 7 \\ \hline \end{array}$

4. $\begin{array}{r} 10 \\ -\ 5 \\ \hline \end{array}$

5. $\begin{array}{r} 6 \\ -\ 0 \\ \hline \end{array}$

6. $\begin{array}{r} 9 \\ +\ 9 \\ \hline \end{array}$

7. $\begin{array}{r} 12 \\ -\ 4 \\ \hline \end{array}$

8. $\begin{array}{r} 10 \\ +\ 10 \\ \hline \end{array}$

9. $\begin{array}{r} 11 \\ -\ 4 \\ \hline \end{array}$

10. $\begin{array}{r} 9 \\ +\ 1 \\ \hline \end{array}$

11. $\begin{array}{r} 8 \\ +\ 0 \\ \hline \end{array}$

12. $\begin{array}{r} 16 \\ -\ 8 \\ \hline \end{array}$

© Pearson Education, Inc. 2

Name _____

Independent Practice ☆ Add or subtract. Use any strategy.

13. $14 - 7 =$ _____

14. $3 + 0 =$ _____

15. $8 + 7 =$ _____

16. $13 - 6 =$ _____

17. $10 + 9 =$ _____

18. $17 - 8 =$ _____

19. $18 - 9 =$ _____

20. $9 - 1 =$ _____

21. $7 + 4 =$ _____

22. $6 + 6 =$ _____

23. $16 - 9 =$ _____

24. $20 - 10 =$ _____

25. $16 - 7 =$ _____

26. $15 - 8 =$ _____

27. $7 + 3 =$ _____

28. $2 + 7 =$ _____

29. $9 + 6 =$ _____

30. $10 - 2 =$ _____

Higher Order Thinking Write the missing number.

31. $6 + \boxed{} = 14 - 5$

32. $12 - 4 = \boxed{} + 2$

33. $14 - \boxed{} = 5 + 4$

34. Math and Science Danielle had 17 pieces of paper. She changed 8 of the pieces by cutting them. How many pieces were not changed? Write an equation to solve.

_____ ◯ _____ = _____

_____ pieces of paper

35. Model Diego saw 5 frogs on a rock. He also saw 7 frogs in the grass. How many frogs did Diego see in all? Write an equation to solve.

_____ ◯ _____ = _____

_____ frogs

36. Higher Order Thinking Glen counts on to solve $9 + \boxed{} = 14$. Explain how he can do this. What is the missing addend?

_____

_____

_____

_____

_____

_____

37. ◐ Assessment Deshawn had some shells. He gave 3 shells to his brother. Now Deshawn has 8 shells. How many shells did Deshawn have to begin with? Solve. Explain your solution.

Which operation will you use to solve this problem?

_____

_____

_____

Name _____

Another Look! You can use strategies to help you practice addition and subtraction facts.

Find 12 − 7.

You can think about the relationship between addition and subtraction and use related facts.

12

7 plus how many more is 12?

or

7 + __5__ = 12

So, 12 − 7 = 5.

HOME ACTIVITY Give your child the following numbers: 5, 6, and 11. Tell your child to write the fact family for these numbers as quickly as he or she can.

Add or subtract. Use any strategy.

1.	2.	3.	4.	5.	6.
11 − 5 6	12 − 6	7 + 6	2 + 1	12 − 3	8 + 8

7. $9 - 3 =$ _____ | **8.** $10 + 9 =$ _____ | **9.** $10 - 1 =$ _____

Higher Order Thinking Fill in the missing numbers so that the sums on the outside are correct.

10.

	3	11
0		3
8	6	

11.

6		10
	9	18
15		

12.

	7	12
8		17
13	16	

13.

6		14
	10	18
	18	

14. Explain What addition doubles fact can help you find $4 + 3$? Explain how you know.

_____

_____

_____

15. ⬤ Assessment Write an addition equation that can help you find $9 - 6$. Explain your answer.

_____

_____

_____

© Pearson Education, Inc. 2

Solve & Share

Diego has 6 apples. Leslie has 9 apples.
How many more apples does Leslie have than Diego?

Will you add or subtract to solve this problem? Explain.

Lesson 1-9

Solve Addition and Subtraction Word Problems

I can ...
use addition and subtraction to solve word problems.

Content Standards 2.CA.2, 2.CA.1
Process Standards PS.1, PS.2, PS.6

add   subtract   ____ ◯ ____ ◯ ____

Leslie has ____ more apples than Diego.

17 books are on a table. 8 books are on a shelf. How many fewer books are on the shelf than on the table?

You can use a bar diagram and an equation to model the problem.

The shelf has fewer books.

books on table

17

8	?

books on shelf   fewer books on shelf

You can write an addition or subtraction equation for the problem.

$17 - 8 = \underline{9}$

$8 + \underline{9} = 17$

17

8	9

So, there are 9 fewer books on the shelf.

Do You Understand?

Show Me! Why can you use addition OR subtraction to solve the problem above?

☆ **Guided Practice** ☆ Write an equation to solve each problem. Use counters, if needed.

1. Sam has 5 red tomatoes and 3 green tomatoes. How many tomatoes does he have in all?

   $\underline{5} \; \bigoplus \; \underline{3} \; \bigodot \; \underline{8}$ $\underline{8}$ tomatoes

2. There are 16 party hats in a box. There are 10 party hats in a bag. How many fewer hats are in the bag than in the box?

   $\underline{} \; \bigcirc \; \underline{} \; \bigcirc \; \underline{}$ $\underline{}$ fewer hats

Independent Practice Write an equation to solve each problem.
Use counters, if needed.

3. Cho has 3 more toy horses than Hakeem.
   Cho has 9 toy horses.
   How many toy horses does Hakeem have?

   ____ ◯ ____ ◯ ____

   ____ toy horses

4. There are 12 peaches in a bowl.
   The children eat some of them.
   Now there are 8 peaches.
   How many peaches did the children eat?

   ____ ◯ ____ ◯ ____

   ____ peaches were eaten.

5. Juan reads 5 books.
   Susan reads some books.
   They read 11 books in all.
   How many books did Susan read?

   ____ ◯ ____ ◯ ____

   ____ books

6. Jack has 13 brushes.
   Igor has 6 brushes.
   How many fewer brushes
   does Igor have than Jack?

   ____ ◯ ____ ◯ ____

   ____ fewer brushes

7. **Number Sense** Jen had 3 animal
   stickers in her collection. Her friend gave her
   5 more stickers. Jen bought 7 more stickers.
   How many stickers does Jen have now?
   Show your work.

Problem Solving

8. **Higher Order Thinking** Sandy has 8 markers.
Alex has 6 fewer markers than Sandy.
Jill has 2 markers.
How many markers do they have in all?

Show your work. Then explain how you found the answer.

_____

_____

_____

Use counters to solve.

9. **Make Sense** Annika saves 13 dimes.
She put some of the dimes in a box and the rest in a jar.

Write an equation to show one way she could have sorted the dimes.

____ ◯ ____ ◯ ____

____ dimes in a jar

____ dimes in a box

10. **◑ Assessment** Maria had 5 rings.
She bought some more rings. Now she has 12 rings.

Choose Yes or No to show if the equation can be used to find how many more rings Maria bought.

$12 - 5 = 7$	◯ Yes	◯ No
$10 + 2 = 12$	◯ Yes	◯ No
$5 + 7 = 12$	◯ Yes	◯ No
$12 - 8 = 4$	◯ Yes	◯ No

© Pearson Education, Inc. 2

Name _____

Another Look! You can use counters to solve this problem.

Francine has made 9 wristbands. Jon has made 5 wristbands. How many more wristbands has Francine made than Jon?

You can use an addition or subtraction strategy to help solve the problem.

Compare blue and red wristbands. Count on from 5 and add to find how many more wristbands Francine made.

$5 + 4 = 9$

You can also subtract. $9 - 5 = 4$

HOME ACTIVITY Make up addition and subtraction word problems. Ask your child to use small objects such as paper clips or pennies to add or subtract to solve the problems. For each problem, have your child write an equation to show how to solve it.

Write an equation to solve each problem. Use counters, if needed.

1. 6 bugs are on a leaf.
   2 bugs join them.
   How many bugs are there in all?

   _____ bugs

2. There are 13 baseballs in a box.
   There are 8 baseballs in a bag.
   How many more baseballs are in a box?

   _____ more baseballs

3. **Be Precise** Devin brought his snail collection to school. He has 10 snails.
How could he put them into 2 tanks so two classes could see them?

Write equations for all the possible ways.
One of the ways is given.

Explain how you know you have found all the ways.

$$10 = 9 + 1$$

_____

_____

_____

Write equations to solve the problem. Use counters, if needed.

4. **Higher Order Thinking** Pat has 9 cards.
Frank has 2 more cards than Steve.
Steve has 3 cards.
How many more cards does Pat have than Frank?

Cards Frank has: ____ ◯ ____ ◯ ____

More cards Pat has than Frank:

Pat has ____ more cards than Frank.

5. **Ⓓ Assessment** Jan has 10 dolls.
Kat has 7 dolls. Choose Yes or No to show if the equation can be used to find how many fewer dolls Kat has than Jan.

$10 - 7 = 3$	◯ Yes	◯ No
$3 + 7 = 10$	◯ Yes	◯ No
$10 + 7 = 17$	◯ Yes	◯ No
$7 + 3 = 10$	◯ Yes	◯ No

© Pearson Education, Inc. 2

Name _____

Solve & Share

How can you use the **make a 10** strategy to find $7 + 9$?

Explain your thinking and work.
Use pictures, numbers, or words.

I can ...
use pictures, numbers, and words to explain why my thinking and work are correct.

Process Standards PS.3 Also PS.1, PS.2, PS.4
Content Standards 2.CA.2, 2.CA.1

Thinking Habits
How can I use math to explain why my work is correct?

Is my explanation clear?

_____

_____

_____

_____

Does 1 more than 6 + 6 have the same sum as 6 + 7?

Make a math argument.

How can I make a math argument and show my work?

I can use pictures, words, or numbers to make a math argument and to show my work.

I can draw pictures and write equations.

6 + 6 = 12

⬤⬤⬤⬤⬤⬤
⬤⬤⬤⬤⬤⬤

6 + 6 + 1 = 6 + 7

⬤⬤⬤⬤⬤
⬤⬤⬤⬤⬤◯

6 + 6 + 1 = 13

6 + 7 = 13

Or I can use words and numbers to make my math argument. My argument is clear and makes sense.

6 + 7 is just one more than 6 + 6.
1 more than 6 + 6 equals
13 and 6 + 7 equals 13.

Do You Understand?

Show Me! Are both math arguments above clear and complete? Explain.

☆ **Guided Practice** ☆ Use the picture to help you solve the problem. Then use words and numbers to make a math argument.

1. Is the sum of 9 + 5 the same as the sum of 10 + 4?

© Pearson Education, Inc. 2

Independent Practice   Solve each problem. Use words, pictures, and numbers to make a math argument.

2. Lynn had 14 grapes. She ate 8 of them. She wants to eat 6 more grapes. Will Lynn have enough grapes? Explain.

3. The Lions scored 11 runs in a baseball game. The Tigers scored 7 runs. Did the Tigers score 3 fewer runs than the Lions? Explain.

4. Complete the explanation below for how to find $8 + 9$. Use pictures, words, or numbers to complete the explanation.

I know that $8 + 8 = 16$

Puppies Sold

The Sunset Pet Store sells puppies. The table shows how many puppies were sold Monday through Thursday.

Is the total number of puppies sold on Tuesday and Wednesday less than the number of puppies sold on Monday?

Number of Puppies Sold			
Monday	Tuesday	Wednesday	Thursday
16	10	7	15

5. **Make Sense** Will you use all the numbers in the table to solve the problem? Explain.

_____

_____

6. **Model** Write an equation to find the total number of puppies sold on Tuesday and Wednesday. Solve.

_____

_____

_____

7. **Explain** Solve the problem. Use words, pictures, and numbers to explain your work and thinking.

Another Look! Tamra has 8 animal books and 4 sports books. Will she be able to give away 9 of her books?

Solve and explain your work and thinking.

You can use words, pictures, and numbers when you explain.

You can also write 8 + 4 = 12 and 12 − 9 = 3. These equations show that Tamara can give away 9 books.

8 animal books   4 sports books

Yes, Tamara can give away 9 of her books.

HOME ACTIVITY Tell your child this story: "Omar has 3 green stickers and 8 blue stickers. If he gives away 5 of these stickers, will Omar have 6 stickers left?" Have your child solve the problem and explain his or her thinking using words, pictures, and numbers.

Solve each problem. Use words, pictures, or numbers to make a math argument.

1. Alan has 17 stickers. He wants to give 6 stickers to Jean and 7 stickers to Matt. How many stickers will Alan give away? Explain.

2. Tasha has 12 minutes. She wants to jump rope for 8 minutes and play tag for 5 minutes. Will Tasha have enough time? Explain.

T-shirts

The number of T-shirts that four students own is given in the table.

Are there three students who have a total of 20 T-shirts? If so, which students are they?

Number of T-Shirts			
Will	Mandy	Greg	Cindy
4	7	12	9

3. **Make Sense** What operation will you use to solve the problem? Explain.

_____

_____

_____

4. **Reasoning** How will you go about solving the problem? Explain.

_____

_____

_____

5. **Explain** Solve the problem. Use words, pictures, and numbers to explain your work and thinking.

Find a Match

Find a partner. Point to a clue. Read the clue.

Look below the clues to find a match. Write the clue letter in the box next to the match.

Find a match for every clue.

I can ...
add and subtract within 20.

Clues

A Near doubles with sums near 8

B Every difference is 6.

C Ways to make 12

D Exactly two differences equal 9.

E Every sum is greater than 14.

F Exactly three differences are equal.

G Near doubles with sums near 6

H Every difference equals $14-7$.

$5 + 7$ $6 + 6$ $8 + 4$ $9 + 3$	$10 - 5$ $11 - 7$ $12 - 7$ $13 - 8$

$11 - 5$ $10 - 4$ $12 - 6$ $9 - 3$	$4 + 3$ $3 + 2$ $2 + 3$ $3 + 4$

$13 - 3$ $9 - 0$ $14 - 6$ $16 - 7$	$3 + 4$ $5 + 4$ $4 + 3$ $4 + 5$

$8 + 9$ $7 + 8$ $8 + 7$ $6 + 9$	$9 - 2$ $13 - 6$ $8 - 1$ $15 - 8$

Glossary

Word List
- addend
- difference
- doubles
- equation
- near doubles
- sum

Understand Vocabulary

1. Circle a doubles fact.

$$7 + 7 = 14$$

$$6 + 7 = 13$$

$$7 + 0 = 7$$

2. Circle a near doubles fact.

$$4 + 4 = 8$$

$$4 + 1 = 5$$

$$4 + 5 = 9$$

3. Write a subtraction equation using numbers and symbols.

_____

4. Find the sum of $8 + 6$.

_____

5. Find the difference of $12 - 5$.

_____

Use Vocabulary in Writing

6. Describe how you can make a 10 to add $7 + 4$. Use a term from the Word List.

_____

_____

_____

_____

Name _____

Set A

You can count on to find a sum.

4 5 6

2 3 4 5 6

4 + 2 = 6

2 + 4 = 6

4 + 2 = 2 + 4

I can add numbers in any order and get the same sum.

Count on to find the sum. Then change the order of the addends.

1. 9 + 3 = ____

____ + ____ = ____

9 + 3 = ____ + ____

2. 6 + 4 = ____

____ + ____ = ____

6 + 4 = ____ + ____

Set B

You can use doubles to help you add a near double.

4 + 4 = 8

So, 3 + 4 = 7.

3 + 4 is one less than 4 + 4.

So, 3 + 4 = 7.

Complete the doubles facts. Use the doubles facts to solve the near doubles.

3. 8 + 8 = ____

So, 7 + 8 = ____.

4. 5 + 5 = ____

So, 6 + 5 = ____.

You can make a 10 to help you add 8 + 6.

8 + 6 = ?

$10 + \underline{4} = \underline{14}$

So, $8 + 6 = \underline{14}$.

Make a 10 to add.

5. 8 + 4 = ?

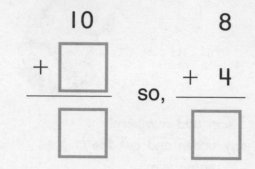

10   8

$+ \square$ so, $+ \ 4$

$\square$ $\square$

You can count on or count back to find 11 − 4.

Start at 4 and count on 7 places to 11.

4, 5, 6, 7, 8, 9, 10, 11   So, 11 − 4 = 7.

Start at 11 and count back 4 places to get to 7.

11, 10, 9, 8, 7   So, $11 - 4 = \underline{7}$.

Count on or count back to subtract. Show your work on the number line.

6. $8 - 5 = \square$

7. $15 - 6 = \square$

Name _____

Set E _____

You can think addition to help you subtract.

Find: $16 - 9 = ?$

Think: $9 + \underline{7} = 16$

So, $16 - 9 = \underline{7}$

Subtract. Write the addition fact that helped you.

8. $13 - 7 = \underline{\hphantom{xx}}$

  $7 + \underline{\hphantom{xx}} = 13$

9. $17 - 9 = \underline{\hphantom{xx}}$

  $9 + \underline{\hphantom{xx}} = 17$

Set F _____

You can make a 10 to subtract.
Find $17 - 8$.

$17 - 7 = 10$

$10 - 1 = 9$

$17 - 8 = \boxed{9}$

Make a 10 to find $13 - 8$.
Draw counters to show your work.

10.

$13 - \underline{\hphantom{xx}} = 10$

$10 - \underline{\hphantom{xx}} = \underline{\hphantom{xx}}$

$13 - 8 = \underline{\hphantom{xx}}$

You can use addition or subtraction to solve word problems.

11 grapes are in a bowl.
9 grapes are in a cup.
How many fewer grapes are in the cup?

$$11 - 9 = 2 \qquad 9 + 2 = 11$$

So, 2 fewer grapes are in the cup.

Write an equation to solve each problem.

11. 13 shirts are in a closet.
8 shirts are in a box.
How many more shirts are in the closet?

_____ ◯ _____ ◯ _____ more shirts

12. Drake has 10 more books than Yuri.
Yuri has 10 books.
How many books does Drake have?

_____ ◯ _____ ◯ _____ books

Thinking Habits

Construct Arguments

How can I use math to explain why my work is correct?

Did I use the correct numbers and symbols?

Solve. Use words, pictures, or numbers to construct arguments.

13. Tyler read 15 pages of a book.
Ann read 9 pages of the same book.
Did Tyler read 4 more pages than Ann? Explain.

Name _____

1. Tom draws 7 bugs. Gina draws 4 bugs. How many bugs did they draw in all?

   Which shows how to *count on* to solve the problem?

   Ⓐ 7, 8, 9, 10, 11

   Ⓑ 4, 5, 6, 7

   Ⓒ 7 + 4

   Ⓓ 4 + 7

2. Lilly has 7 fish. Jack has 1 more fish than Lilly.

   Which equations show how many fish in all? Choose all that apply.

   ☐ $7 + 1 = 8$

   ☐ $7 + 7 + 1 = 15$

   ☐ $7 + 7 = 14$

   ☐ $7 + 8 = 15$

3. Use the ten-frames. Show how to find the sum of $8 + 7$ by making a 10. Then fill in the gray boxes.

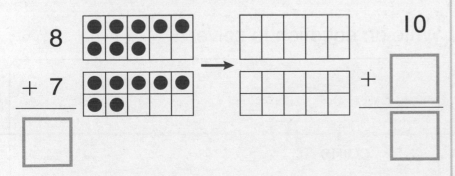

4. Which have a sum of 18? Choose all that apply.

   ☐ $10 + 8$

   ☐ $9 + 8$

   ☐ $9 + 9$

   ☐ $8 + 10$

5. 7 friends go to the movies. They have 4 tickets. How many more tickets do they need?

Draw lines to match each solution to how it was solved.

A. 7, 6, 5, 4   Use an addition
                       fact.

B. 7 − 4 = 3

                       Count back.

C. 4, 5, 6, 7

                       Count on.

D. 4 + 3 = 7

                       Use a subtraction
                       fact.

6. Nita has 14 grapes. She eats 6 grapes.

Which addition fact can help you find how many grapes Nita has left?

Ⓐ   6 + 6 = 12

Ⓑ   6 + 7 = 13

Ⓒ   6 + 8 = 14

Ⓓ   8 + 8 = 16

7. Show how to make a 10 to find 13 − 7. Then complete the equation.

$13 - 7 =$ _____

8. Bruce has some coins.
He gives 4 coins to his brother.
Now Bruce has 9 coins.
How many coins did Bruce have at first?

Write an equation to solve.

_____ ◯ _____ = _____

_____ coins

9. Maria has 4 pears.
She buys some more pears.
Now she has 12 pears.

How many pears does
Maria buy?

Part A
Draw a picture to model
the problem.

Part B
Write an equation to
solve the problem.

_____ $\bigcirc$ _____ = _____

_____ pears

10. The team has 9 players.
Then 2 players quit.
After that, 5 players join the team.

How many players does the team
have now?

Use the numbers on the cards.
Complete both equations to solve the problem.

2	5
7	12

$9 - \boxed{} = \boxed{}$

$7 + \boxed{} = \boxed{}$ $\boxed{}$ players

11. Choose Yes or No to show if 7 will make
each equation true.

$8 + \boxed{} = 16$ ○ Yes ○ No

$7 + \boxed{} = 14$ ○ Yes ○ No

$14 - \boxed{} = 7$ ○ Yes ○ No

$15 - 8 = \boxed{}$ ○ Yes ○ No

12. Matt finds 9 sticks at the park.
Mabel finds 7 sticks.
How many sticks do they find in all?

_____ sticks in all

13. Choose Yes or No to show if 8 will make each equation true.

$$6 + \boxed{} = 14 \qquad 8 + 8 = \boxed{} \qquad 14 - \boxed{} = 6 \qquad 16 - \boxed{} = 8$$

⚪ Yes   ⚪ No   ⚪ Yes   ⚪ No   ⚪ Yes   ⚪ No   ⚪ Yes   ⚪ No

---

14. Josh ate 6 fewer cherries than Gail. Gail ate 15 cherries.

How many cherries did Josh eat?

Part A
Draw a picture to model the problem.

Part B
Write an equation to solve the problem.

_____ ⚪ _____ = _____

_____ cherries

---

15. The table shows how many pictures 3 friends made.

Pictures Made			
	Horses	Cats	Dogs
Brian	9	1	3
Fernando	7	6	2
Laurel	4	0	8

Write an equation to solve the problem.

_____ ⚪ _____ ⚪ _____ = _____

_____ pictures

Choose one of the friends.
Write the name of the friend you choose.

_____

How many pictures did that friend make?

Name _____

Farm Kittens

Many kittens are born each summer at the Sunshine Farm. The table shows the number of kittens born at the farm from June to August.

Number of Kittens Born		
June	July	August
13	8	7

1. During which two months were a total of 20 kittens born?

2. Write an equation to find the total number of kittens born in July and August. Solve.

_____

_____

_____

_____

_____

3. Joy said 5 more kittens were born in June than in August. Do you agree? Circle Yes or No.

Show your work to explain.

Yes   No

4. Use the clues to complete the table below.

- No kittens were born in December, January, and February.

- In March, 6 kittens were born.

- Three kittens were born in April and in September.

- In May, 4 kittens were born.

- Two kittens were born in October and in November.

Kittens Born at the Sunshine Farm		
Season	Months	Number of Kittens Born
Spring	March, April, and May	
Summer	June, July, and August	28
Fall	September, October, and November	
Winter	December, January, and February	

5. Joy says that more kittens were born in the summer than in all other seasons combined. Is she correct? Explain.

_____

_____

_____

_____

_____

_____

6. How many more kittens were born in the spring than in the fall?

Show how to solve the problem with a subtraction equation.

© Pearson Education, Inc. 2

Topic I | Performance Assessment

TOPIC
2

Work with Equal Groups

Essential Questions: How can you show even and odd numbers?
How do arrays relate to repeated addition?

Digital Resources

Solve   Learn   Glossary

Tools   Assessment   Help   Games

Look at these plants and animals!

What plants and animals live in your area?

Wow! Let's do this project and learn more.

Math and Science Project: Plants, Animals, and Arrays

Find Out Make lists of different types of plants and wild animals that you see. Look in your neighborhood or in a nearby park. Look at how the animals and plants come together.

Journal: Make a Book Show what you find out in a book. In your book, also:

- Tell about plants or animals that you see in groups. Look for patterns.

- Make an array of a group of plants and an array of a group of animals.

Name _____

Review What You Know

1. Circle the **addends** in the math below.

$$5 \qquad 8$$
$$\underline{+8} \qquad \underline{-5}$$
$$13 \qquad 3$$

2. Complete the **sum** in the **equation** below.

$$5 + 7 = \underline{\quad}$$

3. Write the **doubles** fact that the model shows.

Near Doubles

4. Find each sum.

$$7 \qquad 4 \qquad 9$$
$$\underline{+6} \qquad \underline{+5} \qquad \underline{+8}$$

Adding in Any Order

5. Change the order of the addends and complete both equations.

$$6 + 8 = \underline{\quad}$$

$$\underline{\quad} + \underline{\quad} = \underline{\quad}$$

Math Story

6. Five brown cows go into the barn. Then 8 black and white cows go into the barn. How many cows are now in the barn?

_____ cows

My Word Cards

Study the words on the front of the card.
Complete the activity on the back.

A-Z
Glossary

even

8 is even.

odd

9 is odd.

array

row

column

bar diagram

15

An _____

is a group of objects set in equal rows and columns that forms a rectangle.

An _____

number cannot be shown as pairs of cubes.

An _____

number can be shown as pairs of cubes.

A model for addition and subtraction that shows the parts and the whole is a

_____.

In an array, objects that are shown up and down are in a

_____.

In an array, objects that are shown across are in a

_____.

Name _____

Solve & Share

Use cubes to make the numbers below. Shade all the numbers that can be shown as two equal groups of cubes.
What do you notice about the numbers you shaded?

I can ...
tell if a group of objects is even or odd.

Content Standards 2.NS.5, 2.CA.1
Process Standards PS.4, PS.5, PS.6, PS.7

1	2	3	4	5	6	7	8	9	10
11	12	13	14	15	16	17	18	19	20

How can you tell if a number is **even** or **odd**?

Use cubes to find out.

8

9

An even number can be shown as two equal parts using cubes.

8 is even.
$4 + 4 = 8$

An odd number cannot be shown as two equal parts using cubes.

9 is odd.
$5 + 4 = 9$

The ones digit tells you if a number is even or odd.

18 is even.
19 is odd.

1	2	3	4	5	6	7	8	9	10
11	12	13	14	15	16	17	18	19	20

Do You Understand?

Show Me! You break apart a tower of cubes to make two equal parts, but there is one cube left over.
Is the number of cubes even or odd? Explain.

Guided Practice Look at the number. Circle even or odd. Then write the equation.

1.

14

odd   (even)

$\underline{7} + \underline{7} = \underline{14}$

2.

19

odd   even

___ + ___ = ___

© Pearson Education, Inc. 2

Name _____

Tools Assessment

☆ **Independent**
☆ **Practice**

Look at the number. Circle even or odd.
Then write the equation. Use cubes to help.

3. 20

odd   even

_____ + _____ = _____

4. 13

odd   even

_____ + _____ = _____

5. 16

odd   even

_____ + _____ = _____

6. 17

odd   even

_____ + _____ = _____

7. 10

odd   even

_____ + _____ = _____

8. 5

odd   even

_____ + _____ = _____

For each number, circle true or false. Then explain your thinking.

9. Higher Order Thinking
Dave says 12 is even.
He says 21 is odd.
True or false?

12
True
or
False

21
True
or
False

_____

_____

_____

Topic 2 | Lesson 1

eighty-three **83**

10. **Model** Gemma fills 2 baskets with 9 berries each. She gives both baskets to Alan. Does Alan have an odd or even number of berries? Draw a picture to solve. Then write an equation.

_____ + _____ = _____

Alan has an _____ number of berries.

11. **Model** Tyrone puts 4 marbles in one jar. He puts 3 marbles in another jar. Does Tyrone have an odd or even number of marbles? Draw a picture to solve. Then write an equation.

_____ + _____ = _____

Tyrone has an _____ number of marbles.

12. **Higher Order Thinking** If you add two odd numbers, will the sum be odd or even? Explain. Use numbers, pictures, or words.

13. ⓘ **Assessment** Use the numbers on the cards below. Write two different addition equations. The sum in each equation needs to be an odd number.

| 3 | 5 | 4 | 2 |

____ + ____ = ____   ____ + ____ = ____

© Pearson Education, Inc. 2

Name _____

Another Look!

An **even** number can be shown as two equal parts using cubes.
An **odd** number cannot be shown as two equal parts using cubes.

There are 6 cubes.
Is 6 an even or odd number?
Draw lines to match the cubes.

 The cubes can be shown as two equal parts.
$3 + 3 = 6$

6 is an ⟨even⟩ number.

There are 7 cubes.
Is 7 an even or odd number?
Draw lines to match the cubes.

 The cubes cannot be shown as two equal parts.
$4 + 3 = 7$

7 is an ⟨odd⟩ number.

HOME ACTIVITY Choose a number from 2 to 20. Have your child tell if it is even or odd. If needed, he or she can use pennies to help solve.

Draw lines to match the cubes.
Then tell if the number is even or odd.

1.

9 is an _____ number.

2.

12 is an _____ number.

3.

15 is an _____ number.

4. 8 is an _____ number.

$4 + \underline{} = 8$

5. 11 is an _____ number.

$6 + \underline{} = 11$

6. 18 is an _____ number.

$\underline{} + 9 = 18$

Number Sense Look at the pictures. Circle the number you will add or subtract.
Then complete the equation.

7. The sum is an **odd** number.

9 or 8

$5 + \underline{} = \underline{}$

8. The difference is an **odd** number.

8 or 9

$15 - \underline{} = \underline{}$

9. The difference is an **even** number.

9 or 10

$19 - \underline{} = \underline{}$

10. **Higher Order Thinking** Shailen is adding three numbers. He gets a sum that is an even number between 10 and 20. Show two addition equations Shailen could have written.

$\underline{} + \underline{} + \underline{} = \underline{}$

$\underline{} + \underline{} + \underline{} = \underline{}$

11. **Assessment** Use the numbers on the cards below. Write two different addition equations. The sum in each equation needs to be an even number.

| 6 | 3 | 8 | 9 |

$\underline{} + \underline{} = \underline{}$ $\underline{} + \underline{} = \underline{}$

Name _____

Solve & Share

Is the sum of $3 + 3$ even or odd?
Circle **odd** or **even**. Explain. You can use cubes.

Write two more equations where the addends are the same. Is the sum even or odd? What patterns do you see? Use cubes to show each equation.

I can …
use different ways to tell if a group of objects shows an even or odd number.

Content Standards 2.NS.5, 2.CA.1
Process Standards PS.2, PS.4, PS.6, PS.7, PS.8

$3 + 3 = $ _____   even   odd

_____ $+$ _____ $=$ _____   even   odd

_____ $+$ _____ $=$ _____   even   odd

What patterns do you see?

4   6

even

3   5

odd

Think about pairs of objects and the shape an even number makes.

If you can count the squares by 2s the number is even.

2   **even**

even

2, 4

The sum of two equal addends equals an even number.

   $3 + 3 = 6$

   $4 + 4 = 8$

The pattern in the sums is to skip count by 2s.

$$1 + 1 = 2$$
$$2 + 2 = 4$$
$$3 + 3 = 6$$
$$4 + 4 = 8$$

What is the next even number after 8?

The next even number is 10.

Do You Understand?

Show Me! Is the number 10 even or odd? Draw a picture to show how you know.

Guided Practice

Write the number for each model. Circle even or odd. Then write the equation.

1.

   _7_   even   (odd)

   $4 + 3 = 7$

2.

   ____   even   odd

   ___ + ___ = ___

Independent Practice   Write the number for each model. Circle even or odd. Then write the equation.

3.

_____   even   odd

____ + ____ = ____

4.

_____   even   odd

____ + ____ = ____

5.

_____   even   odd

____ + ____ = ____

6.

_____   even   odd

____ + ____ = ____

7.

_____   even   odd

____ + ____ = ____

8.

_____   even   odd

____ + ____ = ____

9. Number Sense How many squares are shown? Is this an even or odd amount? Draw a picture that shows how you know. Write an equation for your picture.

10. **Look for Patterns** Equations for the first four even numbers are given. What are the next six even numbers? How do you know?

$$1 + 1 = 2$$
$$2 + 2 = 4$$
$$3 + 3 = 6$$
$$4 + 4 = 8$$

11. **Higher Order Thinking** Mack drew a picture of 5 and 3. He says you can add them to get an even number. Do you agree? Explain and write an equation for the sum.

12. **Math and Science** Desert birds are active in the early morning to stay out of the heat. Marcy sees 19 birds. Does Marcy see an odd or even number of birds? Explain with a drawing and equation.

13. ⓓ**Assessment** Which equations have a sum that is an odd number? Choose all that apply.

- ☐ $5 + 7 = 12$
- ☐ $7 + 7 = 14$
- ☐ $7 + 6 = 13$
- ☐ $8 + 7 = 15$

Name _____

Help Tools Games

Homework & Practice 2-2

Continue Even and Odd Numbers

Another Look! The pictures show an even and an odd number.

 ___10___ (even) odd

 ___7___ even (odd)

2, 4, 6, 8, _10_

Write an equation for each picture.

_5_ + _5_ = _10_

The last top square does **NOT** have a pair.

_4_ + _3_ = _7_

HOME ACTIVITY Draw squares to show an even number. Have your child tell if the number is even or odd. Then, ask your child to write an equation that represents the picture and tell why the number is even.

Write the number for the picture. Circle even or odd. Then write the equation.

You can count the squares by 2s to tell if the number is even.

I.

____ even   odd

___ + ___ = ___

2.

____ even   odd

___ + ___ = ___

3.

____ even   odd

___ + ___ = ___

Topic 2 | Lesson 2   Digital Resources at PearsonRealize.com   ninety-one **91**

Solve the problems below.

4. **Reasoning** Liam says he has an even number of baseballs. Do you agree? Explain. Draw a picture and write an equation to help.

5. **Vocabulary** Draw a picture that shows $8 + 8 = 16$. Then circle **even** or **odd**.

even   odd

6. **Vocabulary** Draw a picture that shows $5 + 6 = 11$. Then circle **even** or **odd**.

even   odd

7. **Higher Order Thinking** Jacob says that an even number plus an odd number equals an odd number. Do you agree? Explain.

8. **Assessment** Which equations have a sum that is an even number?

Choose all that apply.

☐ $5 + 5 = 10$

☐ $2 + 3 = 5$

☐ $6 + 6 = 12$

☐ $9 + 9 = 18$

Name _____

Solve & Share

Show and explain two different ways to find how many circles in all.

I can ...
find the total number of objects in a set of rows and columns.

Content Standards 2.CA.5, 2.CA.1
Process Standards PS.1, PS.3, PS.4, PS.7

You can model repeated addition with an array.

Arrays have equal **rows**. Each row has 3 strawberries.

Arrays have equal **columns**. Each column has 2 strawberries.

Write two equations that match the array.

By Rows
$3 + 3 = 6$

By Columns
$2 + 2 + 2 = 6$

Do You Understand?

Show Me! Is this group an array? Explain.

Guided Practice

Write two equations that match each array.

1.

By Rows

$\underline{4} + \underline{4} = \underline{8}$

By Columns

$\underline{2} + \underline{2} + \underline{2} + \underline{2} = \underline{8}$

2.

By Rows

___ + ___ + ___ = ___

By Columns

___ + ___ + ___ = ___

Topic 2 | Lesson 3

Independent Practice   Write two equations that match each array.

3.

By Rows

____ + ____ + ____ + ____ + ____ = ____

By Columns ____ + ____ + ____ = ____

4.

____ + ____ + ____ = ____

____ + ____ + ____ + ____ = ____

5.

By Rows ____ + ____ = ____

By Columns ____ + ____ = ____

6.

____ + ____ + ____ + ____ + ____ = ____

____ + ____ + ____ + ____ + ____ = ____

---

7. Algebra Use the array to find the missing number.

____ + 5 = 10

8. **Look for Patterns** Ross places the berries in an array. Write two equations that match the array. How many berries are there in all?

Look at the rows and columns.

_____

_____

_____ berries

9. The array shows cars in a parking lot. Can you write two different equations that match the array? Explain. How many cars are in the parking lot in all?

_____

_____

_____ cars

10. **Higher Order Thinking** Draw a garden with up to 5 rows and that has the same number of flowers in each row. Then write two equations that match your array.

11. ⓓ **Assessment** Blake sets basketballs in an array. He has 4 rows of basketballs with 3 basketballs in each row. Which equation shows the array Blake made and how many basketballs in all?

Ⓐ $3 + 3 + 3 + 3 = 12$

Ⓑ $3 + 3 = 6$

Ⓒ $4 + 4 = 8$

Ⓓ $3 + 3 + 3 = 9$

Name _____

Another Look! You can use an array to show equal groups.

There are 3 rows.
There are
3 circles in
each row.

There are 3 columns.
There are
3 circles in
each column.

$\underline{3} + \underline{3} + \underline{3} = \underline{9}$

$\underline{3} + \underline{3} + \underline{3} = \underline{9}$

You can add
the objects in an
array by rows
or columns!

HOME ACTIVITY Gather
12 small objects. Have your
child make an array with
4 rows and write an equation
that matches their array.
Then have your child make
an array with 2 columns
and write an equation that
matches their array.

Write two equations that match each array.

1.

By Rows _____ + _____ + _____ = _____

By Columns _____ + _____ = _____

2.

_____ + _____ + _____ + _____ = _____

_____ + _____ + _____ = _____

Model Write two equations that match each array and tell the total number of objects.

3.

_____

_____

Remember to write the sum.

4.

_____

_____

5. **Math and Science** There are 4 rows of plants in the rainforest. Each row has 4 plants. How many plants are in the rainforest in all? Write an equation to solve the problem.

____ + ____ + ____ + ____ = ____

____ plants

6. **⬤Assessment** Gail puts her crayons in a box. She puts them in 3 rows. 5 crayons are in each row. Which equation shows the array Gail made and how many crayons there are in all?

Ⓐ 3 + 3 + 3 = 9

Ⓑ 3 + 3 = 6

Ⓒ 5 + 5 + 5 = 15

Ⓓ 5 + 5 = 10

Name _____

Solve & Share

Rusty places his toy trucks in 4 columns. He places 3 trucks in each column. How many trucks does Rusty have in all?

Show how you know with counters and an equation.

I can ...
make arrays with equal rows or equal columns.

Content Standards 2.CA.5, 2.CA.I
Process Standards PS.2, PS.4, PS.5, PS.8

Equation

_____

_____ trucks

Jackson's garden has 2 rows with 4 carrots in each row.

How many carrots are in his garden?

You can make an array to show the problem.

$4 + 4 = \underline{8}$

Use repeated addition to find out how many carrots are in Jackson's garden.

You can add the number of carrots in each row.

Repeated addition means adding the same number over and over.

You can also add the number of carrots in each column.

$2 + 2 + 2 + 2 = \underline{8}$

$4 + 4 = \underline{8}$

I have 8 carrots!

Do You Understand?

Show Me! If you have 2 rows with different amounts in each row do you have an array? Explain.

☆ Guided ☆ Practice

Draw an array to show each problem. Use repeated addition to solve.

1. Monica has 2 shelves in her pantry. She puts 3 cans of peas on each shelf. How many cans of peas does she have in all?

$\underline{3} + \underline{3} = \underline{6}$ cans of peas

2. Dominick is organizing his stickers in columns. He has 4 columns with 4 stickers in each column. How many stickers does he have in all?

$\underline{} + \underline{} + \underline{} + \underline{} = \underline{}$ stickers

Independent Practice Draw an array to show each problem.
Use repeated addition to solve.

3. Sarah bakes loaves of bread. She places them in
3 rows with 5 loaves in each row. How many loaves
of bread does Sarah have in all?

_____ + _____ + _____ = _____ loaves of bread

4. Kristin has 5 shelves in her bookcase.
She puts 4 books on each shelf.
How many books does Kristin have in all?

_____ + _____ + _____ + _____ + _____ = _____ books

5. Malcolm puts his marbles in two columns.
He put 2 marbles in each column.
How many marbles does Malcolm have in all?

_____ + _____ = _____ marbles

6. **Algebra** Find the missing numbers.
Frank has 10 baseball cards. He places them in 2 equal rows.
Show how many baseball cards are in each row.

☐ + ☐ = 10 baseball cards

7. **Reasoning** Jenny has 5 rows on each page in her photo album. She puts 2 pictures in each row.How many pictures does she have on each page?

_____ + _____ + _____ + _____ + _____ = _____ pictures

8. **Reasoning** Nina has a bookcase with 4 shelves.
She places 5 dolls on each shelf.
How many dolls does Nina have in all?

_____ + _____ + _____ + _____ = _____ dolls

9. **Higher Order Thinking** Write a story problem using repeated addition. Draw an array to match your story.

10. 🔟 **Assessment** Whitney has a muffin tin with 2 rows. Each row has 4 muffins. Write an equation that shows how many muffins Whitney has in all.

_____

How can drawing a picture help?

Name _____

Another Look! Make an array and write an equation for the following problem.

Tia places bowls of soup on a tray in 3 columns with 2 bowls in each column. How many bowls of soup are on the tray?

First, draw three columns with 2 bowls in each column.

3 columns

2 bowls in each column

HOME ACTIVITY Ask your child to show how they would make an array for the equation $3 + 3 + 3 = 9$.

Arrays have equal rows and columns.

Now, write an equation that matches the array.

$$\underline{2} + \underline{2} + \underline{2} = \underline{6}$$ bowls of soup

Draw an array to show each problem. Use repeated addition to solve.

1. Mrs. Smith places the desks in her classroom in 5 columns. She puts 3 desks in each column. How many desks are in her classroom?

_____ + _____ + _____ + _____ + _____ = _____ desks

Draw an array to show each problem.
Use repeated addition to solve.

2. **Reasoning** Jim has 4 columns of marbles.
   He has 3 marbles in each column.
   How many marbles does he have in all?

3. **Reasoning** Mike has 4 rows of crackers.
   He has 5 crackers in each row.How many
   crackers does he have in all?

4. **Higher Order Thinking** Jill has 10 teddy
   bears in all. If she has 2 columns, how
   many teddy bears are in each column?
   Draw an array and complete the equation.

_____ + _____ = 10

5. **Assessment** Brian has 3 columns
   of bugs. Each column has 5 bugs. Write
   an equation that shows how many bugs
   Brian has in all.

Think about
the meaning of the
word column.

Name _____

Solve & Share

There are 4 tables in a classroom. 3 children sit at each table. How many children are there in all?

Draw a picture and write an equation to model and solve the problem.

I can ...
model problems using equations, drawings, arrays, and bar diagrams.

🔵 **Process Standards** PS.4 Also PS.1, PS.3, PS.5, PS.6, PS.7, PS.8
Content Standards 2.CA.2, 2.CA.5

Thinking Habits
How can a picture and an equation help me model problems?

Does my answer make sense?

____ + ____ + ____ + ____ = ____

____ children

Pat has 3 boxes.
Each box has
5 marbles inside.
How many marbles
does Pat have in all?

Use a model to
show and solve the
problem.

How can I use a model to show and solve the problem?

I can draw
an array and write an
equation to show how many
marbles in all.

$5 + 5 + 5 = 15$

So, Pat has 15 marbles.

Or I can
draw a bar diagram
and write an equation
to show how many
marbles in all.

15

$5 + 5 + 5 = 15$

So, Pat has 15 marbles.

My drawings
and equations show
that $5 + 5 + 5$ is 15.

Pat has 15 marbles
in all.

Do You Understand?

Show Me! How does drawing
a picture and writing an
equation help you model a
problem?

☆ **Guided Practice** ☆ Draw an array and complete the bar diagram to help you solve the problem. Then write an equation.

1. Ray has 2 bookshelves in his room.
   He has 5 books on each shelf.
   How many books does Ray have in all?

10

$\underline{5} + \underline{5} = \underline{}$ books

Tools Assessment

Independent Practice

Draw an array or bar diagram to help you solve each problem.
Then write an equation.

2. Mika has 4 groups of playing cards.
If there are 4 playing cards in each
group, how many cards does Mika
have in all?

____ + ____ + ____ + ____ = ____

3. Anita has 3 packs of baseball cards.
If there are 6 cards in each pack,
how many baseball cards does Anita
have in all?

____ + ____ + ____ = ____

4. Algebra Tina drew this bar
diagram to show 2 equal
groups can make 18. What
are the missing numbers?
Explain how you know.

Problem Solving

Window Displays

Mr. Miller's Hobby Shop has 3 window displays. One is for posters, one is for paint cans, and one is for crayon boxes. The displays are described at the right.

Which display has the least number of items?

Posters	Paint Cans	Crayon Boxes
3 rows	4 rows	2 rows
6 posters in each row	3 paint cans in each row	8 crayon boxes in each row

5. **Make Sense** What are you asked to find?

_____

_____

_____

6. **Explain** Mr. Miller says he will add 3 + 6 to find the total number of posters in the posters display. Do you agree with his plan? Explain.

_____

_____

_____

_____

7. **Model** Use a model to help you find which display has the least number of items. Be prepared to explain which model you used and why.

© Pearson Education, Inc. 2

Name _____

Another Look! You can draw an array or bar diagram to model and help solve problems.

Terri has 3 baskets. Each basket has 2 toys.
How many toys does Terri have in all?

The equation
2 + 2 + 2 = 6
also models the problem.

So, Terri has 6 toys in all.

HOME ACTIVITY Have your child draw an array and then write an equation to model this problem: Joel has 2 bags. Each bag has 3 apples. How many apples does Joel have in all?

Draw an array or bar diagram to help you solve each problem. Then write an equation.

1. Beth has 3 rows of sunflowers in her garden. Each row has 5 flowers. How many sunflowers does Beth have in all?

____ + ____ + ____ = ____ sunflowers

2. Curtis makes 2 books. Each book has 7 pages. How many pages does Curtis make in all?

____ + ____ = ____ pages

Topic 2 | Lesson 5   Digital Resources at PearsonRealize.com   one hundred nine **109**

Planting Flowers

Mrs. Dunlap is planting some flowers in her garden. She has 10 tulips, 5 roses, and 10 daffodils. She wants to plant the flowers in an array, where each row has 5 flowers. How many rows of flowers will be in her garden?

Think about what a row means.

3. **Make Sense** What do you know? What are you asked to find?

_____

_____

_____

_____

4. **Explain** Mrs. Dunlap thinks she should plant the flowers in 4 rows of 5 flowers. Does her plan make sense? Explain why or why not.

_____

_____

_____

_____

5. **Model** Draw an array to show how Mrs. Dunlap should plant her flowers. Label the flowers. How many rows are in her garden?

Name _____

Follow the Path

Color a path from **Start** to **Finish**. Follow the sums and differences that are odd numbers. You can only move up, down, right, or left.

Start

5 + 6	14 − 6	13 − 9	7 − 3	1 + 9	10 − 5	2 + 9	9 + 8	16 − 7
3 + 4	14 − 7	2 + 5	11 − 6	4 + 8	8 − 3	12 − 6	1 + 5	11 − 4
7 − 1	4 + 4	12 − 4	12 − 7	14 − 9	4 + 7	15 − 7	2 + 5	1 + 8
9 + 9	1 + 7	6 − 4	2 + 8	6 + 2	1 + 9	13 − 9	15 − 6	2 + 4
17 − 9	3 + 9	7 + 5	8 + 8	16 − 6	9 − 5	10 − 6	5 + 4	10 − 3

Finish

A-Z
Glossary

Word List
- addends
- array
- bar diagram
- column
- doubles
- equation
- even
- odd
- row
- sum

Understand Vocabulary

Choose a term from the Word List to complete each sentence.

1. An _____ number cannot be shown as pairs of cubes.

2. An _____ is a group of objects set in equal rows and columns.

3. In an array, objects that are shown across are in a _____.

4. A model for addition and subtraction that shows the parts and the whole is called a _____.

Write T for *true* or F for *false*.

5. _____ 9 is an even number.

6. _____ 13 is an odd number.

7. _____ You can model repeated addition with an array.

8. _____ In an array, objects that are shown up and down are in a column.

Use Vocabulary in Writing

9. Which model could you use to show 4 groups of 5 objects in each group? Use at least 1 term from the Word List.

_____
_____
_____
_____

Name _____

Set A

You can use cubes to tell if a number is even or odd.

12

 The number of cubes is even if you can pair or count them by 2s.

odd (even)

$6 + 6 = 12$

Circle even or odd. Then write the equation. Use cubes to help.

1.

11

(odd)   even

___ + ___ = ___

2.

18

odd   even

___ + ___ = ___

Set B

You can use repeated addition to find the total number of loaves.

Write two equations that match the array.

Rows: $3 + 3 = 6$

Columns: $2 + 2 + 2 = 6$

Write two equations that match the array.

3.

Rows: ___ + ___ + ___ + ___ = ___

Columns:

___ + ___ + ___ + ___ + ___ = ___

You can draw arrays and use repeated addition to solve problems.

Alli has 3 shelves in her pantry.
She puts 4 cans of beans on each shelf.
How many cans of beans does Alli have in all?

$\underline{4} + \underline{4} + \underline{4} = \underline{12}$ cans

Thinking Habits

Model with Math

Can I use a drawing, diagram, table, or graph to model the problem?

Can I write an equation to show the problem?

Draw an array to show the problem.
Use repeated addition to solve.

4. Steven puts 3 rows of apples on a table. Each row has 6 apples. How many apples does Steven put on the table?

_____ + _____ + _____ = _____ apples

Draw a model and solve the problem.

5. There are 2 rows of cars.
   Each row has 8 cars.
   How many cars are in the parking lot?

_____ + _____ = _____ cars

Name _____

1. José writes an equation. The sum is an even number greater than 14.

Which equation does José write?

Ⓐ $6 + 6 = ?$

Ⓑ $6 + 7 = ?$

Ⓒ $8 + 8 = ?$

Ⓓ $8 + 7 = ?$

2. Jen has 2 rows of apples with 4 apples in each row.

Which equation shows how many apples Jen has in all?

Ⓐ $4 + 2 = 6$

Ⓑ $2 + 2 + 2 = 6$

Ⓒ $4 + 4 = 8$

Ⓓ $4 + 4 + 4 = 12$

3. Choose Yes or No to tell if the sum in the equation is an even number.

$3 + 4 = 7$ ○ Yes   ○ No

$5 + 5 = 10$ ○ Yes   ○ No

$7 + 6 = 13$ ○ Yes   ○ No

$9 + 7 = 16$ ○ Yes   ○ No

4. Will has 3 rows of trees in his yard. Each row has 4 trees. How many trees in all?

Draw a picture to show the array of trees.

Then write an equation for your picture.

_____ + _____ + _____ = _____

There are _____ trees in all.

5. How many squares are shown? Is the number even or odd?

Draw a picture to show how you know.

6. Ben has 8 pennies. Look at each equation. Choose Yes or No to tell if Ben can use the equation to make an array with his pennies.

$2 + 2 + 2 + 2 = 8$ ○ Yes   ○ No

$5 + 3 = 8$ ○ Yes   ○ No

$4 + 4 = 8$ ○ Yes   ○ No

$6 + 2 = 8$ ○ Yes   ○ No

7. Becky drew this bar diagram to show 2 equal groups can make 14.

Part A
Draw a picture to show what the "?" stands for.

Part B
Change 14 to 16 in the bar diagram. What does the "?" stand for now? Tell how you know.

_____

_____

_____

Name _____

School Garden

Students are planting a garden at school.
The pictures show the number of some plants
in the garden.

Number of Tomato Plants

Number of Corn Plants

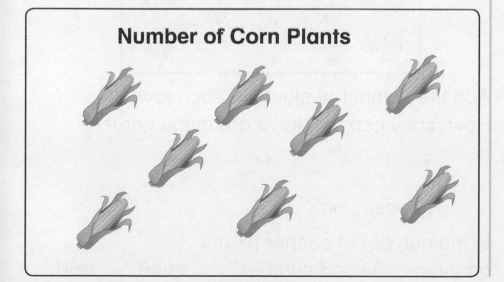

1. Is there an even or odd
   number of tomato plants
   in the garden?

   Circle your answer.   **even**   **odd**

   Show or tell how you know.

2. Tom says the number of corn plants is an
   even number. Do you agree? Draw a picture
   to show why or why not.

3. David plants peas in the school garden. He plants 4 rows of peas with 3 plants in each row.

Part A

Draw an array to show how David planted the peas.

Part B

Write an equation to match the array. How many pea plants does David plant?

4. Jesse says there are other ways to make an array of 12 plants. Show an array of 12 plants that is different from the array David used.

5. The array below shows the number of pepper plants in the garden.

Number of Pepper Plants

Add the number of plants in each row. How many pepper plants are in the garden?

____ + ____ + ____ + ____ + ____ = ____

_____ pepper plants

Is the number of pepper plants an even or an odd number?   **even**   **odd**

© Pearson Education, Inc. 2

Add Within 100 Using Strategies

Essential Question: What are strategies for adding numbers to 100?

Digital Resources

Solve Learn Glossary

Tools Assessment Help Games

The Earth is always changing!

Some changes can happen quickly. Others take a long time.

Wow! Let's do this project and learn more.

Math and Science Project: Earth Changes and Addition Strategies

Find Out Find and share books about how the Earth changes. Talk about changes that people can see, hear, and feel. Talk about changes that people cannot see happening.

Journal: Make a Book Show what you learn in a book. In your book, also:

• Write new science words you learn. Draw pictures that help show what the words mean.

• Write new math words you learn. Draw pictures that help show what the words mean.

Name _____

Review What You Know

A-Z Vocabulary

1. Draw a circle around each **even** number. Use cubes to help.

15   7   14

2   19   18

2. Draw a square around each **odd** number. Use cubes to help.

12   3   6

17   11   4

3. Complete the **bar diagram** to show the sum of $3 + 5$.

Arrays

Write an equation to show the number of circles in each array.

4.

By rows

_____ + _____ = _____

5.

By columns

_____ + _____ + _____ = _____

Math Story

6. Joe has 5 apples. He picks 3 more apples. How many apples does Joe have now?

_____ apples

Does Joe have an even or an odd number of apples?

_____ number

120 one hundred twenty   © Pearson Education, Inc. 2   **Topic 3**

My Word Cards

Study the words on the front of the card.
Complete the activity on the back.

A-Z
Glossary

tens

$54 + 14 = 68$

↑   ↑   ↑

ones

$54 + 14 = 68$

↑   ↑   ↑

open number line

$26 + 20 = 46$

mental math

Start at 23. Count on 2 tens. 33, 43

$23 + 20 = 43$

break apart

$27 + 35 = ?$

Tens: | 20 | 30
Ones: | 7 | 5

compensation

$38 + 24 = ?$
$+2 \quad -2$

You add 2 to 38 to make 40. Then subtract 2 from 24 to get 22. 40 + 22 = 62.

So, 38 + 24 = 62.

My Word Cards

Use what you know to complete the sentences.
Extend learning by writing your own sentence using each word.

An _____

_____

is a tool that can help you
add or subtract. It can begin
at any number.

The digit that shows how
many ones are in a number
is called the

_____ digit.

The digit that shows how
many groups of 10 are in a
number is called the

_____ digit.

_____

is a mental math strategy
you can use when you add
or subtract.

You can _____

a number into its place
value parts.

_____

is math you do in your head.

Name _____

Solve & Share

How can you use the hundred chart to help you find 32 + 43? Explain.

Write an equation to show the sum.

1	2	3	4	5	6	7	8	9	10
11	12	13	14	15	16	17	18	19	20
21	22	23	24	25	26	27	28	29	30
31	32	33	34	35	36	37	38	39	40
41	42	43	44	45	46	47	48	49	50
51	52	53	54	55	56	57	58	59	60
61	62	63	64	65	66	67	68	69	70
71	72	73	74	75	76	77	78	79	80
81	82	83	84	85	86	87	88	89	90
91	92	93	94	95	96	97	98	99	100

I can ...
add within 100 using place-value strategies.

Content Standard 2.CA.1
Process Standards PS.1, PS.2, PS.3, PS.5

_____

_____

_____

_____

_____

_____ + _____ = _____

You can add on a hundred chart. Find 54 + 18.

Start at 54. You need to add the tens from 18. Move down 1 row to show 1 ten.

51	52	53	54	55	56	57	58	59	60
61	62	63	64	65	66	67	68	69	70
71	72	73	74	75	76	77	78	79	80

Now add the **ones.**

You are already at 64. Now move ahead 8 to show 8 ones. You need to go to the next row to add them all. So, 54 + 18 = 72.

51	52	53	54	55	56	57	58	59	60
61	62	63	64	65	66	67	68	69	70
71	72	73	74	75	76	77	78	79	80

Do You Understand?

Show Me! How can you use a hundred chart to find 53 + 24?

☆ Guided ☆ Practice

Add using the hundred chart. Draw arrows on the chart if needed.

11	12	13	14	15	16	17	18	19	20
21	22	23	24	25	26	27	28	29	30
31	32	33	34	35	36	37	38	39	40
41	42	43	44	45	46	47	48	49	50

1. 17 + 32 = 49

2. 28 + 21 = _____

3. _____ = 19 + 20

4. 18 + 8 = _____

© Pearson Education, Inc. 2

Tools   Assessment

Independent Practice ☆ Add using the hundred chart.

1	2	3	4	5	6	7	8	9	10
11	12	13	14	15	16	17	18	19	20
21	22	23	24	25	26	27	28	29	30
31	32	33	34	35	36	37	38	39	40
41	42	43	44	45	46	47	48	49	50
51	52	53	54	55	56	57	58	59	60
61	62	63	64	65	66	67	68	69	70
71	72	73	74	75	76	77	78	79	80
81	82	83	84	85	86	87	88	89	90
91	92	93	94	95	96	97	98	99	100

5. $33 + 9 =$ _____

6. _____ $= 12 + 73$

7. $38 + 21 =$ _____

8. $56 + 42 =$ _____

9. $47 + 28 =$ _____

10. $39 + 17 =$ _____

11. _____ $= 61 + 19$

12. **Higher Order Thinking** Write the digit that makes each equation true.

☐ $+ 83 = 90$ $34 + 2$☐ $= 57$ 1☐ $+ 51 = 67$ $62 +$ ☐$1 = 83$

13. Sara has 48 buttons. Luis has 32 buttons. How many buttons do they have in all?

_____ buttons

31	32	33	34	35	36	37	38	39	40
41	42	43	44	45	46	47	48	49	50
51	52	53	54	55	56	57	58	59	60
61	62	63	64	65	66	67	68	69	70
71	72	73	74	75	76	77	78	79	80
81	82	83	84	85	86	87	88	89	90
91	92	93	94	95	96	97	98	99	100

14. Mika had 70 buttons. Then she found 19 more buttons. How many buttons does Mika have now?

_____ buttons

15. Higher Order Thinking Write the steps you take to add 43 and 39 on a hundred chart.

_____

_____

_____

_____

_____

16. ⓘ**Assessment** Which weights will balance the weights already on the scale? Use a hundred chart to help.

Ⓐ 18 20

Ⓑ 15 20

Ⓒ 16 30

Ⓓ 30 17

© Pearson Education, Inc. 2

Name _____

Help Tools Games

Another Look!

Find 16 + 23.

1. Start on square 16.

2. Move down 2 rows to show the tens in ⬜2 3.

3. Move 3 squares to the right to add the ones in 2 ⬜3 .

4. Where did you stop? _39_

So, _16_ + _23_ = _39_ .

1	2	3	4	5	6	7	8	9	10
11	12	13	14	15	16	17	18	19	20
21	22	23	24	25	26	27	28	29	30
31	32	33	34	35	36	37	38	39	40
41	42	43	44	45	46	47	48	49	50
51	52	53	54	55	56	57	58	59	60
61	62	63	64	65	66	67	68	69	70
71	72	73	74	75	76	77	78	79	80
81	82	83	84	85	86	87	88	89	90
91	92	93	94	95	96	97	98	99	100

The numbers increase by 10 as you move down each row.

HOME ACTIVITY Ask your child to describe how to add 37 and 16 on a hundred chart.

Add using the hundred chart.

1. 12 + 11 = _____

2. 31 + 45 = _____

3. 81 + 14 = _____

Algebra Write the digits that make each equation true.

4. ☐4 + 1☐ = 39

5. 4☐ + ☐9 = 82

6. 74 + ☐4 = 8☐

---

7. **Math and Science** There are 21 active volcanoes in California and 17 active volcanoes in Hawaii. How many active volcanoes are in California and Hawaii?

_____ active volcanoes

8. **Make Sense** Kenji threw two bean bags at the target. He scored 79 points. One bean bag landed on 61. Which number did the other bean bag land on?

53	28
61	18

The other bean bag landed on _____.

---

9. **Higher Order Thinking** Explain how you could use a hundred chart to find the missing number.

63 + ⬚? = 87

The missing number is _____.

10. **⓵Assessment** Which weights can you put on the scale to make it balance? Use a hundred chart to help.

Ⓐ 29 32

Ⓑ 30 29

Ⓒ 34 29

Ⓓ 30 34

© Pearson Education, Inc. 2

Topic 3 | Lesson 1

Name _____

Solve & Share

How can you use the number line to help you find 30 + 40? Explain.

Write an equation to show the sum.

I can ...
add tens on an open number line.

Content Standard 2.CA.1
Process Standards PS.1, PS.3, PS.4, PS.5, PS.6

_____ + _____ = _____

Find 36 + 30.

You can add tens on an **open number line**.

First, place 36 on the number line.

36

You need to add the tens in 30.

30 is 3 tens. So, count on by 10 three times. Show each 10 on the number line.

+10   +10   +10

36   46   56   66

You land on 66. So, 36 + 30 = ___66___.

Do You Understand?

Show Me! How could you use an open number line to find 10 + 40?

Guided Practice   Use an open number line to find each sum.

1. 53 + 40 = _____

+10   +10   +10   +10

53   63   73   83   93

2. 35 + 20 = _____

© Pearson Education, Inc. 2

Topic 3 | Lesson 2

Independent Practice ☆ Use an open number line to find each sum.

3. 30 + 10 = _____

4. 55 + 30 = _____

5. 23 + 20 = _____

6. 46 + 40 = _____

7. **Higher Order Thinking** Susan found 50 + 20 using this open number line. She said that 20 + 50 = 70, too. Is she correct? Explain.

8. **Use Tools** Sam has 38 golf balls.
He gets 20 more golf balls.
How many golf balls does Sam have now?
Use the open number line to solve.

_____ golf balls

9. **A-Z Vocabulary** Complete each
sentence using one of the terms below.

equation   open number line   addend

Numbers are written in order from left to

right on an _____.

$34 + 60 = 94$ is an _____.

34 and 60 are _____.

10. **Higher Order Thinking** Geno used
the open number line below to solve a
problem. What is the missing number
in the equation?

$28 + \_\_\_\_ = 78$

11. **Assessment** Which equation does
this open number line show?

Ⓐ $12 + 20 = 32$

Ⓑ $12 + 30 = 42$

Ⓒ $12 + 40 = 52$

Ⓓ $12 + 50 = 62$

Count the jumps!

Help   Tools   Games

Another Look! Find 64 + 20 using an open number line.

Place 64 on the number line. Then count on by 10 twice.

+10   +10

64   74   84

64 + 20 = 84

Start with 64, then count on by 10 twice. 74, 84

HOME ACTIVITY Ask your child to find 45 + 30 on an open number line.

Use an open number line to find each sum.

1. 63 + 30 = _____

2. 47 + 20 = _____

Use an open number line to solve each problem.

3. **Use Tools** Bridget has 34 books. She gets 30 more books. How many books does Bridget have now?

☐ + ☐ = ☐

4. **Algebra** Find the missing number.

57 + 20 = ☐

5. **Higher Order Thinking** Mary did 20 jumping jacks on Monday, 30 jumping jacks on Tuesday, and 20 jumping jacks on Wednesday.

How many jumping jacks did she do on all three days?

_____ jumping jacks

6. ⓘ **Assessment** Which equation does this number line show?

Ⓐ 70 + 10 = 80

Ⓑ 70 + 20 = 90

Ⓒ 70 + 30 = 100

Ⓓ 70 + 40 = 110

How many times is 10 counted on from 70?

© Pearson Education, Inc. 2

Name _____

Solve & Share

How can you use the open number line to find 35 + 24?

Write an equation to show the sum. Explain your work.

_____ + _____ = _____

I can ...
use an open number line to add tens and ones within 100.

Content Standard 2.CA.1
Process Standards PS.2, PS.3, PS.4, PS.5, PS.6

Find 48 + 23. Use an open number line.

One Way

This way shows jumps by 10s and 1s.

Another Way

So, 48 + 23 = 71.

This way shows how you can make bigger jumps. Both ways are correct.

Do You Understand?

Show Me! Explain how you can use an open number line to find 56 + 35.

☆ **Guided Practice**   Use an open number line to find each sum.

1. 59 + 24 = _____

2. 47 + 25 = _____

© Pearson Education, Inc. 2

Topic 3 | Lesson 3

Tools Assessment

Independent Practice ☆ Use an open number line to find each sum.

3. 34 + 15 = _____

4. 46 + 34 = _____

5. 28 + 16 = _____

6. 59 + 26 = _____

7. Number Sense Matt found 55 + 28 using the open number line below. Is his work correct? Explain.

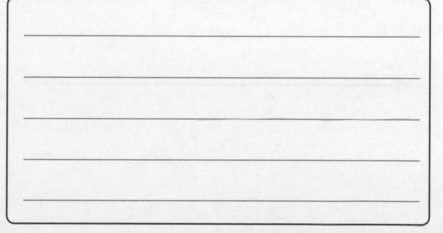

_____

_____

_____

_____

_____

8. Use Tools There are 24 apples in a basket. There are 19 apples on a tray. How many apples are there in all?

_____ apples

9. Use Tools Jamie has 27 more berries than Lisa. Lisa has 37 berries. How many berries does Jamie have?

_____ berries

10. Higher Order Thinking Use two different number lines to show that $34 + 23$ has the same value as $23 + 34$.

11. Assessment Use the numbers on the cards. Write the missing numbers under the number line to show how to find the sum.

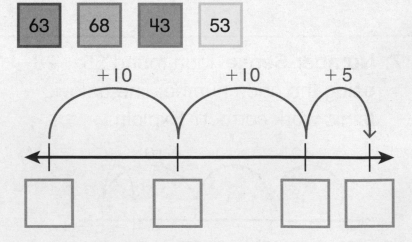

$43 + 25 =$ _____

© Pearson Education, Inc. 2
Topic 3 | Lesson 3

Name _____

Another Look! You can add two-digit numbers by counting on an open number line. 46 + 27 = ?

I can use this strategy to add any numbers.

Place 46 on an open number line.

Count on 2 tens from 46.

46   56   66

Count on 7 ones from 66.

So, 46 + 27 = 73.

46   56   66   70   73

HOME ACTIVITY Ask your child to show how he or she would find 28 + 13 using an open number line.

Use an open number line to find each sum.

1. 34 + 25 = _____

2. 57 + 18 = _____

3. **Use Tools** Jimmy sees 10 baby sea turtles on the shore. He then sees 23 more baby sea turtles. How many sea turtles does Jimmy see in all?

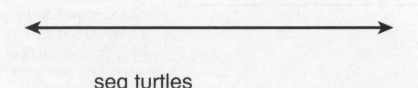

_____ sea turtles

4. **Use Tools** Ebony has 45 beads. Ivory gives her 26 more beads. How many beads does Ebony have in all?

_____ beads

5. **Higher Order Thinking** Bill has 58 crayons. Steve gives him 10 more crayons and Mika gives him 14 more crayons. How many crayons does Bill have in all?

_____ crayons

An open number line can show more than two addends.

6. **Assessment** Use the numbers on the cards. Write the missing numbers under the number line to show how to find the sum.

| 86 | 60 | 80 | 70 |

$50 + 36 =$ _____

© Pearson Education, Inc. 2

Solve

☆ **Solve & Share** ☆

Monica has 24 crayons. Paul has 64 crayons. How many crayons do they have in all?

Solve any way you choose. Explain your work.

I can … add within 100 using place-value strategies.

 Content Standard 2.CA.1
Process Standards PS.2, PS.4, PS.5, PS.7, PS.8

24 + 64 = _____

_____ crayons

$27 + 35 = ?$

You can use place value to **break apart** numbers into **tens** and **ones**.

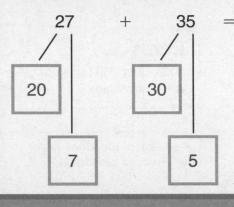

27 + 35 = ?

| 20 | 30 |
| 7 | 5 |

I can then use mental math to find the sum.

Add the tens.
20 + 30 = 50

Add the ones.
7 + 5 = 12

Then add the sums.
50 + 12 = 62

So, $27 + 35 = $ ___62___ .

Think: 50 + 12
                /\
              10 2

$50 + 10 + 2 = 62$

Do You Understand?

Show Me! Explain how you can break apart numbers to find $14 + 32$.

Guided Practice   Break apart numbers to find each sum. Use blocks to help, if needed.

1. $17 + 42 = $ _59_

| 10 | 40 |
| 7 | 2 |

$$\begin{array}{r} 50 \\ +\ 9 \\ \hline 59 \end{array}$$

2. ____ $= 53 + 23$

| ☐ | ☐ |
| ☐ | ☐ |

© Pearson Education, Inc. 2

Topic 3 | Lesson 4

Tools Assessment

Independent Practice Break apart numbers to find each sum.
Use blocks to help, if needed.

3.   23   +   26 = _____

□ □
□ □

4.   9   +   42 = _____

□ □
□ □

5.   _____ = 51   +   16

□ □
□ □

6. 56 + 15 = _____

7. _____ = 76 + 11

8. 33 + 49 = _____

Add tens and ones to solve.

9. **Algebra** One number makes both equations true.
Find the missing number.

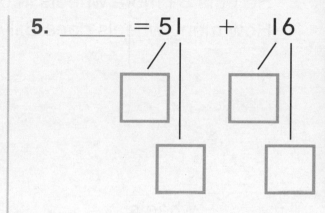

$17 + \boxed{} = 28$

$\boxed{} + 28 = 39$

10. Billy puts 34 skateboard wheels in a pile. He puts 34 more wheels in another pile. How many wheels does Billy have in all?

_____ wheels

11. **Math and Science** A new office and house was built after a hurricane. 24 windows are needed for the office. 18 windows are needed for the house. How many windows are needed in all?

_____ windows

12. **Higher Order Thinking** Write a story problem about 14 + 41. Then solve the problem.

$$14 + 41 = \underline{\hspace{1cm}}$$

13. **Assessment** Cindy has 15 more toy planes than Julie. Julie has 12 toy planes. How many toy planes does Cindy have?

Ⓐ 3

Ⓑ 15

Ⓒ 25

Ⓓ 27

© Pearson Education, Inc. 2

Name _____

Another Look!

Find 34 + 24.

You can draw a picture to show the tens and ones.

34 + 24

30   4   20   4

Add the tens.

$30 + 20 = \underline{50}$

Add the ones.

$4 + 4 = \underline{8}$

Add the sums.

$50 + 8 = \underline{58}$

So, $34 + 24 = \underline{58}$.

HOME ACTIVITY Ask your child to show how he or she would break apart tens and ones to find 23 + 46.

Break apart numbers to find each sum.
Show your work. Draw pictures, if needed.

1. $34 + 6 = \underline{\hspace{1cm}}$

2. $35 + 48 = \underline{\hspace{1cm}}$

3. $67 + 28 = \underline{\hspace{1cm}}$

4. $57 + 19 = \underline{\hspace{1cm}}$

5. 32 + 12 = _____

6. 54 + 7 = _____

7. 37 + 43 = _____

8. **Higher Order Thinking** Carla buys two packages of pens. She buys 49 pens in all. Which color pens does Carla buy? Show how you found the answer.

Pen Packages	
Pen Color	Number of Pens
Blue	25
Black	12
Red	24
Green	33

9. Toby has 63 grapes. There are 33 red grapes and the rest are green grapes. How many of Toby's grapes are green?

10. ⓘ **Assessment** Tad has 72 seashells. He finds 15 more seashells. How many seashells does Tad have in all?

77　　　87　　　88　　　97
Ⓐ　　　Ⓑ　　　Ⓒ　　　Ⓓ

_____ grapes

Name _____

Solve & Share

Josh has 34 cans to recycle. Jill has 27 cans. How many cans do they have in all?

Solve any way you choose. Use drawings and equations to explain your work.

I can ...
break apart numbers into tens and ones to find their sum.

Content Standard 2.CA.1
Process Standards PS.1, PS.4, PS.7

_____ + _____ = _____ cans

$37 + 25 = ?$

You can break apart just the second addend into **tens** and **ones**.

37   +   25   =   ?

| 37 | | 20 | 5 |

$37 + 25 = 37 + 20 + 5$

Add the tens of the second addend.

$37 + 20 = 57$

Add the ones of the second addend.

$57 + 5 = 62$

So, $27 + 35 = \underline{62}$.

57… 58, 59, 60, 61, 62

Do You Understand?

Show Me! Explain how you can break apart 28 to find $33 + 28$.

★ **Guided Practice** ★ Break apart the second addend to find the sum. Show your work. Use blocks to help, if needed.

1. $57 + 32 = \underline{}$

| 57 | 30 | 2 |

$\underline{57} + \underline{30} = \underline{87}$

$\underline{87} + \underline{2} = \underline{89}$

2. $24 + 13 = \underline{}$

| | | |

© Pearson Education, Inc. 2

Independent Practice

Break apart the second addend to find the sum.
Show your work. Use blocks, if needed.

3. 42 + 16 = _____

☐	☐	☐

4. 36 + 44 = _____

☐	☐	☐

5. 41 + 37 = _____

☐	☐	☐

6. 35 + 47 = _____

7. 32 + 28 = _____

8. 48 + 27 = _____

9. **Number Sense** Write the digit that makes each equation true.

3☐ + 58 = 94

28 + 4☐ = 75

1☐ + 43 = 61

53 + 2☐ = 82

It helps to break apart the numbers.

10. Amir planted 35 trees.
Juan planted 27 trees.
How many trees did they plant in all?

_____ trees

11. Carmen has 18 pennies.
Patrick has 12 more pennies than Carmen.
How many pennies does Patrick have?

_____ pennies

12. **Higher Order Thinking** Use the numbers on the cards. Use each number once to write a true equation.

| 3 | 2 | 8 |

$5\boxed{} + \boxed{}4 = \boxed{}6$

13. **⬤ Assessment** Which has a sum of 67? Choose all that apply.

☐ 15 + 52
☐ 15 + 62
☐ 38 + 29
☐ 11 + 55

Remember, you can add numbers in any order.

Another Look!

Find 25 + 34.

Think 25 plus 3 tens and 4 ones.

```
  25      +      34
   |            /   \
┌────┐     ┌────┐ ┌───┐
│ 25 │     │ 30 │ │ 4 │
└────┘     └────┘ └───┘
```

Count on by tens to add 3 tens.

25, <u>35</u>, <u>45</u>, <u>55</u>

Then count on by ones to add 4 ones.

55, <u>56</u>, <u>57</u>, <u>58</u>, <u>59</u>

So, 25 + 34 = 59.

You can break apart the second addend to find the sum.

HOME ACTIVITY Ask your child to explain how to add 43 + 26 in his or her head.

Break apart numbers to find the sums. Show your work. Draw pictures, if needed.

1. 16 + 22 = _____

2. 47 + 29 = _____

3. 56 + 35 = _____

Break apart numbers to find each sum. Show your work. Draw pictures, if needed.

4. $14 + 28 = $ _____

5. $26 + 48 = $ _____

6. $43 + 17 = $ _____

7. Look for Patterns Break apart numbers to solve. Show your work.

Lily has 46 songs on her music player. Tonya has 53 songs on her music player. How many songs do they have in all?

_____ songs

8. Algebra Write the missing number.

$50 + \triangle = 75$

$\triangle + 25 = 50$

$\triangle = $ _____

$\blacksquare + 38 = 80$

$30 + \blacksquare = 72$

$\blacksquare = $ _____

9. Higher Order Thinking Use the numbers on the cards. Use each number once to write a true equation.

| 6 | 7 | 8 |

1 ☐ + ☐ 5 = ☐ 2

10. ⬤ Assessment Which has a sum of 60? Choose all that apply.

☐ $30 + 30$

☐ $35 + 35$

☐ $45 + 15$

☐ $50 + 10$

© Pearson Education, Inc. 2

Name _____

Solve & Share

35 + 8 = _____

Solve the problem by changing the 8 so that it is easier to find the sum of 35 + 8.

Explain your work.

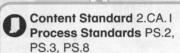

I can ...
break apart addends and combine them in different ways to make numbers that are easy to add mentally.

Content Standard 2.CA.1
Process Standards PS.2, PS.3, PS.8

35 + 8 = _____

Find 38 + 23.

You can use compensation to make numbers that are easier to add.

40   21

---

38 is close to 40. It's easier to add 40 than 38.

So, take 2 from 23 and give it to 38 to make 40.

38   +   23

+ 2   − 2

40   +   21 = ?

Add mentally.

40 + 21 = ?

40 + 21

| 20 | 1 |

40 + 20 + 1 = 60 + 1 = 61

So, 40 + 21 = 61.

If you give an amount to one addend, you must take away the same amount from the other addend, so the sum stays the same.

40 + 21 = 38 + 23

So, 38 + 23 = 61.

Do You Understand?

Show Me! Solve.

$19 + 26 = \boxed{}$

Explain how you can change the addends to make them easier to add.

☆ **Guided Practice** ☆ Use compensation to make numbers that are easier to add. Then solve. Show your work.

1. 17 + 9 = _____

    + 3 − 3

    20 + 6 = 26

2. 23 ◯ + 12 ◯ = _____

    _____ + _____ = _____

3. 25 ◯ + 47 ◯ = _____

    _____ + _____ = _____

Tools Assessment

Independent Practice Use compensation to make numbers that are easier to add. Then solve. Show your work.

4. 33 + 19 = _____

◯ ___ ◯ ___

___ + ___ = ___

5. 28 + 8 = _____

◯ ___ ◯ ___

___ + ___ = ___

6. 27 + 36 = _____

◯ ___ ◯ ___

___ + ___ = ___

7. **Number Sense** Explain how you can use compensation to make numbers that are easy to add. Solve. Show your work.

28 + 37 = ☐

_____ + _____ = ☐

_____
_____
_____

8. **Higher Order Thinking** Show two different ways you could use compensation to make numbers that are easy to add. Solve. Show your work.

17 + 26 = ☐

9. **Explain** Bella said there is only one way to rewrite this problem to make the numbers easier to add. Is she correct? Explain. Then solve.

$42 + 29 = \boxed{}$

_____

_____

_____

_____

10. **A-Z Vocabulary** Show two different ways to use **compensation** to find the sum. Then solve.

$46 + 47 = \boxed{}$

What number is close to 46 or 47?

11. **Higher Order Thinking** Show two different ways to use compensation to find the sum. Then solve.

$37 + 16 + 5 = \boxed{}$

12. **Assessment** Is the amount equal to $42 + 4 + 8$? Choose Yes or No.

$50 + 4$	○ Yes	○ No
$40 + 4 + 10$	○ Yes	○ No
54	○ Yes	○ No
$40 + 12$	○ Yes	○ No

© Pearson Education, Inc. 2

Name _____

Another Look! You can use compensation to make numbers that are easy to add mentally.

Use compensation to find 47 + 28.

- Give 3 to 47 to make 50.
  Give 2 to 28 to make 30.

  47 + 28
  + 3 + 2

- Then it is easy to add in your head.   50 + 30 = 80

- You added 3 + 2 = 5. So subtract 5 from 80 to find the answer.   80 − 5 = 75

  You can count back 5 from 80 to check your answer.   80, <u>79</u>, <u>78</u>, <u>77</u>, <u>76</u>, <u>75</u>

So, 47 + 28 = 75.

Compensation is a way to make numbers that are easy to add in your head!

HOME ACTIVITY Ask your child to explain how to use compensation to add 17 + 38 mentally.

Use compensation to make numbers that are easier to add. Then solve. Show your work.

1. 26 + 6 = _____
   ◯_____ ◯_____
   ____ + ____ = ____

2. 17 + 19 = _____
   ◯_____ ◯_____
   ____ + ____ = ____

3. 39 + 54 = _____
   ◯_____ ◯_____
   ____ + ____ = ____

Use compensation to make numbers that are easier to add. Then solve. Show your work.

4. 24 + 18 = _____
    ◯ _____ ◯ _____
      _____ + _____ = _____

5. 25 + 27 = _____
    ◯ _____ ◯ _____
      _____ + _____ = _____

6. 43 + 32 = _____
    ◯ _____ ◯ _____
      _____ + _____ = _____

7. **Reasoning** Use compensation to solve. Show your work.

Wendy found 13 bugs and Wally found 27 bugs. How many bugs did they find in all?

_____ bugs

8. **Higher Order Thinking** Use compensation to write 3 different equations with the same sum as $38 + 16$. Then solve.

$38 + 16 =$ _____

A. _____ + _____ = _____

B. _____ + _____ = _____

C. _____ + _____ + _____ = _____

9. **⬤Assessment** Which is equal to $14 + 8$? Choose all that apply.

☐ $12 + 6$

☐ $12 + 10$

☐ $10 + 12$

☐ $10 + 4 + 8$

10. **⬤Assessment** Is the amount equal to $26 + 16$? Choose Yes or No.

$30 + 10 + 2$ ◯ Yes ◯ No

$30 + 12$ ◯ Yes ◯ No

$25 + 20$ ◯ Yes ◯ No

$20 + 22$ ◯ Yes ◯ No

© Pearson Education, Inc. 2

Name _____

Solve & Share

Tameka has 39 blocks. Kim has 43 blocks. How many blocks do they have in all?

Choose any strategy. Solve. Show and explain your work.

Practice Adding Using Strategies

I can ...
choose a strategy to help me add two-digit numbers.

Content Standards 2.CA.1, 2.CA.6
Process Standards PS.2, PS.4, PS.5

$43 + 39 =$ _____

_____ blocks

Find 66 + 25.

You can break apart numbers or use compensation.

One Way

Break apart 25 into 20 + 5.

66 + 25

66 + 20 + 5

86 + 5 = 91

Another Way

You can use compensation.

66 + 25
− 5   + 5
61 + 30 = 91

You get the same answer both ways!

So, 66 + 25 = 91.

Do You Understand?

Show Me! In 66 + 25 above, why was 5 subtracted from 66 and then added to 25?

Guided Practice Find each sum. Use any strategy. Show your work.

1.   14 + 32 = _____

14 + 30 + 2

44 + 2 = 46

2. 67 + 26 = _____

© Pearson Education, Inc. 2

Name _____

Tools   Assessment

Independent Practice ☆ Find each sum. Use any strategy. Show your work.

3. 33 + 52 = _____

4. 27 + 6 = _____

5. _____ = 49 + 45

6. 57 + 12 = _____

7. _____ = 63 + 20

8. 14 + 58 = _____

9. 45 + 55 = _____

10. 87 + 9 = _____

11. 19 + 61 = _____

Number Sense Write the digit that makes each equation true.

12. 45 + 1 [ ] = 61

13. 84 = [ ] 8 + 56

14. 3 [ ] + 19 = 56

15. Reasoning Martin has 44 marbles. Carol has 39 marbles. Steve has 90 marbles. How many marbles do Martin and Carol have in all? Do they have more or fewer marbles than Steve?

_____ marbles

Circle: more   fewer

31	32	33	34	35	36	37	38	39	40
41	42	43	44	45	46	47	48	49	50
51	52	53	54	55	56	57	58	59	60
61	62	63	64	65	66	67	68	69	70
71	72	73	74	75	76	77	78	79	80
81	82	83	84	85	86	87	88	89	90
91	92	93	94	95	96	97	98	99	100

16. Higher Order Thinking José collected 32 leaves on Saturday. On Sunday, he collected 14 more leaves than he did on Saturday. How many leaves did José collect in all?

_____ leaves

Move down one row to show adding tens. Move ahead to show adding ones.

17. ⓘ Assessment Lucita wants to use an open number line to find 53 + 18. Show and explain how Lucita can use an open number line to find 53 + 18.

© Pearson Education, Inc. 2

Help   Tools   Games

Another Look!

Find 24 + 56.

Step 1: Remember, 24 + 56 = 56 + 24.

Step 2: Place _56_ on an open number line.

Step 3: Count on _2_ tens from 56 to get to _76_.

Step 4: Then, count on _4_ ones from 76 to get to _80_.

So, 24 + 56 = _80_.

+10   +10   +4

56   66   76 80

HOME ACTIVITY Ask your child to show and describe how to find 46 + 27 using an open number line.

You can add numbers in any order and get the same sum.

Add using an open number line or another strategy. Show your work.

1. 38 + 6 = _____

2. 29 + 67 = _____

3. 48 + 34 = _____

4. **Reasoning** There were 43 students on the playground. Some more students joined them. Now there are 63 students on the playground. How many students joined?

_____ students

5. Roger has 14 grapes. Lisa has 49 grapes. How many grapes do Roger and Lisa have in all?

_____ grapes

6. **Higher Order Thinking** Two teams collected cans for a food drive. How many cans did they collect in all? Show your work.

Red Team		Blue Team	
Boys	**Girls**	**Boys**	**Girls**
23	28	12	30

7. **① Assessment** Ali wrote this first step in how to add 27 + 12 on a hundred chart.

Start at 27 on the chart.

Write the other steps.

_____

_____

_____

_____

Name _____

Solve & Share

The Red Team has 15 more points than the Blue team. The Blue Team has 36 points. How many points does the Red Team have?

Solve and explain your answer using counters, drawings, or equations.

I can ...
use drawings and equations to solve one-step and two-step problems.

Content Standard 2.CA.2
Process Standards PS.1, PS.2, PS.4, PS.6

★★★★★★ **10:00** ☆☆☆☆☆☆

Red Team   **Blue Team**
   ?   Period   **36**
              3

Matt sold 17 tickets.
Jenn sold 8 fewer tickets than Matt.
Amy sold 3 more tickets than Jenn.

How many tickets did each person sell?

Step 1

tickets Matt sold

17

8	9

fewer tickets   tickets Jenn sold

$17 - 8 = 9$
Jenn sold 9 tickets.

Step 2

tickets Amy sold

12

9	3

tickets Jenn sold   more tickets

$9 + 3 = 12$
Amy sold 12 tickets.

Matt: 17 tickets
Jenn: 9 tickets
Amy: 12 tickets

Look back! Does your answer make sense?

Do You Understand?

Show Me! What steps did you take to find the number of tickets Amy sold? Explain.

☆ Guided Practice   Solve the two-step problem. Show your work.

1. Steve read 15 books. Sam read 9 fewer books than Steve. Dixon read 8 more books than Sam.

How many books did Sam read?

$\underline{15} - \underline{9} = \underline{}$

How many books did Dixon read?

$\underline{6} + \underline{8} = \underline{}$

15

____	9

Sam read _____ books.

____

6	8

Dixon read _____ books.

© Pearson Education, Inc. 2

Topic 3 | Lesson 8

Independent Practice ⭐ Solve the problems below. Show your work.

2. Brian has 17 fewer marbles than Kyle. Brian has 21 marbles. How many marbles does Kyle have?

_____ marbles

3. Clint catches 7 frogs. 3 frogs hop away. Then Clint catches 6 more frogs. How many frogs does Clint have now?

_____ frogs

4. Erwin sees 23 birds in a tree. Then 18 more birds come. How many birds does Erwin see now?

_____ birds

5. There are 31 blue fish in a pond. There are also 8 gold fish and 3 red fish in the pond. How many fish are in the pond?

_____ fish

6. Higher Order Thinking Mr. Leu buys 6 bananas. Then he buys 8 more bananas. He gives some bananas to Mr. Shen. Now Mr. Leu has 5 bananas. How many bananas did Mr. Leu give to Mr. Shen?

_____ bananas

7. There are 21 more green crayons than blue crayons. There are 14 blue crayons. How many green crayons are there?

_____ green crayons

8. **Make Sense** Dan swims 4 laps on Monday. He swims 5 laps on Tuesday. Then he swims 9 laps on Wednesday. How many laps does Dan swim in all?

_____ + _____ = _____

_____ + _____ = _____

_____ laps

9. **Higher Order Thinking** Robert has 20 blueberries. He has 10 more blueberries than Janessa. He has 14 fewer blueberries than Amari. How many blueberries does Janessa have? How many blueberries does Amari have?

_____ − _____ = _____

_____ + _____ = _____

Janessa has _____ blueberries.

Amari has _____ blueberries.

10. **Assessment** Billy saw 19 animals at Grayson Zoo in the morning. He saw 17 more animals after lunch. How many animals did Billy see in all?

_____ + _____ = _____ animals

Taylor saw 41 animals at Richmond Zoo. How many animals did Billy and Taylor see in all?

_____ + _____ = _____

Billy and Taylor saw _____ animals in all.

Help Tools Games

Another Look! Write equations to solve two-step problems.

Allison collected 23 rocks.
Jason collected 15 more rocks than Allison.
Phil collected 3 fewer rocks than Allison.

How many rocks does Jason have?
How many rocks does Phil have?

Be sure to solve each part of the problem!

Number of Rocks Jason has: $23 + 15 = ?$

$23 + 10 = 33$ and $33 + 5 = 38$

So, Jason has ___38___ rocks.

You can count back 3 from 23 to find the number of rocks Phil has.

23, __22__, __21__, __20__ So, Phil has __20__ rocks.

HOME ACTIVITY Make up story problems that take two questions, or steps, to solve. Ask your child to solve both steps of each problem.

Write equations to solve the problems.

1. There are 4 fewer students in Ms. Jagger's class than Mr. Curley's class. Mr. Curley's class has 20 students. How many students are in Ms. Jagger's class?

_____ − _____ = _____

_____ students

2. There are 13 green grapes and 7 red grapes in a bowl. Joe ate 5 of the grapes. How many grapes are in the bowl now?

_____ + _____ = _____

_____ − _____ = _____

_____ grapes

Algebra Find the missing numbers.

3. ■ + 42 = 58

   ■ = _____

4. 33 + 49 = ▲

   ▲ = _____

5. 76 + ◯ = 89

   ◯ = _____

Write equations to solve each problem.

6. **Make Sense** There are 6 girls at a park. 6 boys join them. Then 4 girls go home. How many children are at the park now?

   _____ + _____ = _____

   _____ − _____ = _____

   _____ children.

7. **Higher Order Thinking** Mr. Villa's class has 23 students. Ms. Anderson's class has 3 more students than Mr. Villa's class. How many students are there in all?

Check your work. Does your answer make sense?

_____ students

8. **⬤ Assessment** Mike used 27 nails to build a chair. He used 14 more nails to build a table than he used to build the chair. How many nails did Mike use to build the table? Use any strategy to solve. Explain your solution.

_____ nails

© Pearson Education, Inc. 2

Name _____

Solve & Share

There are 23 red balloons in a bag. There are 38 blue balloons in the same bag. How many balloons are in the bag?

Use a tool to solve the problem. Be ready to explain which tool you used and why.

I can ...
choose a tool and use it to solve a problem.

Process Standards PS.5 Also PS.1, PS.2, PS.3
Content Standards 2.CA.2, 2.CA.1

Thinking Habits
Which of these tools can I use?

Tools

Cubes   Paper and
Counters   pencil
Hundred chart   Place-value
Technology   blocks

Is there a different tool I can use?

Ted's puzzle has 37 more pieces than Mia's puzzle. Mia's puzzle has 48 pieces. How many pieces does Ted's puzzle have?

Which tool can I use?

Tools
- cubes
- counters
- hundred chart
- technology
- paper and pencil
- place-value blocks

Which tool is a good choice?

Ted has 37 more pieces than Mia. I can use place-value blocks to find 48 + 37.

48 + 37 = 85

Ted's puzzle has 85 pieces.

If I used counters, I'd need to count each one.

With place-value blocks, I can add the tens quicker.

I can break apart 37 and add each part to 48 to check.

48 + 30 = 78

78 + 7 =
78 + 2 + 5 = 85

My answer makes sense.

Do You Understand?

Show Me! Explain why a ten-frame is not the best tool to use to solve the problem above.

☆ **Guided Practice** ☆ Choose a tool to help you solve the problem. Show your work. Explain why you chose that tool and how you solved the problem.

1. There are 16 chickens in the yard. There are 19 chickens in the barn. How many chickens are there in all?

   Will you use place-value blocks or counters to solve the problem? Explain.

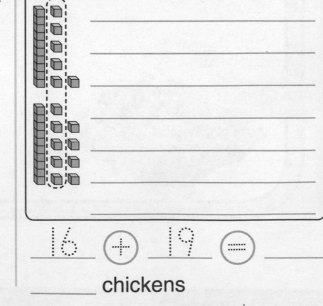

16 ⊕ 19 ⊜ ____

____ chickens

© Pearson Education, Inc. 2

Tools Assessment

Choose a tool to help solve each problem. Show your work. Explain your tool choice and how you solved the problem.

2. Greg had 45 sports cards. Jamal gives him 26 more cards. How many sports cards does Greg have now?

AWESOME MAVERICKS
P. LOVE

_____
_____
_____
_____

____ ◯ ____ ◯ ____

_____ sports cards

3. Denise drew 8 stars with crayons. Then she drew 6 more stars. Trina drew 5 stars. How many fewer stars did Trina draw than Denise?

_____
_____
_____
_____

____ ◯ ____ ◯ ____
____ ◯ ____ ◯ ____

_____ fewer stars

Problem Solving

Bean Bag Toss

Evan and Pam want to choose the best tool to solve this problem.

Evan and Pam each throw two bean bags. Points are added for a score. Pam's total score is 100. Which two numbers did Pam's bean bags land on?

Bean Bag Toss Game Board

4. **Make Sense** What information is given? What do you need to find?

_____

_____

_____

_____

5. **Explain** Which numbers did Pam's bags land on? Explain how you know.

_____

_____

_____

_____

6. **Use Tools** Which tool did you use? How could you use a hundred chart to solve the problem? Explain.

_____

_____

_____

1	2	3	4	5	6	7	8	9	10
11	12	13	14	15	16	17	18	19	20
21	22	23	24	25	26	27	28	29	30
31	32	33	34	35	36	37	38	39	40
41	42	43	44	45	46	47	48	49	50
51	52	53	54	55	56	57	58	59	60
61	62	63	64	65	66	67	68	69	70
71	72	73	74	75	76	77	78	79	80
81	82	83	84	85	86	87	88	89	90
91	92	93	94	95	96	97	98	99	100

© Pearson Education, Inc. 2

Name _____

Another Look! What tool would you use to solve this problem?

Jamie read 23 pages of a book last week.
This week, she read 26 more pages.
How many pages did Jamie read in all?

(23)	24	25	26	27	28	29
33	34	35	36	37	38	39
(43)	44	45	46	47	48	(49)

A hundred chart is a good tool to use. You can start at 23 and count on 2 tens, and then 6 ones. You land on 49. So, 23 + 26 = 49.

23 (+) 26 (=) 49   pages. Jamie read 49 pages in all.

HOME ACTIVITY Take turns adding two 2-digit numbers. Use drawings of tens and ones to show how you found each sum.

Choose a tool to help you solve the problem. Show your work.
Explain your tool choice and how you solved the problem.

1. A year ago, Maggie's puppy weighed 16 pounds. Now her puppy weighs 37 pounds more. How much does Maggie's puppy weigh now?

_____ ◯ _____ ◯ _____ pounds

Rubber Bands

Juan is trying to find the best tool to solve this problem.

Juan wants to buy 1 large bag and 1 small bag of rubber bands. How many rubber bands will he buy?

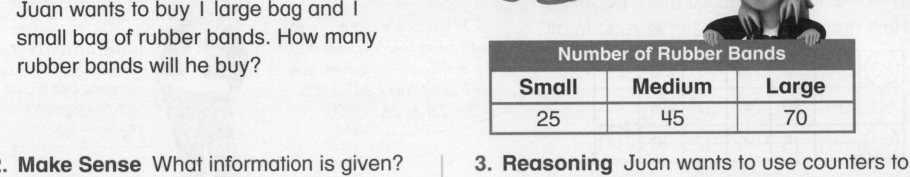

Number of Rubber Bands		
Small	**Medium**	**Large**
25	45	70

2. **Make Sense** What information is given? What do you need to find?

_____

_____

_____

3. **Reasoning** Juan wants to use counters to solve the problem. Do you think Juan's tool choice is a good one? Why or why not?

_____

_____

_____

4. **Use Tools** Use a tool to solve the problem. Which tool did you use? Is there a different tool you could have used to solve the problem? Explain.

_____

_____

_____

_____

_____

Name _____

Find a Match

Find a partner. Point to a clue. Read the clue.

Look below the clues to find a match. Write the clue letter in the box next to the match.

Find a match for every clue.

I can …
subtract within 20.

Clues

A Every difference equals 3.

B Every difference is less than 2.

C Every difference equals 11 − 5.

D Exactly two differences are equal.

E Every difference is greater than 8.

F Exactly three differences are odd.

G Every difference equals 16 − 8.

H Exactly three differences are even.

☐	6 − 5 8 − 8 10 − 10 9 − 9	☐	8 − 6 12 − 8 15 − 8 4 − 0	☐	18 − 9 16 − 7 11 − 2 10 − 1	☐	10 − 8 9 − 4 6 − 2 14 − 9
☐	17 − 9 9 − 1 13 − 5 12 − 4	☐	14 − 8 12 − 6 8 − 2 13 − 7	☐	11 − 6 5 − 3 14 − 7 12 − 3	☐	12 − 9 9 − 6 11 − 8 10 − 7

A-Z
Glossary

Word List
- bar diagram
- break apart
- compensation
- mental math
- ones
- open number line
- tens

Understand Vocabulary

1. Circle the numbers that have a 3 in the ones place.

33   45   13   38

2. Cross out the numbers that do **NOT** have an 8 in the tens place.

80   18   78   89

3. Write an equation to show how to break apart 54 by place value.

_____

4. Use the open number line to find 38 + 23. Add the tens and then add the ones.

Use Vocabulary in Writing

5. Describe a way to find 47 + 18. Use terms from the Word List.

Name _____

Set A

You can use a hundred chart to help you add. Find 62 + 12.

Start at 62.
Move down
I row to add
the one ten
in 12.

51	52	53	54	55	56	57	58	59	60
61	62	63	64	65	66	67	68	69	70
71	72	73	74	75	76	77	78	79	80
81	82	83	84	85	86	87	88	89	90
91	92	93	94	95	96	97	98	99	100

Then move over
2 columns to add
the 2 ones in 12. So, 62 + 12 = __74__.

Reteaching

Use a hundred chart to find each sum.

1. 85 + 15 = _____

2. 60 + 23 = _____

Set B

You can use an open number line to find 64 + 20.

Place 64 on the number line.

Count on by 10 two times from 64.

So, 64 + 20 = __84__.

Use an open number line to find each sum.

3. 50 + 30 = _____

4. 16 + 40 = _____

You can use an open number line to
find 49 + 32.

Place 49 on the number line. There are 3 tens
in 33. So, count on by 10 three times. There
are 2 ones in 32. So, count on 2 from 79.

So, 49 + 32 = ___81___.

Use an open number line to
find each sum.

5. 35 + 13 = _____

6. 47 + 26 = _____

Find 32 + 19.
Break apart the tens and ones.

32   +   19 = ___51___

Tens | 30 | | 10 |

Ones | 2 | | 9 |

Add the tens: ___30___ + ___10___ = ___40___

Add the ones: ___2___ + ___9___ = ___11___

Add the sums: 40 + 11 = ___51___

Break apart numbers to find each sum.
Show your work.

7. 24 + 55 = _____

8. 64 + 27 = _____

© Pearson Education, Inc. 2

Name _____

Set E _____

Find 55 + 17.

Break apart 17 into 10 + 7.

55   +   17 = ?

| 55 | | 10 | 7 |

Add tens: 55 + 10 = 65

Add ones: 65 + 7 = 72

So, 55 + 17 = _72_.

Break apart the second addend to find the sum. Show your work.

Reteaching

9. 53 + 28 = _____

10. 78 + 19 = _____

Set F _____

Find 48 + 27.

48 is close to 50. So, take 2 from 27 and give it to 48 to make 50.

48 + 27 = ?

+ 2   − 2

50 + 25 = ?

| 20 | 5 |

_50_ + _20_ + _5_ = _75_

So, 48 + 27 = _75_

Use compensation to make numbers that are easier to add. Then solve. Show your work.

11. 17 + 46 = _____

12. 29 + 57 = _____

Marla walks 12 blocks on Monday.
On Tuesday she walks 4 fewer blocks.
How many blocks does Marla walk in all?

Blocks Marla walks on Tuesday:

_12_ – _4_ = _8_

Blocks Marla walks on Monday and Tuesday:

_12_ + _8_ = _20_

_20_ blocks

Solve the two-step problem.

13. Wyatt has 16 crayons.
His father buys him 24 new crayons.
Then Wyatt's sister gives him 7 more crayons.
How many crayons does Wyatt have now?

_____ + _____ = _____

_____ + _____ = _____

_____ crayons

Thinking Habits

Use Tools

Which of these tools can I use?

Cubes   Paper and
Counters   pencil
Hundred chart   Place-value
Technology   blocks

Is there a different tool
I can use?

Choose a tool to help solve the problem. Show your work.
Explain your tool choice.

14. 42 people are at a park before lunch. 29 people join those people after lunch.
How many people are at the park in all?

© Pearson Education, Inc. 2

Name _____

1. Use mental math. Which weights can you put on the scale to make it balance?

(A) 10 40

(C) 40 33

(B) 10 21

(D) 33 10

2. Terry has 63 crayons. She gets 25 more crayons. How many crayons does Terry have in all? Show your work.

_____ crayons

---

3. Which equation does this number line show?

(A) $50 + 30 = 80$ (C) $50 + 50 = 100$

(B) $50 + 40 = 90$ (D) $50 + 90 = 140$

---

4. Use the numbers on the cards. Write the missing numbers under the number line to show how to find the sum of $40 + 35$.

75   60   50   70

5. Colin has 54 pennies and 28 nickels. How many coins does Colin have?

Break apart the numbers to solve. Show your work.

_____ coins

6. Show how to add 68 + 16 using the open number line.

68 + 16 = _____

7. Part A Show how you can use an open number line to find 44 + 27.

44 + 27 = _____

Part B In words, tell how you used the open number line to find the sum.

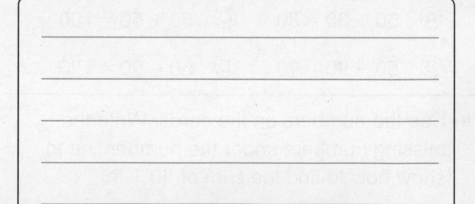

8. Which has a sum of 70? Choose all that apply.

☐ 35 + 35   ☐ 40 + 30   ☐ 45 + 45   ☐ 50 + 20

9. Lisa has 18 markers.
Adam has 22 markers.
How many markers are there in all?

Choose a tool to solve the problem.

_____ markers

10. Ted has 52 cards in a box.
Tyrone has 48 more cards
than Ted. How many cards
does Tyrone have?

_____ cards

11. Which is equal to 47 + 25? Choose all that apply.

☐   40 + 20 + 7 + 5   ☐   40 + 20 + 12   ☐   50 + 12   ☐   50 + 22

12. Emma has 46 rocks.
She gets 25 more rocks from Gus.
How many rocks does Emma
have now?

_____ ◯ _____ = _____

_____ rocks

41	42	43	44	45	46	47	48	49	50
51	52	53	54	55	56	57	58	59	60
61	62	63	64	65	66	67	68	69	70
71	72	73	74	75	76	77	78	79	80

13. Is each sum 64? Choose Yes or No.

22 + 34 + 8   ◯ Yes   ◯ No

32 + 32   ◯ Yes   ◯ No

28 + 34 + 2   ◯ Yes   ◯ No

42 + 14 + 8   ◯ Yes   ◯ No

14. Break apart numbers to find 56 + 38.
Show your work.

56 + 38 = _____

15. Write an equation to solve each part
of the two-step problem.

Ken has 45 stamps.
He uses 20 stamps.
Then he buys 7 more stamps.
How many stamps does he have now?

_____ ◯ _____ = _____

_____ ◯ _____ = _____

Ken has _____ stamps.

16. Show two different ways
to find 28 + 49.

Way 1

Way 2

Name _____

Popcorn Sales

A second-grade class is selling popcorn to help pay for a field trip.

This table shows how many boxes some students have sold.

Number of Popcorn Boxes Sold	
Ted	21
Nancy	19
Darnell	28
Mary	34
Elena	43

1. How many boxes of popcorn did Ted and Mary sell in all? Use the open number line to solve. Show your work.

⟵——————————————⟶

_____ boxes

2. James says that Mary and Nancy sold more boxes in all than Darnell and Ted sold in all. Do you agree with him?

Circle   **yes**   **no**

Explain your answer.

_____

_____

_____

_____

3. Which two students sold a total of 55 boxes? Use any strategy to solve. Show your work.

Circle the names of the two students.

Ted   Nancy   Darnell

Mary   Elena

Which tool can I use?

Tools
- cubes
- counters
- hundred chart
- technology
- paper and pencil
- place-value blocks

4. Nancy sold 18 fewer boxes than Lucas. How many boxes did Lucas sell?

Part A Solve the problem. Show your work and explain your thinking.

_____ boxes

Part B Emily wants to use a tool to solve the problem. Look at the list of tools at the left. Which tool would be a good choice? Which tool would **NOT** be a good choice? Explain.

© Pearson Education, Inc. 2

Topic 3 | Performance Assessment

Fluently Add Within 100

Essential Question: What are strategies for adding numbers to 100?

Digital Resources

Solve   Learn   Glossary

Tools   Assessment   Help   Games

The islands of Hawaii began as volcanoes!

You can still see some volcanoes if you visit Hawaii.

Wow! Let's do this project and learn more.

Math and Science Project: Making and Using Models

Find Out Find and share books about Hawaii and volcanoes. Make a model of a volcano that becomes an island. Tell about how the island can change over a long time.

Journal: Make a Book Show what you learn in a book. In your book, also:

• Draw pictures to show how volcanoes can become islands.

• Show how you can use models to help you add numbers to 100.

Name _____

Review What You Know

A-Z Vocabulary

1. Circle the **tens** digit in each number.

73

53

82

2. Circle the **ones** digit in each number.

34

43

97

3. **Break apart** 23 into tens and ones.

23 = _____ tens and

_____ ones

Mental Math

4. Use mental math to find each sum.

34 + 10 = _____

50 + 5 = _____

20 + 40 = _____

Open Number Line

5. Use the open number line to find 39 + 15.

39 + 15 = _____

Math Story

6. Stacy has 17 marbles. Diana gives her 22 marbles. How many marbles does Stacy have now?

_____ marbles

© Pearson Education, Inc. 2

My Word Cards

Study the words on the front of the card.
Complete the activity on the back.

A-Z
Glossary

partial sum

Tens	Ones
5	7
+ 2	8
7	0	← partial sum
+ 1	5	← partial sum
8	5	← sum

regroup

compatible numbers

8 + 2
20 + 7
53 + 10

Use what you know to complete the sentences.
Extend learning by writing your own sentence using each word.

_____

_____

are numbers that are easy to add or subtract using mental math.

You can _____

10 ones to make 1 ten.

You can _____

1 ten to make 10 ones.

When you add numbers, the sum of one of the place values is called a

_____.

Solve & Share

Use place-value blocks to find 47 + 22.
Then draw a picture to show your work.

47 + 22 = _____

Find 57 + 28.

> I can use place-value blocks to check my work.

Tens	Ones
5	7
+ 2	8

First, add the tens.

That's one **partial sum**.

	Tens	Ones
	5	7
+	2	8
50 + 20 =	7	0

Then add the ones.

That's another partial sum.

	Tens	Ones
	5	7
+	2	8
50 + 20 =	7	0
7 + 8 =	1	5

Then add the partial sums to find the sum.

	Tens	Ones
	5	7
+	2	8
50 + 20 =	7	0
7 + 8 =	1	5
Sum =	8	5

So, 57 + 28 = 85.

Do You Understand?

Show Me! How can you use partial sums to add 23 + 8? Explain.

☆ Guided Practice ☆

Add. Use partial sums. Show your work. Use place-value blocks, if needed.

1. 24 + 13

	Tens	Ones
	2	4
+	1	3
20 + 10 =	3	0
4 + 3 =		7
Sum =		

2. 68 + 7

	Tens	Ones
	6	8
+		7
60 + 0 =		
8 + 7 =		
Sum =		

© Pearson Education, Inc. 2

Name

Independent Practice ☆ Add. Use partial sums. Use place-value blocks, if needed.

3. 34 + 25

Tens	Ones
3	4
+ 2	5
___ + ___ =		
___ + ___ =		
Sum =		

4. 68 + 18

Tens	Ones
6	8
+ 1	8
___ + ___ =		
___ + ___ =		
Sum =		

5. 37 + 8

Tens	Ones
3	7
+	8
___ + ___ =		
___ + ___ =		
Sum =		

6. 52 + 38

Tens	Ones
5	2
+ 3	8
___ + ___ =		
___ + ___ =		
Sum =		

7. 45 + 29

Tens	Ones
4	5
+ 2	9
___ + ___ =		
___ + ___ =		
Sum =		

8. 28 + 39

Tens	Ones
2	8
+ 3	9
___ + ___ =		
___ + ___ =		
Sum =		

Number Sense Write each missing tens or ones digit.

9. 23 + 1☐ = 37

10. 59 = ☐8 + 31

11. Model 34 students are on the playground. 17 students are in the gym. How many students are there in all?

12. Sarah put 8 white roses in a vase. Then she added 7 red roses and 12 yellow roses to the vase. How many roses are in the vase now?

Why does the partial sums method work? Think about it!

_____ students

_____ roses

13. Higher Order Thinking Write each missing tens or ones digit. What strategy did you use?

$$\begin{array}{r} 12 \\ + 3\square \\ \hline 50 \end{array}$$

$$\begin{array}{r} 24 \\ + 3\square \\ \hline 60 \end{array}$$

$$\begin{array}{r} 35 \\ + 3\square \\ \hline 70 \end{array}$$

14. Assessment Sasha has 28 pennies. Her sister gives her 36 more pennies. How many pennies does she have now? Use partial sums to solve.

Ⓐ 8

Ⓑ 12

Ⓒ 54

Ⓓ 64

Name _____

Help   Tools   Games

Another Look! Use partial sums to find 32 + 45.

Write the problem this way.   32 + 45 = ?

Step 1: Add the tens   30 + 40 = 70

Step 2: Add the ones.   2 + 5 = 7

Step 3: Add the
partial sums.   70 + 7 = 77

So, 32 + 45 = __77__.

> Break apart the numbers into tens and ones.

HOME ACTIVITY Ask your child to show you how to add 24 + 33 using partial sums.

Add. Use partial sums. Show your work.

1. 23 + 16 = _____

Add the tens.

_____ + _____ = _____

Add the ones.

_____ + _____ = _____

Add the partial sums.

_____ + _____ = _____

2. 37 + 61 = _____

Add the tens.

_____ + _____ = _____

Add the ones.

_____ + _____ = _____

Add the partial sums.

_____ + _____ = _____

3. 35 + 29 = _____

Add the tens.

_____ + _____ = _____

Add the ones.

_____ + _____ = _____

Add the partial sums.

_____ + _____ = _____

4. Make Sense 28 leaves fell from a tree. Then 32 more leaves fell. How many leaves fell in all?

_____ leaves

5. Liam put 6 cars on his empty toy racetrack. Then Joe put 8 cars on the track. Then Kim put 4 cars on the track. How many cars are on the track now?

_____ cars

6. Higher Order Thinking Write each missing number. What pattern do you see?

```
  34        44        54
+ [  ]    + [  ]    + [  ]
────      ────      ────
  44        54        64
```

7. ⓘAssessment Amir had 37 stamps. Then Tim gave him 16 more stamps. How many stamps does Amir have now? Use partial sums to solve.

Ⓐ 16

Ⓑ 21

Ⓒ 43

Ⓓ 53

Name _____

Solve & Share

Wendy picked 37 pears. Toni picked 46 pears. How many pears did they pick in all?

Solve the problem using partial sums.
Draw place-value blocks to help explain your work.

I can ...
add numbers using partial sums.

 Content Standard 2.CA.1
Process Standards PS.1, PS.2, PS.3, PS.4, PS.6

	Tens	Ones
+		
+ =		
+ =		
Sum =		

_____ pears

Find 38 + 59.

Tens	Ones
3	8
+ 5	9

You can use mental math to find partial sums.

First, add the tens.

Tens	Ones
3	8
+ 5	9
Tens: 8	0

Then, add the ones.

Tens	Ones
3	8
+ 5	9
Tens: 8	0
Ones: 1	7

Last, add the partial sums.

Tens	Ones
3	8
+ 5	9
Tens: 8	0
Ones: 1	7
Sum: 9	7

So, 38 + 59 = 97.

Do You Understand?

Show Me! Ken adds 43 + 27. His sum is 60. Is he correct? Explain.

☆ Guided Practice   Add. Use partial sums. Show your work.

1. 12 + 23

Tens	Ones
1	2
+ 2	3
Tens: 3	0
Ones:	5
Sum:	

2. 18 + 42

Tens	Ones
1	8
+ 4	2
Tens:	
Ones:	
Sum:	

3. 33 + 48

Tens	Ones
3	3
+ 4	8
Tens:	
Ones:	
Sum:	

Tools Assessment

Independent Practice ☆ Add. Use partial sums. Show your work.

4. 18 + 24

Tens	Ones
1	8
+ 2	4
Tens:	
Ones:	
Sum:	

5. 47 + 38

Tens	Ones
4	7
+ 3	8
Tens:	
Ones:	
Sum:	

6. 26 + 47

Tens	Ones
2	6
+ 4	7
Tens:	
Ones:	
Sum:	

7. 34 + 58

Tens	Ones
3	4
+ 5	8
Tens:	
Ones:	
Sum:	

Higher Order Thinking Read the sum above each box.
Circle all the pairs of numbers in the box that match the sum.

8. Sum 33

13	21	12
20	27	11
13	6	22

9. Sum 48

28	40	22
20	8	38
23	25	10

10. Sum 64

48	15	49
16	40	24
42	26	38

11. Toby planted 28 trees. Juan planted 36 trees. How many trees did they plant in all?

Tens	Ones
+	

Tens: ☐

Ones: ☐

Sum: ☐

_____ trees

12. Make Sense Jenny has 13 tennis balls. Sal had 19 tennis balls, but he gave 7 of them to Joe. How many tennis balls do Jenny and Sal have now?

_____ tennis balls

13. Higher Order Thinking Write an addition story using two 2-digit numbers. Then solve the problem for your story.

14. ☐**Assessment** Which is the same amount as 28 + 16? Choose all that apply.

☐ 20 + 10 + 8 + 6

☐ 30 + 14

☐ 34

☐ 44

Is there more than one correct answer?

Name _____

Continue to Add with Partial Sums

Another Look! Find 36 + 28.

Step 1
Add the tens.
3 tens + 2 tens
30 + 20 = 50

Tens	Ones

Step 2
Add the ones.
6 + 8 = 14

Tens	Ones

Make 1 ten with 10 ones.

Step 3
Add the partial sums.

	Tens	Ones
	3	6
+	2	8
Tens:	5	0
Ones:	1	4
Sum:	6	4

So, 36 + 28 = 64.

HOME ACTIVITY Write 27 + 44 on a sheet of paper. Ask your child to use partial sums to find the total.

Add. Use partial sums. Show your work.

1. 24 + 35

	Tens	Ones
	2	4
+	3	5
Tens:		
Ones:		
Sum:		

2. 17 + 44

	Tens	Ones
	1	7
+	4	4
Tens:		
Ones:		
Sum:		

3. 58 + 24

	Tens	Ones
	5	8
+	2	4
Tens:		
Ones:		
Sum:		

4. 25 + 65

	Tens	Ones
	2	5
+	6	5
Tens:		
Ones:		
Sum:		

Be Precise Add. Use partial sums. Show your work.

5. 53 + 23

Tens	Ones
5	3
+ 2	3

Tens:

Ones:

Sum:

6. 35 + 28

Tens	Ones
3	5
+ 2	8

Tens:

Ones:

Sum:

7. 39 + 48

Tens	Ones
3	9
+ 4	8

Tens:

Ones:

Sum:

8. 69 + 27

Tens	Ones
6	9
+ 2	7

Tens:

Ones:

Sum:

9. Higher Order Thinking Draw the second addend. Write the number.

First Addend

Second Addend

Sum

There is more than one correct answer!

10. Algebra Write each missing number.

28 + = 48

 = _____

△ + 18 = 68

△ = _____

11. Assessment Which is the same amount as 12 + 9 + 8? Choose all that apply.

☐ 20 + 9

☐ 12 + 10 + 7

☐ 29

☐ 39

Leslie collects 36 rocks. Her brother collects 27 rocks. How many rocks do they collect in all?

Use place-value blocks to help you solve. Draw your place-value blocks.

I can …
use models to add 2-digit numbers and then explain my work.

Content Standard 2.CA.1
Process Standards PS.2, PS.3, PS.4, PS.5, PS.6

Tens	Ones
+	

_____ rocks

Let's add!

37 + 19 = ?

Show 37.
Then show 19.

Tens	Ones
3	7
1	9

+

Add the ones.

7 ones + 9 ones = 16 ones

Tens	Ones
3	7
1	9

+

There are 16 ones.
Regroup 16 ones as
1 ten and 6 ones.

Tens	Ones
3	7
1	9
	6

+

Write **6** ones.
Write **1** to show 1 ten.

Add the tens.

3 tens + 1 ten = 4 tens
4 tens + 1 ten = 5 tens

Tens	Ones
1	
3	7
1	9
5	6

+

Write **5** to show 5 tens.

Do You Understand?

Show Me! When do you have to regroup when adding?

☆ **Guided Practice** ☆ Add. Draw place-value blocks to show your work. Regroup if needed.

1.

Tens	Ones
⬚	
3	2
2	9
6	

+

Tens	Ones

2.

Tens	Ones
⬚	
2	4
5	2

+

Tens	Ones

3.

Tens	Ones
⬚	
1	5
3	8

+

Tens	Ones

Name _____

 Independent Practice ☆   Add. Draw place-value blocks to show your work. Regroup if needed.

4.

Tens	Ones
☐	
3	6
+ 2	9

Tens	Ones

5.

Tens	Ones
☐	
2	7
+ 2	3

Tens	Ones

6.

Tens	Ones
☐	
5	9
+ 1	3

Tens	Ones

7.

Tens	Ones
☐	
2	4
+ 3	5

Tens	Ones

8. Higher Order Thinking Draw the second addend.

First Addend   Second Addend   Sum

Topic 4 | Lesson 3   two hundred seven **207**

9. **Model** Chen counts 47 buttons. Then he counts 20 more buttons. How many buttons does Chen count in all?

_____ buttons

10. **Math and Science** There were 24 earthquakes in the U.S. one year. There were 23 earthquakes the next year. How many earthquakes were there in those two years?

_____ earthquakes

11. **Higher Order Thinking** Write an addition story about the desks and chairs in your classroom. Use pictures, numbers, or words.

12. ⬤ **Assessment** Do you have to regroup to find each sum? Choose Yes or No.

$62 + 34 = ?$　　○ Yes　○ No

$72 + 19 = ?$　　○ Yes　○ No

$43 + 49 = ?$　　○ Yes　○ No

$26 + 60 = ?$　　○ Yes　○ No

Name _____

Another Look! You can use these steps to add. Add 46 + 18.

Way I:

Step I: Draw the tens and ones.
Make I ten with 10 ones.

Tens	Ones

Step 2: Count the tens. Count the ones.

Tens	Ones

Way 2:

Tens	Ones
☐	
4	6
+ 1	8
6	4

46 + 18 = ___64___

HOME ACTIVITY Ask your child to show you how to add 27 + 34. Have your child explain each step of the addition.

Follow the steps to add. Draw place-value blocks to show your work. Regroup if needed.

1.

Tens	Ones
☐	
2	4
+ 2	9

2.

Tens	Ones
☐	
3	8
+ 4	5

Higher Order Thinking Write the missing numbers.
Draw place-value blocks if you need to.

3.

Tens	Ones
☐ 5	7
2	7
+	

4.

Tens	Ones
☐ 6	2
1	5
+	

5.

Tens	Ones
☐ 1	9
3	3
+	

Remember to write the regrouped numbers.

6.

Tens	Ones
☐ 2	7
◯	8
+	
4	5

7.

Tens	Ones
☐ 2	◯
5	7
+	
8	0

8.

Tens	Ones
☐ 3	8
◯	4
+	
6	2

9. Reasoning Lia has 38 red cups.
She has 25 blue cups.
How many cups does Lia have in all?

_____ cups

10. Assessment Do you have to regroup to find each sum? Choose Yes or No.

$22 + 41 = ?$ ◯ Yes   ◯ No

$19 + 60 = ?$ ◯ Yes   ◯ No

$64 + 28 = ?$ ◯ Yes   ◯ No

$39 + 52 = ?$ ◯ Yes   ◯ No

© Pearson Education, Inc. 2

Topic 4 | Lesson 3

Name _____

Solve & Share

Add 46 + 26.

Draw place-value blocks, if needed.
Explain how you solved the problem.

Tens | **Ones**

+

I can ...
add 2-digit numbers and then explain my work.

Content Standard 2.CA.1
Process Standards PS.1,
PS.2, PS.3, PS.4, PS.6

_____

_____

_____

Find 56 + 17.
Show 56. Then show 17.
Start by adding the ones.

Tens	Ones
5	6
1	7

6 ones + 7 ones = 13 ones

Regroup 13 ones
as 1 ten and 3 ones.

Tens	Ones
☐	
5	6
1	7
	3

Write **3** ones.
Write **1** to show
1 ten.

---

5 tens + 1 ten = 6 tens
6 tens + 1 ten = 7 tens

Add the tens.

Tens	Ones
1	
5	6
1	7
7	3

Write **7** to show 7 tens.

So, 56 + 17 = 73.

Do You Understand?

Show Me! Roger found
54 + 27. His sum was 71. Is
he correct? Why or why not?
Draw place-value blocks to
check.

☆ **Guided Practice** ☆ Write the addition problem. Find the sum.
Use drawings if you need to.

1. 34 + 17

Tens	Ones
1	
3	4
1	7
5	1

2. 52 + 31

Tens	Ones
☐	
+	

3. 35 + 26

Tens	Ones
☐	
+	

© Pearson Education, Inc. 2

Name _____

Independent Practice

Write the addition problem. Find the sum.
Use drawings if you need to.

4. 15 + 28

Tens	Ones
☐	

+

5. 29 + 20

Tens	Ones
☐	

+

6. 63 + 29

Tens	Ones
☐	

+

7. 37 + 48

Tens	Ones
☐	

+

8. 67 + 17

Tens	Ones
☐	

+

9. 15 + 18

Tens	Ones
☐	

+

10. 43 + 49

Tens	Ones
☐	

+

11. 62 + 28

Tens	Ones
☐	

+

Higher Order Thinking Write the missing ones or tens digits.

12. 27 + 2☐ = 50

13. 3☐ + 16 = 48

14. ☐4 + 49 = 93

15. Make Sense

Amir plants 25 trees. Juan plants 27 trees. How many trees do they plant in all?

Tens | Ones

+

_____ trees

16. On Monday, Sasha puts 32 pennies in her bank. On Tuesday, she puts 57 more pennies in her bank. How many pennies does she put in her bank on both days?

Tens | Ones

+

_____ pennies

17. Higher Order Thinking Write an addition story using 2 two-digit numbers. Then solve the problem for your story.

Tens | Ones

+

18. ⬤Assessment 52 acorns fall from a tree. Then 37 more acorns fall. How many acorns in all fall from the tree? Show how you solved the problem.

_____ acorns

Name _____

Another Look! Remember these steps for adding.

Step 1:
Add the ones.

Step 2:
Regroup if you need to.

Step 3:
Add the tens.

$34 + 27 = ?$
Regroup
11 ones as
1 ten and
1 one.

Tens	Ones
1	
3	4
+ 2	7
6	1

$12 + 36 = ?$
You do
not need
to regroup
8 ones.

Tens	Ones
1	2
+ 3	6
4	8

HOME ACTIVITY Write $28 + 45$ on a sheet of paper. Have your child find the sum using paper and pencil. Once finished, have your child explain why regrouping was needed.

Write the addition problem. Find the sum. Use drawings, if needed.

1. $15 + 26$

Tens	Ones
+	

2. $32 + 24$

Tens	Ones
+	

3. $28 + 15$

Tens	Ones
+	

4. $49 + 13$

Tens	Ones
+	

5. $75 + 13$

Tens	Ones
+	

Higher Order Thinking Read the sum. Circle all of the number pairs in the box that match that sum.

6. Sum 22

10	4	18
12	15	14
20	21	13

7. Sum 55

25	30	14
18	14	45
15	21	10

8. Sum 83

30	45	30
56	19	64
27	29	20

9. 🔵**A-Z** **Vocabulary** Paul has a stack of 47 cards. He also has a stack of 36 cards. How many cards does Paul have in all?

_____ cards

Be precise.

10. 🔵**J** **Assessment**
One box has 38 blue paper clips.
Another box has 43 green paper clips.
A third box has 6 red paper clips.
How many paper clips are in all the boxes?
Show how you solved the problem.

Fill in the blanks.

I **regrouped** _____ ones for _____ ten.

_____ paper clips

© Pearson Education, Inc. 2

Topic 4 | Lesson 4

Name _____

Solve & Share

Make three 2-digit numbers. The tens digit for each number is shown below. Toss a number cube three times to find the ones digit for each number.

How can you add your three numbers? Explain.

Tens	Ones
2	
1	
+ 2	

I can ...
add three or four 2-digit numbers.

Content Standard 2.CA.6
Process Standards PS.2, PS.3, PS.4, PS.6, PS.8

_____

_____

_____

Start by adding the ones. Add in any order.

```
  2 4
  1 6
  1 4
+ 1 5
```

You can use doubles.

```
  2 ⟨4⟩
  1 6
  1 ⟨4⟩
+ 1 5
    9
```

4 + 4 = 8
6 + 5 = 11
11 + 8 = 19

Or you can make 10.

```
  2 4
  1 ⟨6⟩
  1 ⟨4⟩
+ 1 5
    9
```

6 + 4 = 10
4 + 5 = 9
10 + 9 = 19

Then add the tens.

```
  2 4
  1 6
  1 4
+ 1 5
  6 9
```

The sum is 69!

Do You Understand?

Show Me! When you add more than three numbers, can you always make 10 to help you add the ones digits? Explain.

☆ Guided Practice   Add. Circle the two digits you added first.

1.
```
  1⟨8⟩
  1⟨2⟩
+ 1 5
  4 5
```

2.
```
  1 4
  1 1
+  9
```

3.
```
  2 1
  1 4
  4 1
+  2
```

4.
```
  2 1
  1 5
  3 2
+ 2 5
```

Remember, you can add numbers in any order.

Topic 4 | Lesson 5

Tools Assessment

Independent Practice ☆ Add. Circle the two digits you added first.

5.
```
   22
   14
 + 22
```

6.
```
   16
   23
 + 26
```

7.
```
   27
   13
 + 21
```

8.
```
   13
   33
 + 25
```

9.
```
   25
   21
 + 32
```

10.
```
   55
    7
   24
 +  2
```

11.
```
   32
   16
   18
 + 31
```

12.
```
   16
   42
   12
 + 22
```

13.
```
   17
   41
   27
 + 13
```

14.
```
   37
   11
   15
 + 28
```

Algebra Find the missing numbers.

15. $8 + 3 + \boxed{} + 2 = 18$

16. $5 + \boxed{} + 6 + 5 = 19$

17. $7 + 27 + 23 + \boxed{} = 61$

18. $\boxed{} + 24 + 18 + 4 = 52$

19. Generalize

28 trucks are blue.
32 trucks are yellow.
17 trucks are green.
11 trucks are pink.
How many trucks are
there in all?

Are there shortcuts
you can take to
solve the problems?

_____ trucks

20. Higher Order Thinking Henry is adding
the numbers 24, 36, and 18. He makes a
ten to add. Which ones digits does Henry
add first? Explain.

_____

_____

_____

21. ⓘ **Assessment** Find the sum.
Explain your work.

```
    25
    16
    15
 +   8
```

_____

_____

_____

_____

_____

Name _____

Another Look! You can add three or four numbers in any order. Remember to add the ones first. Then, add the tens.

Look for doubles.

```
 14    4 + 4 = 8
 35    8 + 5 = 13
+24
 73
```

Make a ten.

```
 13
 26
 24    6 + 4 = 10
+12    3 + 2 = 5
 75    10 + 5 = 15
```

Count on.

```
 53
 19
+22    Count on from 12.
 94    13, 14
```

9 + 3 = 12

HOME ACTIVITY Ask your child to find the sum of 16 + 14 + 6 using two different strategies.

Add. Circle the two digits you added first.

1. Look for doubles.

```
  21
  10
  34
 +24
```

2. Count on.

```
  12
  17
 +24
```

3. Make a ten.

```
  15
  28
 +22
```

4. Choose a way to add.

```
  26
  22
 +36
```

Model Look at the sum. Read the clues. Circle the three numbers that add up to that sum. Show the addition you used to find the sum.

5. Sum: 83

5   44   12   19   10   20

One number is the sum of 22 + 22.
One number is one less than 20.
One number is greater than
19 and less than 44.

6. Sum: 72

36   12   25   7   33   14

One number has two of the
same digits.
One number is greater than 12 and
less than 25.
One number is 20 more than 5.

7. Higher Order Thinking Mac's family donates clothes to charity. Mac donates 16 shirts. His brother donates 14 shirts, and his mother donates 9 more shirts than Mac. How many shirts does Mac's family give to charity?

_____ shirts

8. ⓓAssessment There are 37 ants, 39 worms, 12 moths, and 11 beetles living in a big garden. Find the sum. Explain your work.

```
   37  _____
   39  _____
   12  _____
+  11
       _____
```

© Pearson Education, Inc. 2

Topic 4 | Lesson 5

Solve

Solve & Share

Maria has 39 stickers. Sally has 28 stickers. They found 14 more stickers. How many stickers do they have in all?

Show your work. Explain how you found the answer.

I can ...

use mental math strategies and models to add more than two numbers.

 Content Standards 2.CA.1, 2.CA.6
Process Standards PS.2, PS.3, PS.4, PS.6, PS.7

_____ stickers

Find 27 + 38 + 12 + 3.
One Way: Use partial sums.

Tens	Ones
2	(7)
3	8
1	2
+	(3)

Tens: 6 0
Ones: 2 0
Sum: 8 0

Look for compatible numbers to make tens.
7 + 3 = 10
8 + 2 = 10
10 + 10 = 20

Another Way: Add the ones. Regroup, if needed. Then add the tens.

I get the same sum either way!

Tens	Ones
2	
2	(7)
3	8
1	2
	(3)
8	0

Check your work.

You can add the numbers in a different order to check your work.

30

27 + 38 + 12 + 3 =

50

30 + 50 = 80
So, 27 + 38 + 12 + 3 = 80.

Do You Understand?

Show Me! Find the sum of 14 + 28 + 33 + 22. Explain.

☆ Guided Practice   Add.

1.
```
  18
  43
+ 12
 73
```

How can you check your work?

2.
```
  29
+ 47
```

3.
```
   9
  34
+ 21
```

4.
```
  33
  27
  18
+ 13
```

© Pearson Education, Inc. 2

Independent Practice ☆ Add.

5.   28
      + 8
      ____

6.   8
      + 17
      ____

7.   5
        31
      + 29
      ____

8.   36
         4
      + 28
      ____

9.   20
         16
      + 16
      ____

10. 27
        13
        12
      + 5
      ____

11.   9
         29
          5
      + 35
      ____

12. 18
         23
          7
      + 42
      ____

13. 27
         15
         33
      + 24
      ____

14. 13
          7
         20
      + 55
      ____

Number Sense Solve each problem. In which order did you add the numbers? Explain.

15. 22 + 17 + 8 + 3 = _____

_____

_____

_____

16. 5 + 12 + 15 + 3 = _____

_____

_____

_____

17. **Model** Kim has 38 seashells. Mike has 27 seashells. Use **partial sums** to find how many shells they have in all. Then check your answer by adding another way.

_____ seashells

18. **Math and Science** Fossils form slowly over millions of years. Many fossils come from the sea. Kyle has 9 fossils, Jorie has 12 fossils, Leah has 6 fossils, and Joshua has 8 fossils. How many fossils did they have in all?

_____ fossils

19. **Higher Order Thinking** Find the sum. Explain why your strategy works.

22
13
18
+ 7

20. 🄳**Assessment** Kate has 7 balloons. Claire has 9 balloons. Billy has 6 balloons. How many balloons do they have in all? Show your work.

_____ balloons

© Pearson Education, Inc. 2
Topic 4 | Lesson 6

Name _____

Another Look! Find the sum.

34
29
18
+ 6
‾‾‾‾
60
+27
‾‾‾‾
87

Step 1: Add the tens in any order.
$30 + 20 + 10 = 50 + 10 = 60$

Step 2: Add the ones in any order.

(4) + 9 + 8 + (6) = ?

$10 + 17 = 27$

Step 3: Add the partial sums.
Think: $60 + 27 = ?$
$60 + 20 + 7 = 87$
So, $34 + 29 + 18 + 6 = 87$.

Add in any order.
It helps to make a 10.
$4 + 6 = 10$

HOME ACTIVITY Write
$22 + 33 + 18 + 7$ on a
sheet of paper. Ask your
child to show you how to
find the sum.

Add using partial sums.

1.

Tens	Ones
2	8
1	(3)
+	(7)
Tens: 3	0
Ones: 1	8
Sum:	

2.

Tens	Ones
3	4
2	6
+	7
Tens:	
Ones:	
Sum:	

3.

Tens	Ones
3	1
2	4
1	1
+	9
Tens:	
Ones:	
Sum:	

4.

Tens	Ones
2	3
3	7
	8
+ 2	8
Tens:	
Ones:	
Sum:	

Be Precise Add any way you choose. Show your work.

5. $\begin{array}{r} 26 \\ + 48 \\ \hline \end{array}$

6. $\begin{array}{r} 8 \\ 13 \\ + 22 \\ \hline \end{array}$

7. $\begin{array}{r} 5 \\ 11 \\ + 59 \\ \hline \end{array}$

8. $\begin{array}{r} 16 \\ 4 \\ 28 \\ + 48 \\ \hline \end{array}$

9. $\begin{array}{r} 20 \\ 6 \\ 17 \\ + 46 \\ \hline \end{array}$

Number Sense Find each missing number.

10. $6 + 13 + 4 + 7 = \boxed{}$

11. $5 + 15 + 12 + \boxed{} = 38$

12. **Higher Order Thinking** Write an addition story problem with 3 or more addends. Then solve the problem. Show your work.

13. **Assessment** Ricky is building a toy. He uses 27 red blocks. He uses 10 blue blocks and 36 brown blocks. How many blocks in all? Show your work.

_____ blocks

© Pearson Education, Inc. 2

Name _____

Solve & Share

The second graders take a trip to a nature center. The Green Class sees 23 animals. The Blue Class sees 14 animals. The Yellow Class sees 32 animals. How many animals do they see in all?

Solve using drawings, models, or an equation.
Be prepared to explain your work.

I can ...
use drawings, models, and equations to solve one- and two-step problems.

Content Standard 2.CA.2
Process Standards PS.1, PS.4, PS.5, PS.8

_____ animals

Aimee and Devin count 36 butterflies. Suddenly, more butterflies join them. Now, there are 53 butterflies.

How many new butterflies join them?

The total is 53. The first group has 36 butterflies. I will use a bar diagram to model the problem.

53

| 36 | ? |

$36 + ? = 53$

I can use mental math to find $36 + ? = 53$.

Think: $36 + 10 = 46$
$46 + 4 = 50$
$50 + 3 = 53$

$10 + 4 + 3 = 17$

So, $36 + \underline{17} = 53$.

So, 17 butterflies join them.
Check your work.

$$\begin{array}{r} 3\,6 \\ + 1\,7 \\ \hline 5\,3 \end{array}$$

The answer makes sense.
$36 + 17 = 53$

Do You Understand?

Show Me! Suppose you count 28 butterflies. Then suddenly there are 54. How could you use mental math to find how many join?

Guided Practice

Use the bar diagram and mental math to solve each problem. Then check your work.

1. There are 29 red marbles, 7 green marbles, and 11 blue marbles in a bag.

How many marbles are in the bag?

$\underline{29} + \underline{7} + \underline{11} = \underline{}$

_____ marbles

| 29 | 7 | 11 |

$$\begin{array}{r} 2\,9 \\ 7 \\ + 1\,1 \\ \hline \end{array}$$

© Pearson Education, Inc. 2

Independent Practice Use the bar diagram and mental math to solve each problem. Then check your work.

2. 29 students are on the bus.
Then some more students get on the bus.
Now, there are 46 students on the bus.
How many students got on the bus?

Check:

+

_____ + _____ = _____

_____ students

3. Ella has 34 more buttons than Julio.
Julio has 49 buttons. How many buttons does Ella have?

Check:

+

_____ + _____ = _____

_____ buttons

4. Wendy has 14 more crayons than Oscar.
Oscar has 54 crayons.
How many crayons does Wendy have?

The bar diagram helps you see how the numbers are related.

Check:

+

_____ + _____ = _____

_____ crayons

Problem Solving ☆ Solve each problem. Show your work.

5. Make Sense Mariah has 17 figs. Kendra has 20 more figs than Mariah. Toby has 33 more figs than Kendra. How many figs do Kendra and Toby each have?

Step 1:
How many figs does Kendra have?

_____ ◯ _____ = _____ _____ figs

Step 2:
How many figs does Toby have?

_____ ◯ _____ = _____ _____ figs

6. Higher Order Thinking 8 girls and some boys are in the pool. In all, 17 children are in the pool. Then some more boys jump in the pool. Now there are 13 boys in the pool. How many more boys jumped in the pool?

Step 1:

_____ ◯ _____ = _____

Step 2:

_____ ◯ _____ = _____

_____ more boys jumped in the pool

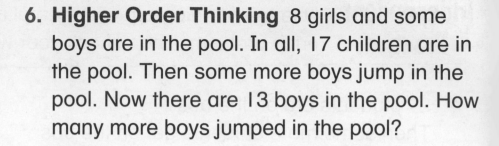

Solve one step at a time.

---

7. ⓘ Assessment The soccer coach has 18 shirts. Then she gets 9 more shirts. There are 22 players on her team. She gives a shirt to each player. How many shirts does the coach have left?

Use the numbers on the cards. Complete both equations to solve the problem.

| 5 | 27 | 9 | 22 |

Step 1:

18 + ☐ = ☐

Step 2:

27 − ☐ = ☐

The coach has _____ shirts left.

Name _____

Another Look! You can write the numbers in a chart to solve the problem.

There are 33 red cars, 27 gray cars, and 25 tan cars in the parking lot.
How many cars in all?

Tens	Ones
3	③
2	⑦
+ 2	5
Tens: 7	0
Ones: 1	5
Sum: 8	5

85

33	27	25

Add in any order.
It helps to make a 10.
3 + 7 = 10
10 + 5 = 15

HOME ACTIVITY Write 39 + 14 + 11 on a sheet of paper. Ask your child to show you how to find the sum.

_____ cars

Solve the problem. Show your work.

1. On Monday, Matt puts 32 cents in his bank. On Tuesday, he puts in 25 cents. On Wednesday, he puts in 18 cents. How much money does Matt put in his bank on those three days?

Tens	Ones
+	
Tens:	
Ones:	
Sum:	

_____ cents

Solve each problem. Show your work.

2. **Generalize** Alexis has 16 peaches, 18 apples, and 12 pears to bring to school for the class snack. How many pieces of fruit does Alexis have in all?

_____ + _____ + _____ = _____

_____ pieces of fruit

3. **Higher Order Thinking** Chris has 16 party hats. Then he gets 27 more hats. He gives away 20 hats at his birthday party. How many hats are left?

Step 1:

_____ ◯ _____ = _____

Step 2:

_____ ◯ _____ = _____

_____ hats

4. **Assessment** The dance team has 13 dancers. Then 7 more dancers join. The next week 5 dancers quit. How many dancers are now on the team?

Use the numbers on the cards. Complete both equations to solve the problem.

| 20 | 15 | 13 | 5 |

Step 1:

☐ + 7 = ☐

Step 2:

20 − ☐ = ☐

The team now has _____ dancers.

© Pearson Education, Inc. 2

Name _____

Solve & Share

Kim puts 25 toys into an empty toy box. Then she puts 17 more toys in the toy box. How many toys are in the box in all?

Use a model to show the problem. Be ready to explain how your model helps you solve the problem.

_____ toys

I can ...
make models to help solve math problems.

 Process Standards PS.4 Also PS.1, PS.2, PS.3
Content Standards 2.CA.2, 2.CA.1

Thinking Habits

Can I use a drawing, diagram, table, graph, or objects to show the problem?

Can I write an equation to show the problem?

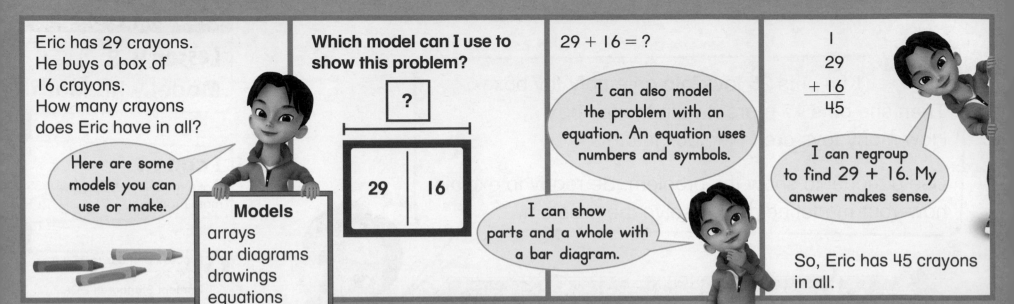

Eric has 29 crayons. He buys a box of 16 crayons. How many crayons does Eric have in all?

Here are some models you can use or make.

Models
arrays
bar diagrams
drawings
equations

Which model can I use to show this problem?

I can show parts and a whole with a bar diagram.

$29 + 16 = ?$

I can also model the problem with an equation. An equation uses numbers and symbols.

$$\begin{array}{r} 1 \\ 29 \\ + 16 \\ \hline 45 \end{array}$$

I can regroup to find $29 + 16$. My answer makes sense.

So, Eric has 45 crayons in all.

Do You Understand?

Show Me! How does drawing a bar diagram or writing an equation model a problem? Is there another way to model the problem?

☆ **Guided Practice** ☆ Complete the bar diagram and write an equation to model and solve each problem.

1. Flora has 24 books about birds. She has 18 books about bugs. How many books is that?

   $24 + 18 = ?$ books

2. Barb saw 14 cars on one street. She saw 15 cars on another street. How many cars did Barb see on both streets?

   _____ + _____ = _____ cars

© Pearson Education, Inc. 2

Tools Assessment

Independent Practice Make a model to show each problem. Then use the model to solve. Show your work.

3. Avi takes 16 pictures.
   Then he takes 17 more pictures.
   How many pictures does Avi take?

Remember, you can use different models. Be ready to explain how your model shows the problem!

4. Tina picks 55 blueberries.
   Then she picks 27 more.
   How many blueberries does Tina pick?

5. Raj finds 47 acorns in his front yard.
   He finds 29 acorns in his back yard.
   How many acorns does Raj find in all?

Problem Solving

African Safari

The Santos family are on an African safari. The chart at the right shows the number of animals they see.

How many animals do they see?

Number of Animals	
Giraffes	15
Elephants	9
Lions	16
Zebras	11

6. Make Sense What do you know? What are you asked to find?

_____

_____

_____

_____

7. Reasoning Make a model to help you find the number of animals they see. Be ready to explain why you chose the model you did.

8. Model What other model could you use to show the problem? Make another model. Explain which model you think is better.

_____

_____

© Pearson Education, Inc. 2

Name _____

Help   Tools   Games

Homework & Practice 4-8
Model with Math

Another Look! Complete the bar diagram and equation to model and solve the problem.

Paul has 23 counters.

He gets 27 more counters.

How many counters does Paul have in all?

You can show pictures or numbers in a bar diagram.

HOME ACTIVITY Ask your child to model and find $14 + 19$ by drawing a bar diagram and writing an equation.

$23 + 27 = ?$

Paul has 50 counters in all.

Make a model to show the problem. Then use the model to solve. Show your work.

Be ready to explain how your model shows the problem!

1. There were 38 yo-yos at a toy store.
   Then the store got 12 more yo-yos.
   How many yo-yos are at the store now?

Topic 4 | Lesson 8   Digital Resources at PearsonRealize.com   two hundred thirty-nine **239**

Problem Solving

On the Path

The diagram shows the distances, in feet, of paths between each farm animal. What is the total distance of the paths from the cow to the chicken, to the horse, to the pig, to the cow?

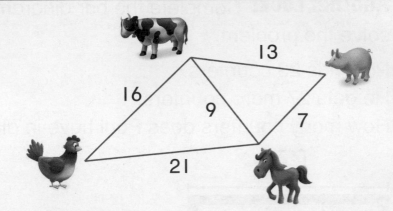

2. **Make Sense** What do you know? What are you asked to find?

_____

_____

_____

_____

3. **Reasoning** Make a model to help you find the total distance in the problem.
Be ready to explain why you chose the model you did.

4. **Model** What other model could you use to show the problem? Make another model. Explain which model you think is better.

© Pearson Education, Inc. 2

Name _____

Point & Tally

Find a partner. Get paper and a pencil.
Each partner chooses a different color: light blue or dark blue.

Partner 1 and Partner 2 each point to a black number at the same time. Both partners add those numbers.

If the answer is on your color, you get a tally mark.
Work until one partner gets twelve tally marks.

Partner 1							Partner 2
7	13	17	14	10	9	12	8
4							6
9							5
6	15	11	8	18	13	16	4
8							7
5							9

Tally Marks for Partner 1

Tally Marks for Partner 2

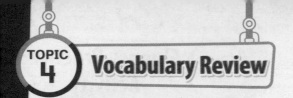

A-Z
Glossary

Word List
• compatible numbers
• ones
• partial sum
• regroup
• sum
• tens

Understand Vocabulary

Use the problem at the right.
Write *partial sum* or *sum* for each.

Tens	Ones
6	8
+ 1	9
7	0
1	7
8	7

1. 70 is a _____ .

2. 17 is a _____ .

3. 87 is the _____ .

4. Use the ones column in the problem at the right.
   Which compatible numbers can you add to make
   a ten?
   Write two different equations.

Tens	Ones
3	8
1	4
2	2
+	6

Use Vocabulary in Writing

5. Solve the addition problem.
   Tell how you solved it. Use terms
   from the Word List.

   27
   + 35
   _____

   _____
   _____
   _____

© Pearson Education, Inc. 1

Name _____

Set A

You can use partial sums to find the sum. Find $46 + 37$.

	Tens	Ones	
	4	6	
+	3	7	
$40 + 30 =$	7	0	Add the tens.
$6 + 7 =$	1	3	Add the ones.
Sum $=$	8	3	Add the partial sums.

Reteaching

Add. Use partial sums. Use place-value blocks, if needed.

1.

	Tens	Ones
	3	3
+	5	7
___ + ___ =		
___ + ___ =		
Sum =		

Set B

You can show partial sums another way. Find $29 + 63$.

	Tens	Ones	
	2	9	
+	6	3	
Tens:	8	0	Add the tens.
Ones:	1	2	Add the ones.
Sum:	9	2	Add the partial sums.

Add. Use partial sums. Show your work.

2.

	Tens	Ones
	1	4
+	4	5
Tens:		
Ones:		
Sum:		

3.

	Tens	Ones
	1	7
+	7	7
Tens:		
Ones:		
Sum:		

You can regroup to find a sum.
Find 28 + 34.

8 ones + 4 ones = 12 ones.
So regroup 12 as 1 ten and 2 ones.

Tens	Ones

	Tens	Ones
	1	
	2	8
+	3	4
	6	2

Add. Draw place-value blocks to
show your work. Regroup if needed.

4.

	Tens	Ones
	☐	
	3	2
+	4	8

Tens	Ones

Line up the tens and the ones to add.
45 + 29 = ?

	Tens	Ones
	1	
	4	5
+	2	9
	7	4

Regroup 14 ones
as 1 ten and 4 ones.

Write each addition problem. Find each sum.
Use drawings, if needed.

5.   67 + 26

	Tens	Ones
	☐	
+		

6.   38 + 25

	Tens	Ones
	☐	
+		

© Pearson Education, Inc. 2

Name _____

Set E

You can add more than two
2-digit numbers. Add the ones in
any order. Make a 10 to help.

Then add the tens.

```
  1 5
  3 7
  2 2
+ 2 3
─────
  8 7
```

Add. Circle the two digits you
added first.

Reteaching
Continued

7.
```
   1 5
     9
+ 2 1
─────
```

8.
```
   3 3
   4 6
     2
+ 1 4
─────
```

Set F

Use partial sums to find
$45 + 7 + 21 + 13$.

Tens	Ones
4	5
	7
2	1
+ 1	3
Tens: 7	0
Ones: 1	6
Sum: 8	6

Look for
compatible
numbers
to make tens.
$7 + 3 = 10$

So, $45 + 7 + 21 + 13 =$ ___86___

Add using partial sums.

9.

Tens	Ones
2	2
2	1
	9
+ 1	8
Tens:	
Ones:	
Sum:	

27 students are eating lunch.
More students join them.
Now 63 students are eating lunch.
How many students joined them?

Write an equation: $27 + ? = 63$
Count on to find the missing addend:

$27 + 30 = 57$ | $30 + 3 + 3 = $ _36_
$57 + 3 = 60$ | $27 + $ _36_ $= 63$
$60 + 3 = 63$

So, 36 students joined them.

Thinking Habits

Model with Math

Can I use a drawing, diagram, table, graph, or objects to show the problem?

Can I write an equation to show the problem?

Complete the bar diagram and solve.

10. Lana has 24 crayons.
Then she gets some
more crayons.
Now she has 42 crayons.
How many crayons does
Lana get?

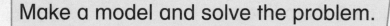

$24 + ? = 42$

Make a model and solve the problem.

11. Students ride buses to the museum.
28 students ride in Bus A.
27 students ride in Bus B.
How many students ride in both buses?

Name _____

1. Kelly has 46 beads.
Her sister gives her 28 more beads.
How many beads does Kelly have now?

Ⓐ 18

Ⓑ 22

Ⓒ 64

Ⓓ 74

2. Which is the same amount as $45 + 38$? Choose all that apply.

☐ $40 + 30 + 5 + 8$

☐ $70 + 13$

☐ 83

☐ 93

3. Do you have to regroup to find each sum? Choose Yes or No.

$42 + 56 = ?$ ◯ Yes ◯ No

$52 + 29 = ?$ ◯ Yes ◯ No

$37 + 50 = ?$ ◯ Yes ◯ No

$63 + 19 = ?$ ◯ Yes ◯ No

4. Circle the addition problem that you can use regrouping to solve.
Then explain how you know.

$30 + 29$ $54 + 38$ $43 + 44$

_____

_____

_____

_____

5. Ryan has 57 stones in his collection.
Joy gives him 15 more stones.
How many stones does Ryan
have now?

Ⓐ 82

Ⓑ 72

Ⓒ 62

Ⓓ 42

6. Which is the same amount as
$13 + 8 + 7$? Choose all that apply.

☐ $20 + 8$

☐ $10 + 10 + 8$

☐ 18

☐ 28

7. One zoo has 26 dolphins.
Another zoo has 53 dolphins.
A third zoo has 7 dolphins.
How many dolphins in all?

Show your work.

_____ dolphins

8. Faith has 23 shells.
Then she finds 19 more shells.
Faith gives 10 of the shells to a friend.
How many shells does Faith have now?

Show your work.

_____ shells

© Pearson Education, Inc. 2

Name _____

9. Part A Find the sum.
Show your work.

```
   25
   37
   15
 +  8
```

Part B
Tell how you found the sum.

_____

_____

_____

_____

_____

---

10. Ms. Wise has 12 tablets.
Then she gets 9 more tablets.
Ms. Wise has 20 students in her class.
She gives each student one tablet.
How many tablets does she have left?

Use the numbers on the cards below.
Complete both equations to solve the problem.

| 1 | 9 | 20 | 21 |

Step 1: $12 + \boxed{} = \boxed{}$

Step 2: $21 - \boxed{} = \boxed{}$

_____ tablet

11. Pearl has 8 medals.
Grace has 9 medals.
Timmy has 6 medals.
How many medals do they have in all?

Solve and show your work in the blue
box at the right.

_____ medals

12. Match each number card to an equation to find the missing addend.
Draw lines to match. Then write the missing addend in the gray box.

| 5 | ○ $6 + 14 + \boxed{} + 3 = 30$ |

| 6 | ○ $3 + 32 + 7 + \boxed{} = 50$ |

| 7 | ○ $25 + 25 + \boxed{} + 5 = 60$ |

| 8 | ○ $5 + \boxed{} + 15 + 14 = 40$ |

13. Corey has 17 more marbles than Tony.
Tony has 64 marbles.
How many marbles does Corey have?

Use the bar diagram to model and solve the
problem. Show your work.

_____ marbles

© Pearson Education, Inc. 2

Topic 4 | Assessment

Name _____

Our Pets

Students draw pictures of their pets. The chart shows the number of pets the students have.

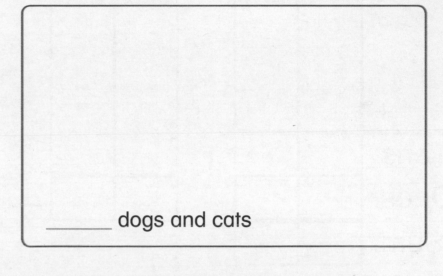

Number of Pets		
Dogs		41
Cats		29
Rabbits		6
Fish		24

1. How many dogs and cats do the students have?
Show your work.

_____ dogs and cats

2. How many cats and fish do the students have?
Show your work.

_____ cats and fish

3. Use partial sums to find how many cats, rabbits, and fish the students have.
Then use regrouping to check your work.

Check:

Tens	Ones
+	
Tens:	
Ones:	
Sum:	

Tens	Ones
☐	

How many cats, rabbits, and fish in all?

_____ cats, rabbits, and fish

4. Explain why you can use regrouping when you add.

_____

_____

_____

5. The students also draw pictures of 10 hamsters, 19 birds, and 5 mice.

Part A

Complete the model to show how to find the total number of hamsters, birds, and mice.

Part B

Complete the equation to show how many hamsters, birds and mice they draw. Then write the total.

_____ ◯ _____ ◯ _____ = _____

_____ hamsters, birds, and mice

TOPIC 5 Subtract Within 100 Using Strategies

Essential Question: What are strategies for subtracting numbers to 100?

Digital Resources

Solve Learn Glossary

Tools Assessment Help Games

Look at the big pieces of ice in the water!

How can heating and cooling change water and ice?

Wow! Let's do this project and learn more.

Math and Science Project: Heating, Cooling, and Subtraction

Find Out Have an adult help you heat and cool water and other materials. Find out if water and ice can change back and forth. Find out if heating and cooling an egg can change it back and forth.

Journal: Make a Book Show what you learn in a book. In your book, also:

• Tell about how heating and cooling are related.

• Tell about how addition and subtraction are related.

Name _____

Review What You Know

A-Z Vocabulary

1. Circle each **difference** in the math problems shown below.

$15 - 5 = 10$

$$\begin{array}{r} 23 \\ + 32 \\ \hline 55 \end{array} \qquad \begin{array}{r} 14 \\ - 7 \\ \hline 7 \end{array}$$

2. Circle the statement if it describes **mental math**.

Math that is done with paper and pencil.

Math that you can do in your head.

3. Circle the statement if it describes **compatible numbers**.

Numbers that are close to numbers that you want to add or subtract.

Numbers that you can add or subtract using mental math.

Addition and Subtraction Facts

4. Complete the related addition and subtraction facts below.

$6 + \boxed{} = 13$

$13 - \boxed{} = 6$

5. Write each sum or difference.

$$\begin{array}{r} 4 \\ + 7 \\ \hline \end{array} \qquad \begin{array}{r} 12 \\ - 3 \\ \hline \end{array} \qquad \begin{array}{r} 9 \\ + 6 \\ \hline \end{array} \qquad \begin{array}{r} 16 \\ - 8 \\ \hline \end{array}$$

You can use addition facts to help you subtract.

Math Story

6. Tim has 25 stamps. Roy gives him 51 more stamps. How many stamps does Tim have now?

_____ stamps

Name _____

Solve & Share

How can you use the hundred chart to help you find 57 − 23? Explain. Write an equation.

I can ...
use a hundred chart to subtract tens and ones.

Content Standard 2.CA.1
Process Standards PS.1, PS.3, PS.5, PS.6, PS.7

1	2	3	4	5	6	7	8	9	10
11	12	13	14	15	16	17	18	19	20
21	22	23	24	25	26	27	28	29	30
31	32	33	34	35	36	37	38	39	40
41	42	43	44	45	46	47	48	49	50
51	52	53	54	55	56	57	58	59	60
61	62	63	64	65	66	67	68	69	70
71	72	73	74	75	76	77	78	79	80
81	82	83	84	85	86	87	88	89	90
91	92	93	94	95	96	97	98	99	100

____ ◯ ____ = ____

Find 43 − 28 using a hundred chart.

I need to find the difference between 28 and 43.

Start at 28. Count to the next number that matches the ones in 43.

21	22	23	24	25	26	27	28	29	30
31	32	33	34	35	36	37	38	39	40
41	42	43	44	45	46	47	48	49	50

Count by ones! I counted 5 ones to get from 28 to 33.

Count by tens to 43.

21	22	23	24	25	26	27	28	29	30
31	32	33	34	35	36	37	38	39	40
41	42	43	44	45	46	47	48	49	50

That's 1 ten, or 10 more.

I added 5 and 10. That makes 15.

$28 + 15 = 43$
So, $43 − 28 = 15$.

Do You Understand?

Show Me! How can you use a hundred chart to find $60 − 18$?

☆ Guided Practice ☆

Subtract using the hundred chart. Draw arrows if you need to.

21	22	23	24	25	26	27	28	29	30
31	32	33	34	35	36	37	38	39	40
41	42	43	44	45	46	47	48	49	50
51	52	53	54	55	56	57	58	59	60
61	62	63	64	65	66	67	68	69	70

1. $69 − 36 = \underline{33}$

2. $54 − 24 = \underline{}$

3. $\underline{} = 65 − 34$

4. $47 − 22 = \underline{}$

Tools   Assessment

Independent Practice   Subtract using the hundred chart. Draw arrows if you need to.

1	2	3	4	5	6	7	8	9	10
11	12	13	14	15	16	17	18	19	20
21	22	23	24	25	26	27	28	29	30
31	32	33	34	35	36	37	38	39	40
41	42	43	44	45	46	47	48	49	50
51	52	53	54	55	56	57	58	59	60
61	62	63	64	65	66	67	68	69	70
71	72	73	74	75	76	77	78	79	80
81	82	83	84	85	86	87	88	89	90
91	92	93	94	95	96	97	98	99	100

5. $54 - 7 =$ _____

6. _____ $= 96 - 63$

7. $45 - 22 =$ _____

8. $82 - 61 =$ _____

9. $65 - 21 =$ _____

10. _____ $= 79 - 47$

11. $84 - 6 =$ _____

Algebra Write the digit that makes each equation true.

12. $73 - \boxed{}2 = 41$

$5\boxed{} - 32 = 26$

13. $46 - \boxed{}1 = 15$

$78 - 36 = \boxed{}2$

14. $53 - \boxed{}2 = 31$

$99 - \boxed{}3 = 16$

Problem Solving

Use Tools Use the hundred chart to solve the problems below.

15. Darren's puzzle has 98 pieces. Darren fits 55 pieces together. How many more pieces does Darren still need to fit to complete the puzzle?

_____ − _____ = _____ pieces

16. A test has 86 questions. Glenda needs to answer 23 more questions to finish the test. How many test questions has Glenda answered already?

_____ questions

The hundred chart is a good tool to use. Count by ones and tens to subtract.

41	42	43	44	45	46	47	48	49	50
51	52	53	54	55	56	57	58	59	60
61	62	63	64	65	66	67	68	69	70
71	72	73	74	75	76	77	78	79	80
81	82	83	84	85	86	87	88	89	90
91	92	93	94	95	96	97	98	99	100

17. **Higher Order Thinking** Chris wants to subtract $76 - 42$. Write the steps he can take to subtract 42 from 76 on the hundred chart.

_____

_____

_____

18. ⓳ **Assessment** Lu has 75 buttons. 49 of the buttons are green. The rest of the buttons are red. How many of the buttons are red?

Ⓐ 16 Ⓑ 20 Ⓒ 26 Ⓓ 36

© Pearson Education, Inc. 2

Topic 5 | Lesson 1

Name _____

Homework & Practice 5-1
Subtract Tens and Ones on a Hundred Chart

Another Look! Here is another way to subtract on a hundred chart.

Find 36 − 24.

1. Start at 36.

2. Move up 2 rows to subtract
   __2__ tens.

3. Move left 4 columns to subtract
   __4__ ones.

So 36 − 24 = 12.

1	2	3	4	5	6	7	8	9	10
11	⟨12⟩	13	14	15	⟨16⟩	17	18	19	20
21	22	23	24	25	26	27	28	29	30
31	32	33	34	35	⟨36⟩	37	38	39	40
41	42	43	44	45	46	47	48	49	50
51	52	53	54	55	56	57	58	59	60
61	62	63	64	65	66	67	68	69	70
71	72	73	74	75	76	77	78	79	80
81	82	83	84	85	86	87	88	89	90
91	92	93	94	95	96	97	98	99	100

HOME ACTIVITY Ask your child to subtract 58 − 23 on a hundred chart and explain how he or she subtracted.

Subtract using the hundred chart.

1. 87 − 7 = _____

2. 79 − 48 = _____

3. 65 − 41 = _____

4. 99 − 52 = _____

5. 35 − 13 = _____

6. _____ = 84 − 33

7. $\boxed{}3 - 2\boxed{} = 71$

8. $5\boxed{} - \boxed{}1 = 14$

9. $78 - \boxed{}5 = 4\boxed{}$

10. **Look for Patterns** A treasure is hidden under one of the rocks. Follow the clues to find the treasure. Color each rock you land on.

A. Start at 55.   B. Subtract 20.

C. Add 5.   D. Add 20.

E. Add 10.   F. Subtract 5.

G. Subtract 20.   H. Add 5.

I. Subtract 20.   J. Subtract 5.

The treasure is hidden under the last rock that you colored. What is the number of that rock? _____
Describe the pattern you see in the numbers you colored.

11. **⬤Assessment** A pan holds 36 biscuits. Kiana put 12 biscuits on the pan. How many more biscuits will fit on the pan?

Ⓐ 24   Ⓑ 23   Ⓒ 22   Ⓓ 21

12. **⬤Assessment** A garden has room for 22 flowers. Dan needs to plant 11 more flowers to fill the garden. How many flowers did Dan already plant?

Ⓐ 10   Ⓑ 11   Ⓒ 12   Ⓓ 13

Count Back to Subtract on an Open Number Line

Name _____

Solve & Share

Jesse had 50 balloons at the fair.
A strong wind blew away 30 balloons.
How many balloons does Jesse have left?
Use the number line below to show your work.

I can …
use an open number line to subtract tens.

Content Standard 2.CA.1
Process Standards PS.2, PS.3, PS.5, PS.8

POPCORN

← ————————————————————————— →

_____ ◯ _____ = _____

Find 56 − 20.

You can subtract tens on an open number line. First, place 56 on the number line.

56

One Way

20 is 2 tens. So, count back by 10 two times. Show each 10 on the number line as you count.

−10   −10

36   46   56

Another Way
Moving back 2 tens from 56 is the same as 56 − 20.

−20

36   56

You land on 36. So, 56 − 20 = __36__.

Do You Understand?

Show Me! How can an open number line help you subtract numbers?

★ **Guided Practice** ★ Use an open number line to find each difference.

1. 70 − 20 = _____

−10   −10

50   60   70

2. 67 − 30 = _____

Independent Practice

Use an open number line to find each difference.

3. 60 − 40 = _____

4. 85 − 20 = _____

5. 99 − 40 = _____

6. 42 − 30 = _____

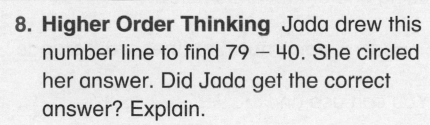

7. 34 − 10 = _____

The number you are subtracting from should be put on the right side of the line.

8. Higher Order Thinking Jada drew this number line to find 79 − 40. She circled her answer. Did Jada get the correct answer? Explain.

−10   −10   −10   −10

29   39   59   69   79

9. Reasoning Evan has 62 baseball cards. He gives 30 cards to Bridget. How many cards does Evan have left?

_____ baseball cards

10. Math and Science 45 icicles hang from a roof. 20 icicles melt and fall. How many icicles are left?

_____ icicles

11. 🅐🅩 Vocabulary Complete each sentence using one of the terms below.

sum   open number line   difference

You can use an _____

_____

to solve addition and subtracton problems. Counting back is a way to find the

_____.

The _____ is the answer to an addition problem.

12. 🄳 Assessment Which does the number line show? Choose all that apply.

☐ Count back by 10 two times from 56.
☐ Count back by 10 three times from 56.
☐ 56 − 30 = 26
☐ 26 + 56 = 82

 Topic 5 | **Lesson 2**

Name _____

Another Look! Find 45 − 20 using an open number line.

You can use an open number line to make subtracting tens easier.

Place 45 on the number line. Then count back by 10 twice to subtract 20.

− 10   − 10

25   35   45

HOME ACTIVITY Draw an open number line on a sheet of paper. Then have your child find 33 − 20 using the number line.

So, 45 − 20 = 25.

Use an open number line to find each difference.

1. 30 − 20 = _____

2. 95 − 30 = _____

3. $21 - 20 =$ _____

4. $15 - 10 =$ _____

5. Lisa has 25 beads.
She gives 10 beads to Maria.
How many beads does Lisa have now?

_____ beads

6. Mike has 43 balloons.
He gives away 20 balloons.
How many balloons does Mike have left?

_____ balloons

7. Higher Order Thinking Jackson drew this number line to solve a subtraction problem. Write the equation he solved.

_____ $-$ _____ $=$ _____

8. ⓓAssessment Which does the number line show? Choose all that apply.

☐ Count back 4 tens from 90.

☐ Count back 40 from 90.

☐ $90 - 30 = 60$

☐ $90 - 40 = 50$

Name _____

Solve & Share

Jeremy had 56 bug stickers.
He gave 24 stickers to Eric.
How many bug stickers does Jeremy have left?
Use the open number line below to show your work.

I can ...
use an open number line to subtract tens and ones.

Content Standard 2.CA.1
Process Standards PS.1, PS.4, PS.5

◄─────────────────────────────►

_____ − _____ = _____

Learn   Glossary

Find 68 − 23.

Let's use an open number line and count back. First, place 68 on the line.

68

One Way

23 is 2 tens and 3 ones.
So, count back 2 tens from 68.
58, 48
Then, count back 3 ones from 48.
47, 46, 45

−1 −1 −1 −10 −10

45 46 47 48   58   68

Another Way

You can subtract 68 − 20 = 48,
then 48 − 3 = 45.

−3   −20

45 48   68

So, 68 − 23 = __45__.

I can check my subtraction by adding 45 + 23 = 68.

Do You Understand?

Show Me! How can the open number line help you keep track as you count back?

☆ **Guided Practice** ☆ Use an open number line to find each difference.

1. 28 − 24 = _____

−4   −10   −10

4   8   18   28

_____

2. 50 − 35 = _____

© Pearson Education, Inc. 2

Topic 5 | Lesson 3

Independent Practice ☆   Use an open number line to find each difference.

3. 45 − 13 = _____

4. 63 − 22 = _____

5. 78 − 46 = _____

6. 92 − 37 = _____

7. 80 − 44 = ?

Break apart the number you are subtracting into tens and ones.

_____ − _____ = _____

8. **Number Sense** How many tens and ones will you count back to solve this problem: 56 − 38 = ? Solve the problem.

_____ tens _____ ones

_____ − _____ = _____

9. **Use Tools** There are 47 raffle tickets to sell for the fair. Ms. Brown's class sells 23 raffle tickets. How many raffle tickets are left to sell?

_____ raffle tickets

10. **Use Tools** Ethan counts 78 carrots. He sells 35 carrots at the farmers market. How many carrots does Ethan have left?

_____ carrots

11. **Higher Order Thinking** Show two different ways to find 63 − 25 using the open number lines.

63 − 25 = _____

12. **⓪ Assessment** Jen solved a subtraction problem using the open number line shown. Write the equation that her work below shows.

_____ − _____ = _____

Name _____

Another Look! Find 83 − 35.

35

3 tens   5 ones

How many tens and ones do you need to subtract?

First place 83 on an open number line. Then count back 3 tens and 5 ones to subtract 35.

−5   −10   −10   −10

48   53   63   73   83

So, 83 − 35 = 48.

HOME ACTIVITY Tell your child a subtraction story for 36 − 15. Have your child draw an open number line and use it to solve the problem.

Use an open number line to find each difference.

1. 95 − 23 = _____

2. 30 − 15 = _____

Use Tools Use an open number line to solve each problem.

3. 87 − 23 = _____

4. 54 − 19 = _____

5. Joe has 43 grapes. He gives 17 grapes to Dee. How many grapes does Joe have left?

_____ grapes

6. Izzy has 99 bottle caps. She gives 33 to Max. How many bottle caps does Izzy have left?

_____ bottle caps

7. Higher Order Thinking Write a story problem for 36 − 14. Draw and use an open number line to solve the problem.

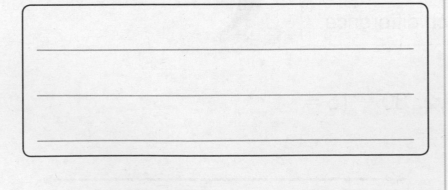

8. Assessment Manuel solved a subtraction problem using the open number line shown. Write the equation his open number line shows.

_____ − _____ = _____

© Pearson Education, Inc. 2

Topic 5 | Lesson 3

Solve

Add Up to Subtract Using an Open Number Line

Solve & Share

There are 50 children at the park. 28 are boys and the rest are girls. How many girls are at the park?

Use the open number line to solve. Show your work.

I can ...
add up to subtract using an open number line.

Content Standard 2.CA.1
Process Standards PS.1, PS.2, PS.5, PS.6

_____ ◯ _____ = _____

Find 57 − 28.

You can add up from 28 to subtract. Place 28 on the number line first.

28

You can add 2 to get to 30.

Then add 10, and 10 again, to get to 50.

Then add 7 to land on 57.

+2 +10   +10   +7

28 30   40   50 57

Add the tens and ones.

$2 + 10 + 10 + 7 = 29$

So, $57 − 28 = 29$.

I can check by adding!
$28 + 29 = 57$

Do You Understand?

Show Me! How can you add up to find $42 − 17$?

☆ **Guided Practice** ☆ Add up to find each difference. Use an open number line.

1. $45 − 27 =$ _____

+3 +10   +5

27 30   40   45

2. $66 − 39 =$ _____

© Pearson Education, Inc. 2

Topic 5 | Lesson 4

Independent Practice

Add up to find each difference.
Use an open number line.

3. 41 − 19 = _____

4. 63 − 34 = _____

5. 83 − 58 = _____

6. 74 − 46 = _____

7. 72 − 34 = _____

8. **Math and Science** Rob had 34 snowballs. Some melted and now he has 18 snowballs. How many snowballs melted?

_____ − _____ = _____

Don't forget to find the sum of the tens and the ones you added up. That is the difference.

Problem Solving

Add up to solve each problem. Use an open number line. Write the equations.

9. Be Precise Dino has 41 crayons. He gives 23 crayons to Bridget, and 7 crayons to Dan. How many crayons does Dino have left? Solve using two steps.

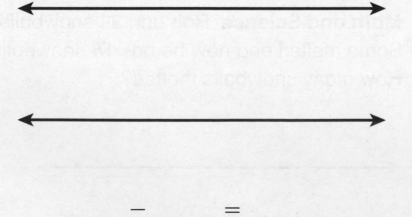

The answer to the first step is needed for the second step. Is your work precise?

Step 1: _____ ◯ _____ = _____

Step 2: _____ ◯ _____ = _____

---

10. Higher Order Thinking Show two different ways to add up to find 72 − 35.

_____ − _____ = _____

11. ⓓ **Assessment** Add up to solve 46 − 25. Show your work on the open number line and then write an equation.

_____ − _____ = _____

© Pearson Education, Inc. 2

Name _____

Help   Tools   Games

Another Look!

You can add up on an open number line to subtract 73 − 45.

+10   +10   +5 +3

45   55   65 70 73

You can start at 45. Add 10, and 10 again, to get to 65.
Then add 5 to get to 70. Then add 3 to get to 73.

Add tens and ones to find the difference:

_10_ + _10_ + _5_ + _3_ = _28_

So, 73 − 45 = 28.

HOME ACTIVITY Have your child tell a story about 52 − 34. Tell your child to solve the problem by adding up on an open number line. Then, have your child write an equation to show the answer.

Add up to find each difference. Use an open number line.

1. 93 − 65 = _____

2. 84 − 67 = _____

Add up to solve each problem. Use an open number line. Write the equations.

3. **Use Tools** Misha has 36 bows. She gives 19 bows to Alice. How many bows does Misha have left?

_____ − _____ = _____

4. **Use Tools** Remi has 80 golf balls. He hits 53 of them. How many golf balls does Remi have left?

_____ − _____ = _____

5. **Higher Order Thinking** Richard found 93 − 67 by adding up on the open number line. Is he correct? Explain. Then write an addition equation to show how you could check his work.

93 − 67 = 26

_____

_____

_____ ⃝ _____ = _____

6. **ⒾAssessment** Use the open number lines. Show two different ways to add up to find 91 − 56.

One way

Another way

91 − 56 = _____

© Pearson Education, Inc. 2

Solve & Share

Don wants to find 42 − 7 by breaking apart the 7 into two numbers. Use and draw place-value blocks to show how Don could find the difference.

Lesson 5-5

Break Apart Numbers to Subtract

I can ...
break apart 1-digit numbers to help me subtract mentally.

Content Standard 2.CA.1
Process Standards PS.3, PS.6, PS.7

33 − 6 = ?

You can break apart the number you are subtracting to find the difference.

Here are 3 ways to break apart 6. Which is best for subtracting 6 from 33?

```
     6         6         6
    / \       / \       / \
   1 + 5     2 + 4     3 + 3
```

33 − 6 = _____ ?

```
      / \
   [3]   [3]
```

Start at 33. Subtract 3 to get to 30. Then subtract 3 more.

11	12	13	14	15	16	17	18	19	20
21	22	23	24	25	26	27	28	29	30
31	32	33	34	35	36	37	38	39	40

33 − 6 = _27_

Do You Understand?

Show Me! Look at the problem above. Why wasn't the 6 broken apart into 1 + 5 to find 33 − 6?

☆Guided Practice☆

Subtract. Break apart the number you are subtracting. Show your work.

1. 43 − 9 = _____

```
   / \
 [ ]  [ ]
```

2. _____ = 24 − 6

```
       / \
     [ ]  [ ]
```

11	12	13	14	15	16	17	18	19	20
21	22	23	24	25	26	27	28	29	30
31	32	33	34	35	36	37	38	39	40
41	42	43	44	45	46	47	48	49	50

© Pearson Education, Inc. 2

Topic 5 | Lesson 5

Name _____

Independent Practice

Subtract. Break apart the number you are subtracting. Show your work. Use a hundred chart if needed.

3. $35 - 8 =$ _____

4. $41 - 5 =$ _____

5. _____ $= 82 - 7$

6. $53 - 7 =$ _____

7. $97 - 8 =$ _____

8. $64 - 9 =$ _____

9. $86 - 8 =$ _____

10. _____ $= 32 - 9$

11. $93 - 6 =$ _____

12. **Algebra** One number makes both equations true.
Find the missing number.

$48 +$ ☐ $= 56$ $56 -$ ☐ $= 48$

Think about how addition and subtraction are related.

The missing number is _____.

13. Explain Karen has 7 pencils. Karen's teacher has 45 pencils. How many fewer pencils does Karen have than her teacher? Explain how you solved the problem.

_____

_____

_____

Is your explanation clear?

_____ fewer pencils

14. Higher Order Thinking Write a story problem about $63 - 8$. Then solve.

_____

_____

_____

_____

$63 - 8 =$ _____

15. ⓘ **Assessment** Duane has 24 seashells. He gives 9 shells to his cousin Rob. How many seashells does Duane have now?

Ⓐ 16   Ⓒ 14

Ⓑ 15   Ⓓ 13

Help Tools Games

Another Look! Find $55 - 8$.

You can break apart 8 to find $55 - 8$.

One way is $8 = 5 + 3$.

There is a 5 in the ones place in 55. It's easy to subtract $55 - 5$.

$$\underline{55} - \underline{5} = \underline{50}$$

Next, subtract $50 - 3$. You can count back 3 from 50.

$$\underline{50} - \underline{3} = \underline{47}$$

So, $55 - 8 = \underline{47}$.

HOME ACTIVITY Ask your child to show you how to break apart the 5 in $43 - 5$ to find the difference.

Subtract. Break apart the number you are subtracting. Show your work.

1. $65 - 9 =$ _____

2. $24 - 7 =$ _____

3. _____ $= 84 - 8$

Explain Subtract. Break apart the number you are subtracting. Show your work to explain your thinking.

4. $41 - 5 =$ _____

5. _____ $= 94 - 8$

6. $25 - 9 =$ _____

7. **Higher Order Thinking** The table shows how many spools of thread Smith's Fabric Store sold on Monday.

Before the sale, there were 34 red spools and 53 black spools. How many red spools were left at the end of Monday? How many black spools were left?

_____ red spools _____ black spools

Spools of Thread Sold	
Thread Color	Number of Spools
Red	8
Blue	7
Black	6

8. 🔵**Assessment** Ron has 21 comic books. He sells 6 of them to a friend. How many comic books does Ron have now?

Ⓐ 17

Ⓒ 15

Ⓑ 16

Ⓓ 14

9. 🔵**Assessment** Yelena has 5 animal stickers. Vera has 41 animal stickers. How many fewer animal stickers does Yelena have than Vera?

Ⓐ 26

Ⓒ 35

Ⓑ 34

Ⓓ 36

© Pearson Education, Inc. 2

Name _____

Solve & Share

Gina wants to find 53 − 28 by breaking apart 28 into two numbers. Use place-value blocks and the hundred chart to show how Gina could find the difference.

I can ...
break apart 2-digit numbers to help me subtract.

Content Standard 2.CA.1
Process Standards PS.1, PS.3, PS.6, PS.7

21	22	23	24	25	26	27	28	29	30
31	32	33	34	35	36	37	38	39	40
41	42	43	44	45	46	47	48	49	50
51	52	53	54	55	56	57	58	59	60
61	62	63	64	65	66	67	68	69	70

$81 - 27 = ?$

You can use place value to break apart the number you are subtracting.

Break apart 27 into tens and ones. Then break apart the ones.

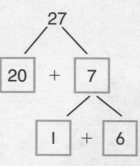

27
20 + 7
1 + 6

$81 - 27 = \underline{}?$

20   7

1   6

Start at 81.
Subtract 20 to get to 61.
Then subtract 1 to get to 60.
Then subtract 6 more.

51	52	53	54	55	56	57	58	59	60
61	62	63	64	65	66	67	68	69	70
71	72	73	74	75	76	77	78	79	80
81	82	83	84	85	86	87	88	89	90

So, $81 - 27 = \underline{54}$.

Do You Understand?

Show Me! How do you decide how to break apart the ones?

Guided Practice

Subtract. Break apart the number you are subtracting. Show your work.

1. $54 - 26 = \underline{}$

2. $43 - 18 = \underline{}$

21	22	23	24	25	26	27	28	29	30
31	32	33	34	35	36	37	38	39	40
41	42	43	44	45	46	47	48	49	50
51	52	53	54	55	56	57	58	59	60

© Pearson Education, Inc. 2

Independent Practice

Subtract. Break apart the number you are subtracting. Show your work. Use a hundred chart if needed.

3. _____ = 32 − 13

4. 74 − 28 = _____

5. _____ = 61 − 47

6. 84 − 46 = _____

7. 46 − 17 = _____

8. _____ = 95 − 38

9. **Higher Order Thinking** Tina found 53 − 27 by breaking apart 27 into 23 and 4. Does Tina's way work?

Show another way you could break apart 27 to find 53 − 27. Then find the difference.

10. Math and Science Kate had 32 ice cubes. She put 14 of them in the sun and they melted. How many ice cubes does Kate have now?

_____ ice cubes

11. Make Sense Mark has 27 stamps. Sam has 82 stamps. Lena has 42 stamps. How many more stamps does Sam have than Mark?

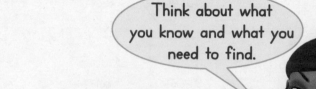

Think about what you know and what you need to find.

_____ more stamps

12. Higher Order Thinking Allison found 51 − 34 by breaking apart 34 into 31 + 3.

Write equations to show how Allison could have found the difference.

13. ⬤ **Assessment** A bakery has 66 loaves of bread. 27 of the loaves are sold. How many loaves are left?

Ⓐ 39

Ⓑ 38

Ⓒ 37

Ⓓ 36

© Pearson Education, Inc. 2

Name _____

Another Look! Find 43 − 27.

To find 43 − 27, you can break apart 27.

One way is 20 + 7.

It's easy to find 43 − 20.

$$\underline{43} - \underline{20} = \underline{23}$$

Next, subtract 23 − 7. You can break apart 7 into 3 + 4.

$$\underline{23} - \underline{3} = \underline{20} \text{ and}$$

$$\underline{20} - \underline{4} = \underline{16}$$

So, 43 − 27 = 16.

HOME ACTIVITY Ask your child to show you how to break apart 38 to find 65 − 38.

Subtract. Break apart the number you are subtracting. Show your work to explain your thinking.

1. 76 − 29 = _____

2. _____ = 82 − 39

3. 92 − 16 = _____

4. 75 − 27 = _____

5. _____ = 61 − 34

6. 87 − 28 = _____

---

7. Higher Order Thinking Brian found 42 − 19 by breaking apart 19 into 12 + 7. Write equations to show how Brian could have found the difference.

How can place value help you solve the problem?

---

8. ⓘ Assessment Rosita has 55 grapes. She gives a friend 26 of her grapes. How many grapes does Rosita have now?

Ⓐ 17

Ⓑ 29

Ⓒ 28

Ⓓ 37

9. ⓘ Assessment Can you use the equations to find 86 − 27? Choose Yes or No.

86 − 20 = 66   ○ Yes   ○ No
66 − 7 = 59

26 − 10 = 16   ○ Yes   ○ No
16 − 6 = 10

86 − 20 = 66   ○ Yes   ○ No
66 − 6 = 60
60 − 1 = 59

© Pearson Education, Inc. 2

Solve & Share

Yuri found 86 − 29 using mental math.
He changed 29 so it would be easier to find the difference.

Show how Yuri could have found the difference.
Explain how he could have used mental math.

I can ...
make numbers that are easier
to subtract, then use mental
math to find the difference.

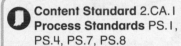
Content Standard 2.CA.1
Process Standards PS.1,
PS.4, PS.7, PS.8

$43 - 18 = ?$

You can use compensation to make numbers that are easier to subtract.

It is easier to subtract 20, than 18.

One Way Add 2 to both numbers. Then subtract using mental math.

$$43 \quad - \quad 18 \quad = \quad ?$$
$$\downarrow +2 \qquad \downarrow +2$$
$$45 \quad - \quad 20 \quad = \quad 25$$

So, $43 \quad - \quad 18 \quad = \quad 25.$

Another Way Add 2 to 18. Then subtract using mental math. Then add 2 to find the answer.

$$43 - 18 = ?$$
$$\downarrow +2$$
$$43 - 20 = 23$$
$$\downarrow +2$$
So, $43 - 18 = 25.$

I subtracted 2 more than 18, so I need to add 2 to 23 to find the answer.

Do You Understand?

Show Me! Marc says to find $61 - 13$, it's easier to subtract 10 instead of 13. He says if you subtract 3 from 13 to get 10, you must subtract 3 more from your answer. Do you agree? Explain.

Guided Practice

Use compensation to make numbers that are easier to subtract. Then solve. Show your work.

1. $52 \quad - \quad 8 \quad = \quad \underline{\hspace{1cm}}$

$\downarrow \boxed{+2} \qquad \downarrow \boxed{+2}$

$54 \quad - \quad 10 \quad = \quad 44$

2. $76 \quad - \quad 27 \quad = \quad \underline{\hspace{1cm}}$

$\downarrow \boxed{} \qquad \downarrow \boxed{}$

$\underline{\hspace{1cm}} \quad - \quad \underline{\hspace{1cm}} \quad = \quad \underline{\hspace{1cm}}$

3. $52 - 15 = \underline{\hspace{1cm}}$

$\downarrow \boxed{+5}$

$52 - 20 = 32 \longrightarrow 37$

$\boxed{+5}$

4. $93 \quad - \quad 39 \quad = \quad \underline{\hspace{1cm}}$

$\downarrow \boxed{}$

$\underline{\hspace{1cm}} \quad \bigcirc \quad \underline{\hspace{1cm}} \quad = \quad \underline{\hspace{1cm}} \longrightarrow 54$

$\boxed{}$

Topic 5 | Lesson 7

Independent Practice

Use compensation to make numbers that are easier to subtract. Then solve. Show your work.

5. 73 − 9 = _____

↓ ☐

_____ ◯ _____ = _____ → 64

☐

6. 35 − 16 = _____

↓ ☐

_____ ◯ _____ = _____ → 19

☐

7. 43 − 28 = _____

↓ ☐

_____ ◯ _____ = _____ → 15

☐

8. 51 − 27 = _____

↓ ☐   ↓ ☐

_____ − _____ = _____

9. 74 − 35 = _____

↓ ☐   ↓ ☐

_____ − _____ = _____

10. 99 − 21 = _____

↓ ☐   ↓ ☐

_____ − _____ = _____

11. Higher Order Thinking Yoshi says that to find 91 − 32, she can subtract 2 from both numbers. Then subtract using mental math. She says the answer is 59. Do you agree?

12. **Make Sense** There were some buttons in a jar. Mrs. Kim puts 19 more buttons in the same jar. Now there are 45 buttons in the jar. How many buttons were in the jar to begin with?

_____ buttons

13. Romi has 42 cards. Lisa has 75 cards. How many more cards does Lisa have than Romi?

_____ more cards

Think about what you are trying to find.

14. **Higher Order Thinking** Greg found 72 − 24. First he subtracted 20 because he thinks it is easier. Use words and numbers to explain how Greg could have found the difference.

15. **Assessment** Use the numbers on the cards. Write the missing numbers to solve the problem.

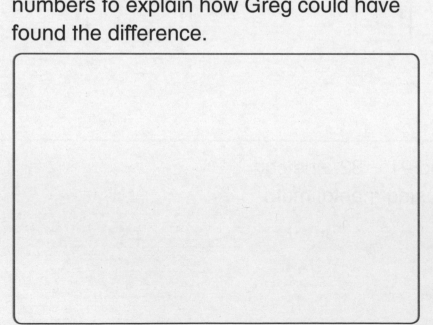

| 2 | 25 | 30 | 55 |

53 − 28 = _____

+ 2   + [ ]

_____ − _____ = _____

© Pearson Education, Inc. 2

Topic 5 | Lesson 7

Name _____

Help   Tools   Games

Another Look! You can use compensation to find $64 - 27$.

27 is close to ___30___.

$27 + $ __3__ $= $ __30__

It's easy to find $64 - 30$.

$64 - 27 = ?$

$\downarrow + 3$

$64 - 30 = 34 \rightarrow 37$

$+ 3$

So, $64 - 27 = $ ___37___.

> Since I subtracted 30, I subtracted 3 more than 27.
>
> So, I need to add 3 to 34 to find the answer.

HOME ACTIVITY Ask your child to show you how to use compensation to find $82 - 49$.

Use compensation to make numbers that are easier to subtract. Then solve. Show your thinking.

I.

$65 - 48 = $ ____

$\downarrow$ ☐

___ ◯ ___ = ___ $\rightarrow 17$

☐

2.

$96 - 37 = $ ____

$\downarrow$ ☐

___ ◯ ___ = ___ $\rightarrow 59$

☐

3.

$24 - 18 = $ ____

$\downarrow$ ☐

___ ◯ ___ = ___ $\rightarrow 6$

☐

Solve each problem. Show your work.

4. Make Sense A store had 45 hats for sale. On Friday, 26 of the hats were still for sale. How many hats sold? Think about what you are trying to find.

_____ hats

5. **A-Z** **Vocabulary** Complete each sentence using one of the terms below.

regroup   **subtract**

To find 56 + 38, you can _____ 14 ones as 1 ten and 4 ones.

You can use compensation to help you add and _____ mentally.

6. Higher Order Thinking Use compensation to find 93 − 78. Use words, pictures, or numbers to explain how you found the difference.

7. 🔘**Assessment** Use the numbers on the cards. Write the missing numbers to solve the problem.

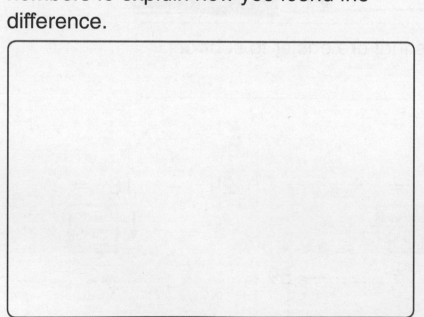

| 2 | 29 | 31 | 50 |

$$81 - 52 = \underline{\quad}$$

$$\downarrow -2$$

81 ◯ ☐ = ☐ → ☐

☐

© Pearson Education, Inc. 2

Name _____

Solve & Share

Some frogs were sitting on a pond.
16 more frogs joined them.
Now there are 49 frogs on the pond.
How many frogs were on the pond at first?
Show how you know.

I can ...
solve one- and two-step
problems using addition or
subtraction.

Content Standard 2.CA.2
Process Standards PS.1,
PS.2, PS.4, PS.5

_____ frogs

Brian had some baseball cards. Eric gave Brian 6 more cards. Now Brian has 15 cards. How many baseball cards did Brian have at first?

You can use a model to keep track of the numbers.

You know the whole and one part.

You can use addition or subtraction to solve the problem.

$$\underline{9} + 6 = 15$$

or

$$15 - 6 = \underline{9}$$

So, Brian had $\underline{9}$ cards at first.

Check that your answer makes sense.

Brian had 9 cards. Then Eric gave him 6 more cards. Now he has 15 cards.

$$9 + 6 = 15$$

My answer makes sense!

Do You Understand?

Show Me! Cory scored some points. Then he scored 8 more points. He scored 14 points in all. How many points did Cory score at first? How can you solve the problem?

☆ Guided Practice ☆

Complete both equations to solve the problem. Use the model to help you.

1. Some people got on the bus at the first stop.
9 more people got on the bus at the second stop.
There are 21 people on the bus now.
How many people got on the bus at the first stop?

$$\underline{12} \oplus \underline{9} = \underline{21}$$

or

$$\underline{21} \ominus \underline{9} = \underline{12}$$

_____ people

Name _____

Tools   Assessment

Independent Practice ✧ Solve each problem. Show your work.

2. Mr. Wing's class collected some cans to recycle on Tuesday. They collected 18 more cans on Wednesday. The class collected 44 cans in all. How many cans did the class collect on Tuesday?

You can use addition or subtraction to solve this problem.

_____ + _____ = _____

or

_____ − _____ = _____

_____ cans

3. Sue took out 5 books from the library on Monday. She took out 6 books from the library on Tuesday. Then she returned 3 books on Wednesday. How many books does Sue have on Thursday?

_____ books

4. **Higher Order Thinking** There are 24 peas on Kim's plate. Kim eats 15 peas. Then Kim's mother puts 8 more peas on her plate. How many peas are on Kim's plate now?

Step 1

_____ − _____ = _____

Step 2

_____ + _____ = _____   _____ peas

Topic 5 | Lesson 8   two hundred ninety-nine   **299**

Write two equations to solve each problem. Show your work.

Think about what you know and what you are trying to find.

5. **Make Sense** Elaine put 13 photos in the album. Ken put some more photos in the album. There are 32 photos in the album in all. How many photos did Ken add?

_____ photos

6. **Make Sense** Kris sees some students in the library. Then 10 more students enter the library. Now Kris sees 20 students in the library. How many students were in the library in the beginning?

_____ students

7. **Higher Order Thinking** There are 15 vocabulary words in Week 1. There are 8 more vocabulary words in Week 2 than in Week 1.

How many words are there in both weeks?

Step 1: _____ + _____ = _____

Step 2: _____ + _____ = _____

_____ words

8. **Assessment** Blake puts 8 marbles in the bag. Cole puts 9 marbles in the bag. Then Blake takes out 7 marbles from the bag. How many marbles are in the bag now?

Solve. Show your work in the table.

Step 1
Step 2
Answer: _____ marbles

Name _____

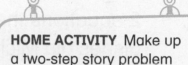
Another Look! You can solve a two-step problem by writing two equations.

Rena counts 6 birds in the tree. 3 birds fly away. Then 8 more birds land in the tree. How many birds does Rena count in the tree now?

Step 1
Subtract to find how many birds are in the tree after 3 birds fly away.

Step 2
Add the number of birds that landed in the tree.

$$6 - 3 = 3$$

$$3 + 8 = 11$$

_____ birds

HOME ACTIVITY Make up a two-step story problem for your child to solve.

Complete both equations to solve each problem.

1. Lucy collects 9 rocks. She gives 4 rocks to Sam. Then Lucy collects 7 more rocks. How many rocks does Lucy have now?

_____ rocks

Step 1:

_____ − _____ = _____

Step 2:

_____ + _____ = _____

2. 4 boys ride their bicycles to the park. 6 more boys ride their bicycles to the park. Then 2 boys go home. How many boys are at the park now?

_____ boys

Step 1:

_____ + _____ = _____

Step 2:

_____ − _____ = _____

Solve each problem. Show your work.

3. **Model** Michael put some of the dishes away. Scott put 17 dishes away. They put away 32 dishes in all. Use the bar diagram to model the story. Then write 2 equations the model shows. How many dishes did Michael put away?

_____ + _____ = _____

_____ - _____ = _____

_____ dishes

4. **Higher Order Thinking** Kina picked 14 green apples. Her dad picked 8 red apples. Then they each ate 2 apples. How many apples do they have now? Explain how you solved the problem.

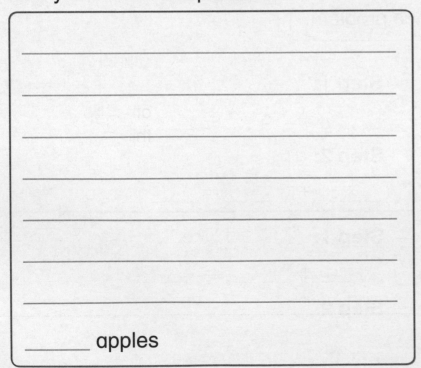

_____ apples

5. **Assessment** 3 black cats were in the alley. 5 cats joined them. Then 6 cats walked away. How many cats are still in the alley?

Solve. Show your work in the table.

Step 1
Step 2
Answer: _____ cats

© Pearson Education, Inc. 2

Name _____

Solve & Share

Bill collects and sells seashells. He has 45 shells, finds 29 shells, and sells 20 shells. How many seashells does Bill have now?

Tara says you have to subtract 45 − 29 and then add 20 to solve the problem. Do you agree with Tara's thinking? Circle your answer. Use pictures, words, or equations to explain.

I can ...
critique the thinking of others by using what I know about addition and subtraction.

Process Standards PS.3 Also PS.1, PS.4, PS.7
Content Standards 2.CA.2, 2.CA.1

Agree	Do Not Agree

Thinking Habits
What questions can I ask to understand other people's thinking?

Are there mistakes in other people's thinking?

Learn   Glossary

42 people are swimming. Some people leave. Now 15 people are swimming.

Kelly added up to subtract and she says 17 people left.

How can I decide if I agree with Kelly?

I can check for mistakes or ask Kelly questions.

I can draw a number line and add up to check for mistakes.

+5   +10   +2

15   20   30 32

$5 + 10 + 2 = 17$,
but $15 + 17$ is only 32.

Kelly's strategy of adding up is good, but her answer is not correct.

+5   +10   +10   +2

15   20   30   40 42

$15 + 27 = 42$
So, 27 people left.

Do You Understand?

Show Me! What question would you ask Kelly to help her check her reasoning?

☆ **Guided Practice** ☆ Circle the answer. Use pictures, words, or equations to explain your reasoning.

1. 51 people were on a train. 33 people left the train. How many people are on the train now?

Ryan says 18 people. He broke apart 33 into 30 and 3. Then he subtracted each number. Does Ryan's reasoning make sense?

Agree   **Do Not Agree**

_____

_____

_____

_____

_____

© Pearson Education, Inc. 2

Independent Practice Circle the answer. Use pictures, words, or equations to explain your reasoning.

2. Jill put 53 buttons in a box. Marci put 17 buttons in another box.

   Jarod says Marci has 33 fewer buttons than Jill. He thinks 53 − 20 is easier to subtract than 53 − 17. He subtracts 53 − 20 and gets 33.

   Do you agree or not agree with Jarod's thinking?

   Agree   **Do Not Agree**

---

3. Rob has 68 more puzzle pieces than Gina. Rob has 90 puzzle pieces.

   Carol says Gina has 22 puzzle pieces. Carol says she found 90 − 68 using an open number line. She added up 2 and 20 more from 68 and got 90.

   Does Carol's reasoning make sense?

   Agree   **Do Not Agree**

Problem Solving

Reading Books

Ricky read the first 3 chapters of a book. Chapter 1 has 11 pages. Chapter 2 has 7 pages. Chapter 3 has 9 pages.

Sally read 46 pages of her book. How many more pages did Sally read than Ricky?

4. Make Sense What steps do you need to take to solve the problem?

_____

_____

_____

5. Look for a Pattern Is there a shortcut to find how many pages Ricky read? Explain.

_____

_____

_____

6. Explain Sally drew this open number line. Sally says she read 21 more pages than Ricky. Do you agree? Explain.

_____

_____

_____

_____

Another Look!

Shane has 62 stamps. Jake has 36 stamps.

Nita says Jake has 26 fewer stamps than Shane, because she can break apart 36 and subtract $62 - 30 = 32$ and $32 - 6 = 26$. Is Nita correct?

$62 - 36 = ?$

> I can break apart 36 into $30 + 6$ and subtract.

$62 - 30 = 32$
$32 - 2 = 30$ and $30 - 4 = 26$
So, $62 - 36 = 26$.
Yes, Nita is correct.

HOME ACTIVITY Take turns writing your own subtraction problems involving two-digit numbers. Make some mistakes in some of your solutions. Then challenge each other to find the mistakes.

Circle the answer. Use pictures, words, or equations to explain.

1. There were 64 runners in a race last year. This year there were 25 fewer runners.

   Latoya says 39 runners were in the race this year. She says $64 - 30$ is easy to subtract. So she added $25 + 5 = 30$. Then she found $64 - 30 = 34$, and added 5 to 34 to get 39.

   Agree   **Do Not Agree**

Landing Planes

Luis says the number of landings in the afternoon equals the number of landings in the morning and evening. Do you agree with Luis?

Morning   **Afternoon**   **Evening**

36 landings   **74 landings**   **38 landings**

2. **Make Sense** What do you know? What do you need to do to tell if Luis is correct?

_____

_____

_____

3. **Model** Use pictures, words, or equations to explain if Luis's thinking is correct.

_____

_____

_____

4. **Explain** Luis got his answer by finding $74 - 38 = 36$.

Do you agree with Luis's thinking? Use pictures, words, or equations to explain.

© Pearson Education, Inc. 2

Topic 5 | Lesson 9

Find a Match

Find a partner. Point to a clue. Read the clue.

Look below the clues to find a match. Write the clue letter in the box next to the match.

Find a match for every clue.

I can …
add and subtract within 20.

Clues

A Every difference is 10.

B Every sum is 11.

C Every sum and difference is 6.

D Exactly three sums are the same.

E Exactly three differences are the same.

F Every sum is the same as $9 + 4$.

G Every difference is odd.

H Exactly three sums are even.

12 − 5 17 − 8 14 − 7 16 − 9	10 − 0 20 − 10 14 − 4 19 − 9	6 + 6 2 + 8 7 + 4 5 + 7	14 − 8 3 + 3 15 − 9 0 + 6
8 + 6 7 + 8 9 + 6 10 + 5	15 − 8 18 − 9 12 − 7 13 − 6	5 + 6 4 + 7 9 + 2 3 + 8	7 + 6 3 + 10 8 + 5 4 + 9

A-Z
Glossary

Word List
- break apart
- compatible numbers
- compensation
- difference
- mental math
- ones
- open number line
- tens

Understand Vocabulary

Choose a term from the Word List to complete each sentence.

1. You can count back or add up to subtract on an

   _____.

2. To find $42 - 7$, you can _____ 7 into $2 + 5$.

3. The answer to a subtraction problem is called the _____.

4. There are 6 _____ in the number 36.

---

5. In 43, there are _____ tens.

6. In 76, there are _____ tens and _____ ones.

7. Break apart 8 to find $65 - 8$.

   _____

Use Vocabulary in Writing

8. Use words to tell how to find $54 - 19$. Use terms from the Word List.

   _____

   _____

   _____

   _____

   _____

© Pearson Education, Inc. 2

Name _____

Set A

You can use a hundred chart to help you subtract. Find 65 − 31.

Start at 31. Move right 4 ones to 35.
Then move down 3 tens to 65.
3 tens and 4 ones is 34.

So, 65 − 31 = __34__ .

31	32	33	34	35	36	37	38	39	40
41	42	43	44	45	46	47	48	49	50
51	52	53	54	55	56	57	58	59	60
61	62	63	64	65	66	67	68	69	70

Reteaching

Use a hundred chart to solve the problems.

1. 67 − 42 = _____

2. 70 − 33 = _____

3. 58 − 42 = _____

4. 63 − 38 = _____

Set B

You can use an open number line to find 85 − 30.

Place 85 on the number line.

30 is 3 tens. Count back by 10 three times from 85.

So, 85 − 30 = __55__ .

Use an open number line to find each difference.

5. 60 − 20 = _____

6. 78 − 40 = _____

You can use an open number line to find 57 − 24.

Place 57 on the number line. There are 2 tens in 24. So, count back by 10 two times. There are 4 ones in 24. Then count back 4 from 37.

So, 57 − 24 = _33_ .

Use an open number line to find each difference.

7. 38 − 13 = _____

8. 93 − 36 = _____

Find 62 − 37.

Place 37 on the line. Add 3 to get to 40. Then add two 10s to get to 60. Then add 2 to get to 62. Add the tens and ones: 3 + 10 + 10 + 2 = 25.

So, 62 − 37 = _25_ .

Add up on an open number line to find each difference.

9. 75 − 47 = _____

10. 52 − 29 = _____

Name _____

Set E

Break apart 17 to find 54 − 17.

21	22	23	24	25	26	27	28	29	30
31	32	33	34	35	36	⟨37⟩	38	39	40
41	42	43	44	45	46	47	48	49	50
51	52	53	⟨54⟩	55	56	57	58	59	60

54 − 17

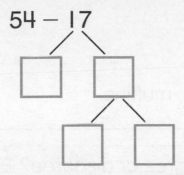

Start at 54. Subtract 10. Then subtract
4 to get to 40. Then subtract 3 more.

So, 54 − 17 = 37 .

Set F

74 − 27 = ?

Use compensation to solve.

74 − 27
        ↓ +3
74 − 30 = 44 �·····▸ 47
              +3

So, 74 − 27 = 47 .

Subtract. Break apart the
number you are subtracting.
Show your work.

11. 52 − 23 = _____

12. 45 − 19 = _____

Use compensation to make numbers
that are easier to subtract. Then solve.

13. 42 − 18 = _____

14. 84 − 37 = _____

Mason reads 34 pages in two days. He reads 8 of the pages on the second day. How many pages does Mason read the first day?

34

? | 8

$26 + 8 = 34$ and
$34 - 8 = 26$

_26_ pages

Thinking Habits

Critique Reasoning

What questions can I ask to understand other people's thinking?

Are there mistakes in other people's thinking?

Add or subtract to solve the problem. Show your work.

15. Gene bakes 60 muffins in one day. He bakes 24 of the muffins before lunch. How many muffins does he bake after lunch?

___ ◯ ___ = ___

_____ muffins

Do you agree or disagree? Explain.

16. Ken has 29 more stamps than Jamie. Ken has 52 stamps. Lisa says Jamie has 23 stamps.

Lisa added up 1 from 29, then 20 more from 30, and 2 more to get to 52. Does Lisa's reasoning make sense?

Name _____

1. A store has 68 candles. Then they sell 29 of the candles. How many candles are left?

Ⓐ 29   Ⓑ 38   Ⓒ 39   Ⓓ 97

2. Which does the number line show? Choose all that apply.

☐ Count back by 10 two times from 48.

☐ Count back by 10 three times from 48.

☐ 48 − 30 = 18

☐ 18 + 48 = 66

3. Tony has 66 rocks.
He gives 23 rocks to Chris.

How many rocks does Tony have now?

_____ ◯ _____ = _____

_____ rocks

21	22	23	24	25	26	27	28	29	30
31	32	33	34	35	36	37	38	39	40
41	42	43	44	45	46	47	48	49	50
51	52	53	54	55	56	57	58	59	60
61	62	63	64	65	66	67	68	69	70

4. Raven solved a subtraction problem using the number line. Write the equation that the number line shows.

_____ − _____ = _____

5. Ella has 7 carrots.
Ann has 34 carrots.
How many fewer carrots does
Ella have than Ann?

(A) 7

(C) 34

(B) 27

(D) 41

6. Keena has 64 balloons.
28 of the balloons are red.
14 balloons are green.
The rest of the balloons are purple.
How many of the balloons are purple?

(A) 22

(C) 42

(B) 36

(D) 50

7. Break apart 48 to solve.
Show your work.

$$73 - 48 = ?$$

$$73 - 48 = \underline{\qquad}$$

8. Joe has 43 stickers.
Then he gives away 9 stickers.
How many stickers does Joe have left?

Can you use the two equations to solve?
Choose Yes or No.

$43 + 7 = 50$ ○ Yes   ○ No
$50 + 2 = 52$

$43 + 10 = 53$ ○ Yes   ○ No
$53 - 1 = 52$

$43 - 3 = 40$ ○ Yes   ○ No
$40 - 6 = 34$

$43 - 10 = 33$ ○ Yes   ○ No
$33 + 1 = 34$

© Pearson Education, Inc. 2

Topic 5 | Assessment

Name _____

9. Which does the number line show? Choose all that apply.

☐ Count back 4 tens from 70.

☐ Count back 4 from 70.

☐ 70 − 30 = 40

☐ 70 − 40 = 30

10. Use the open number line to find the difference.

$$80 - 42 = ?$$

80 − 42 = _____

11. Part A 33 ants are on a leaf. 15 ants leave. How many ants are left?
Jay adds 2 to 33 to make an easier problem, 35−15. He says 20 ants are left. Circle whether you agree or do not agree.

Agree   **Do Not Agree**

Part B Explain why you agree or do not agree with Jay's strategy.

12. Use the open number lines. Show two different ways to find 74 − 28.
Show your work.

One Way

74 − 28 = _____

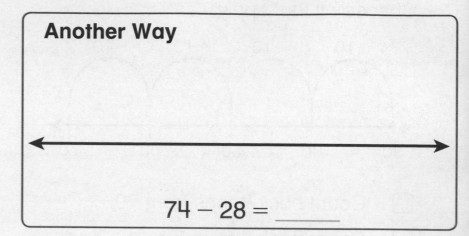

Another Way

74 − 28 = _____

13. Use the numbers on the cards.
Write the missing numbers to solve
the problem.

| 3 | 35 | 40 | 75 |

72 − 37 = _____

+3 [+]

_____ − _____ = _____

14. 5 black cows are at the ranch.
9 brown cows join them.
Then 6 cows leave the ranch.
How many cows are still at the ranch?

Solve. Show your work in the table.

Step 1
Step 2
Answer _____ cows

Name _____

Beautiful Boats

Chen's family goes to the lake for a vacation.
They count the boats that they see.

12 sailboats   28 rowboats   36 motorboats

1. How many more motorboats does
   Chen see than sailboats?

   Use the open number line to
   solve.

_____ more motorboats

2. Maria's family saw 57 rowboats
   on their vacation. How many
   more rowboats did they see
   than Chen's family?

   Use compensation to solve.
   Explain how you found your answer.

   _____

   _____

   _____

   _____

   _____

   _____

   _____ more rowboats

3. Chen's sisters play with toy boats at the lake. They have 21 yellow boats. They have 9 fewer red boats than yellow boats. How many boats do they have in all?

Write two equations to solve the problem.

_____ − _____ = _____

_____ + _____ = _____

_____ boats

4. Julie's family saw 94 boats on their vacation. How many more boats did they see than Chen's family?

Part A What do you need to do to solve the problem?

Part B How many boats did Chen see? Show your work. Then explain how you found your answer.

_____ boats

Part C Julie said that her family saw 18 more boats than Chen's family. She broke apart 76 into $70 + 4 + 2$. Then she subtracted each number from 94. Does Julie's reasoning make sense? Explain.

© Pearson Education, Inc. 2

Fluently Subtract Within 100

Essential Question: What are strategies for subtracting numbers to 100?

More of Earth is covered with water than with land!

And some of the land is covered with snow and ice!

Wow! Let's do this project and learn more.

Math and Science Project: Finding Water and Finding Differences

Find Out Use globes, maps, books, and other sources to find out where water, snow, and ice can be found on Earth. Make a list of different names of bodies of water and names of bodies of snow and ice.

Journal: Make a Book Show what you learn in a book. In your book, also:

• Tell about how globes are models that show where water is found on Earth.

• Tell about how to use a subtraction model to find differences.

Name _____

Review What You Know

A-Z Vocabulary

1. **Break apart** 56 into tens and ones. Draw place value blocks to show the parts.

   $56 = $ _____ $+$ _____

2. Complete the drawing to show how to **regroup** 1 ten as ones.

3. Complete the **bar diagram** to model $64 - 31 = ?$

Open Number Lines

4. Find $40 - 25$ by counting back on an open number line. Show your work.

   $40 - 25 = $ _____

5. Find $45 - 22$ by adding up on an open number line. Show your work.

   $45 - 22 = $ _____

Math Story

6. Lea has 30 cookies. She gives 17 cookies to her friends. How many cookies does Lea have now?

   _____ cookies

© Pearson Education, Inc. 2

Solve & Share

How can you use tens and ones to find 23 − 6?
Use place-value blocks to help you. Show your work.

Solve

Lesson 6-1

Regroup 1 Ten for 10 Ones

I can ...
exchange 1 ten for 10 ones.

Content Standard 2.CA.1
Process Standards PS.1,
PS.3, PS.5, PS.8

_____ − _____ = _____

Find 34 − 6. Show 34. There are not enough ones to subtract 6.

Tens	Ones

You need to regroup.

Regroup 1 ten as 10 ones.

Tens	Ones

Subtract 6.

Tens	Ones

Cross out 6 ones to subtract. Now there are 2 tens and 8 ones left that show the difference.

34 − 6 = __28__

Do You Understand?

Show Me! Do you need to regroup when you subtract 5 from 44? Explain why or why not.

☆ Guided Practice ☆

Subtract. Use your workmat and place-value blocks. Regroup if you need to.

	Show.	Subtract.	Do you need to regroup?	Find the difference.
1.	35	8	Yes No	35 − 8 = __27__
2.	46	3	Yes No	46 − 3 = ___
3.	62	4	Yes No	62 − 4 = ___
4.	50	7	Yes No	50 − 7 = ___

© Pearson Education, Inc. 2

Topic 6 | Lesson 1

Tools Assessment

☆ Independent ☆ Practice

Subtract. Use your workmat and place-value blocks. Regroup if you need to.

Show.	Subtract.	Do you need to regroup?	Find the difference.
5. 81	2	Yes No	81 − 2 = _____
6. 29	1	Yes No	29 − 1 = _____
7. 60	4	Yes No	60 − 4 = _____
8. 24	9	Yes No	24 − 9 = _____
9. 75	3	Yes No	75 − 3 = _____
10. 43	5	Yes No	43 − 5 = _____

11. **Higher Order Thinking** Which one-digit numbers can you subtract from 74 without first regrouping? Explain how you know.

_____

_____

Think about what each digit stands for in 74.

12. Make Sense There are 21 snails in a garden. 6 snails leave. How many snails are still in the garden?

_____ snails

13. Make Sense Kate has 45 marbles. She gives 3 marbles to her brother. How many marbles does Kate have now?

_____ marbles

14. Higher Order Thinking Sammie has 9 fewer rings than Emilio.
Sammie has 7 more rings than Sara.
Emilio has 34 rings.
Complete the sentences below.
Draw a picture to explain your work.

Sammie has _____ rings.

Sara has _____ rings.

15. ⓙ **Assessment** Malcolm has 38 seeds. Juan has 4 fewer seeds than Malcolm. Juan gives 8 seeds to his friend. How many seeds does Juan have now?

Ⓐ 22

Ⓑ 26

Ⓒ 36

Ⓓ 46

Think about what you know and what you are trying to find. Can drawing place-value blocks help?

Name _____

Another Look! Use place-value blocks to find 42 − 7.

Show 42.

Tens	Ones

Regroup.

Tens	Ones

Subtract 7 ones.

Tens	Ones

HOME ACTIVITY Ask your child to show you how to subtract 26 − 7 using small objects such as buttons, marbles, or paper clips. Have your child explain and show you how to regroup.

$12 - 7 = \underline{5}$ ones

$42 - 7 = \underline{35}$

Subtract. Use the pictures to help.

1. Subtract 5 from 31.

Show 31.

Tens	Ones

Regroup.

Tens	Ones

Subtract _____ ones.

Tens	Ones

$11 - 5 = \underline{\hphantom{00}}$ ones

$31 - 5 = \underline{\hphantom{00}}$

2. **A-Z** **Vocabulary** Circle the missing word.

addend   **equation**

$42 - 7 = 35$ is an _____.

3. **Algebra** What number is missing?

_____ $- 5 = 20$

4. **Algebra** What number is missing?

$37 -$ _____ $= 28$

Make Sense Solve. Think about what you know and need to find.

5. Maria buys 36 beads.
She uses 9 of the beads.
How many beads does Maria have left?

_____ beads

6. Luke buys 7 new pencils.
Now he has 21 pencils.
How many pencils did Luke have at first?

_____ pencils

---

7. **Higher Order Thinking** A flag pole is 30 feet tall. A bug crawls 14 feet up the pole. Then it crawls another 4 feet up the pole. How much farther must the bug crawl to get to the top?

30 —

14 —

0 —

_____ feet

8. **Assessment** An old building has 48 big windows.
The building has 12 small windows.
There are 9 broken windows.
How many windows are **NOT** broken?

Ⓐ 51

Ⓑ 48

Ⓒ 41

Ⓓ 37

Solve & Share

There are 22 students drawing pictures. 4 students finish drawing. How many students are still drawing?

Use place-value blocks to help you solve. Show the tens and ones you have.

I can ...

use place value and models to subtract 2-digit and 1-digit numbers.

Content Standard 2.CA.1
Process Standards PS.3, PS.4, PS.5

Tens	Ones

_____ tens   _____ ones

$$22 - 4 = \underline{\hspace{1cm}}$$

Find 32 − 5.

Show 32. There are not enough ones to subtract.

Tens	Ones
||| :	

Tens	Ones
3	2
	5

Regroup 1 ten as 10 ones.

Write 2 to show 2 tens.
Write 12 to show 12 ones.

Tens	Ones
2 3́	12 2́
	5

Subtract the ones.
Then subtract the tens.

Tens	Ones
2 3́	12 2́
	5
2	7

There are 2 tens and 7 ones left.

So, 32 − 5 = ___27___.

Tens	Ones
2 3́	12 2́
	5
2	7

Do You Understand?

Show Me! Why do you need to regroup when you subtract 32 − 5?

☆ **Guided Practice** ☆ Subtract. Draw place-value blocks to show your work. Regroup if needed.

1.

Tens	Ones
3̶	1 4̶
	9
3	5

2.

Tens	Ones
2	3
	5

Tens	Ones

3.

Tens	Ones
3	5
	8

Tens	Ones

Independent Practice

Subtract. Draw place-value blocks to show your work. Regroup if needed.

4.

Tens	Ones
☐	☐
6	3
	2
−	

Tens	Ones

5.

Tens	Ones
☐	☐
9	1
	7
−	

Tens	Ones

6.

Tens	Ones
☐	☐
6	6
	9
−	

Tens	Ones

7.

Tens	Ones
☐	☐
5	2
	6
−	

Tens	Ones

Write the missing numbers in the boxes. Draw a picture to show and explain your work.

8. Algebra What numbers will complete the subtraction equations?

$\boxed{} - 8 = 17$ $34 - \boxed{} = 29$

9. There are 23 students playing tag. 9 students go home. How many students are still playing tag?

Tens	Ones

_____ students

10. There are 67 books on the shelf. Dion takes 5 of them. How many books are left on the shelf?

Tens	Ones

_____ books

11. **Higher Order Thinking** What mistake did Alia make when she subtracted 72 − 4? Show how to fix her mistake.

Alia's Work
```
  72
−  4
  72
```

_____

_____

_____

_____

12. **Assessment** You draw place value blocks to model each subtraction. Would you regroup to show the difference? Choose Yes or No.

29 − 3 = ?   ◯ Yes   ◯ No

30 − 0 = ?   ◯ Yes   ◯ No

77 − 8 = ?   ◯ Yes   ◯ No

55 − 5 = ?   ◯ Yes   ◯ No

Another Look! Regroup when there are not enough ones. Find 52 − 8.

Step 1

Show 52. There are not enough ones to subtract 8.

Step 2

Regroup 1 ten as 10 ones.

Step 3

Subtract the ones. Then subtract the tens.

Tens	Ones
|||||	:

Tens	Ones
|||| ⦶	(dots)

Tens	Ones
||||	• x

Tens	Ones
5	2
−	8

Tens	Ones
4	12
5̶	2̶
−	8

Tens	Ones
4	12
5̶	2̶
−	8
4	4

So, 52 − 8 = __44__.

HOME ACTIVITY Write 22 − 6 in vertical form on a piece of paper. Ask your child to show you how to find 22 − 6 using small objects such as paper clips, buttons, or marbles. Have your child write the difference.

Subtract. Draw place-value blocks to show your work. Regroup if needed.

1.

Tens	Ones
2	6
−	7

Tens	Ones

2.

Tens	Ones
4	3
−	9

Tens	Ones

Model Solve each problem. Draw place-value blocks to model.

3. There are 40 students in the gym. 9 students are jumping rope. How many students are **NOT** jumping rope?

Tens	Ones
☐	☐
−	

_____ students

4. Kate writes on 7 pages in her notebook. There are 34 pages in her notebook. How many pages are blank?

Tens	Ones
☐	☐
−	

_____ pages

5. **Higher Order Thinking** Write a subtraction story about 45 − 8. Then solve.

Tens	Ones
☐	☐
−	

_____

_____

_____

6. **○ Assessment** You draw place value blocks to model each subtraction. Choose all of the problems that need regrouping to show the difference.

☐ 62 − 4 = ?   ☐ 75 − 7 = ?

☐ 58 − 7 = ?   ☐ 35 − 5 = ?

© Pearson Education, Inc. 2

Solve & Share

Ari has 31 stickers.
He puts 8 of his stickers in a scrapbook.
How many stickers are left?

Solve. Explain why your strategy works.

I can ...
use place value and regrouping to subtract.

Content Standard 2.CA.1
Process Standards PS.4, PS.5, PS.6, PS.8

Tens	Ones
−	

_____

_____

_____

_____

_____

_____

Find 42 − 9.

Show 42.

Tens	Ones
||||	:

Tens	Ones
□	□
4	2
	9

Look at the ones. There are not enough ones to subtract.

Regroup!

Tens	Ones
||||	⦿

Tens	Ones
3	12
4	2
	9

Subtract the ones. Then subtract the tens.

Tens	Ones
|||	✗✗ ✗✗ ✗✗

Tens	Ones
3	12
4	2
	9
3	3

There are 3 tens and 3 ones left.

42 − 9 = 33

Tens	Ones
3	12
4	2
	9
3	3

Do You Understand?

Show Me! Look at the regrouping in the problem above. Why is 12 written above the 2 in the ones column?

Guided Practice Subtract. Use drawings if needed.

1.

Tens	Ones
2	16
3	6
	8
2	8

2.

Tens	Ones
2	9
	4

3.

Tens	Ones
4	1
	4

4.

Tens	Ones
6	3
	5

5.

Tens	Ones
5	0
	1

6.

Tens	Ones
4	8
	7

Tools   Assessment

Independent Practice ☆ Subtract. Use drawings if needed.

7.

Tens	Ones
☐	☐
3	2
	6

8.

Tens	Ones
☐	☐
2	0
	3

9.

Tens	Ones
☐	☐
6	7
	6

10.

Tens	Ones
☐	☐
5	2
	4

11.

Tens	Ones
☐	☐
3	5
	0

12.

Tens	Ones
☐	☐
7	5
	3

13.

Tens	Ones
☐	☐
5	6
	7

14.

Tens	Ones
☐	☐
8	5
	1

15.

Tens	Ones
☐	☐
9	8
	9

16.

Tens	Ones
☐	☐
7	7
	9

Use words or a picture to solve.

17. Number Sense What is the missing number? Explain how to solve.

$45 - 9 = 46 - \boxed{}$

18. **Generalize** There are
25 bikes at a bike store.
The store owner sells 7 bikes.
How many bikes are left?

Tens	Ones
−	

You can repeat steps to subtract. First subtract the ones. Regroup if needed. Then subtract the tens. 7 has zero tens.

_____ bikes

19. **Higher Order Thinking** A bike store sold
10 fewer locks on Wednesday than on
Tuesday. How many more locks did the
store sell on Wednesday than on Monday?

Bike Locks Sold	
Monday	9
Tuesday	33
Wednesday	

Tens	Ones
−	

_____ locks

20. **Assessment** Use the numbers on the
cards to find the missing numbers in the
problem. Write the missing numbers.

15	9	3

Tens	Ones
3	
4	5
−	6

Think: How will I regroup to subtract?

© Pearson Education, Inc. 2

Name _____

Another Look! Find 42 − 6. You can subtract the ones first.

Think: Are there enough ones to subtract?

There are **NOT** enough ones to subtract.

Regroup if you need to. Then subtract the tens. Draw pictures if needed.

1-digit numbers have 0 tens.

Tens	Ones
3 12	
4	2
−	6
3	6

Regroup? (Yes)   No

So, 42 − 6 = 36.

HOME ACTIVITY Write 34 − 9 in vertical form on a sheet of paper. Have your child use pencil and paper to solve.

Subtract. Use drawings if needed.

1.
Tens	Ones
2	5
−	4

2.
Tens	Ones
4	1
−	8

3.
Tens	Ones
6	5
−	7

4.
Tens	Ones
7	8
−	9

5.
Tens	Ones
8	3
−	6

6. 53 grapes are on a plate. Andrea eats 5 of them. How many grapes are on the plate now?

Tens	Ones
□	□
−	

_____ grapes

7. Chato reads 7 pages. His book has 67. How many pages does Chato have left to read?

Tens	Ones
□	□
−	

_____ pages

8. Higher Order Thinking Complete the subtraction frame. Subtract a one-digit number from a 2-digit number.

Tens	Ones
□	□
−	
7	6

You know the difference! Work backwards to check your work. There is more than one correct answer.

9. ⓘAssessment Use the numbers on the cards to find the missing numbers in the problem. Write the missing numbers.

| 1 | 8 | 11 |

Tens	Ones
2	1
−	3
1	□

© Pearson Education, Inc. 2

Name _____

☆ Solve & Share ☆

You have 42 pipe cleaners.
You use 19 of the pipe cleaners.
How many pipe cleaners do you have now?

Use place-value blocks to help you solve.
Draw your place-value blocks.
Tell if you need to regroup.

I can ...
use place value and models to subtract 2-digit numbers.

Content Standard 2.CA.1
Process Standards PS.3, PS.4, PS.5, PS.7

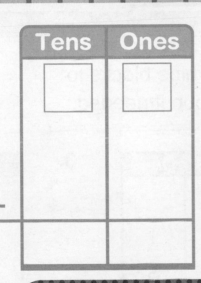

Tens	Ones

−

Regroup?

Yes   No

_____ pipe cleaners

Find 31 − 14.

Show 31. There are not enough ones to subtract.

Tens	Ones
|||	.

−

Tens	Ones
3	1
1	4

Regroup 1 ten as 10 ones.

Write 2 to show 2 tens. Write 11 to show 11 ones.

Tens	Ones
|||(|)	::::

−

Tens	Ones
2	11
3́	4́
1	4

Subtract the ones.

Tens	Ones
||	:: ✗✗ ✗✗ ✗✗

−

Tens	Ones
2	11
3́	4́
1	4
	7

Subtract the tens.

So, 31 − 14 = 17.

Tens	Ones
|✗|	:::

−

Tens	Ones
2	11
3́	4́
1	4
1	7

Do You Understand?

Show Me! Explain why you need to regroup to find 65 − 17.

☆ Guided Practice ☆

Subtract. Draw place-value blocks to show your work. Regroup if needed.

1.

Tens	Ones
4	12
5́	2́
1	3
3	9

2.

Tens	Ones
4	1
2	6

Tens	Ones

3.

Tens	Ones
6	4
4	7

Tens	Ones

Topic 6 | Lesson 4

Tools   Assessment

Independent Practice Subtract. Draw place-value blocks to show your work. Regroup if needed.

4.

Tens	Ones
☐	☐
5	6
− 3	1

Tens	Ones

5.

Tens	Ones
☐	☐
6	6
− 5	8

Tens	Ones

6.

Tens	Ones
☐	☐
8	5
− 4	6

Tens	Ones

7.

Tens	Ones
☐	☐
4	3
− 1	5

Tens	Ones

8. Algebra Write numbers to complete the equations. Draw pictures to help if needed.

$37 - 18 = \boxed{}$

$46 - \boxed{} = 18$

$\boxed{} - 17 = 16$

9. Number Sense
Do these models show the same value? Explain.

_____

_____

_____

_____

10. **Model** Anita has $63. She spends $24 and saves the rest. How much does Anita save?

Tens	Ones
−	

$_____

What kind of picture can you draw to model the subtraction?

11. **Higher Order Thinking** Write a subtraction story about 36 − 17. Explain how to solve the problem.

_____

_____

_____

_____

_____

_____

12. ⭘**Assessment** Sara has 70 beads. There are 11 beads that are **NOT** round. The rest are round. How many round beads does Sara have?

Ⓐ 59

Ⓑ 49

Ⓒ 47

Ⓓ 11

Help   Tools   Games

Another Look! Find 43 – 16.

Step 1	Step 2	Step 3
Show 43. There are not enough ones to subtract 6.	Regroup 1 ten as 10 ones.	Subtract the ones. Then subtract the tens.

Tens	Ones
4	3
1	6

Tens	Ones
3	13
4̶	3̶
1	6

Tens	Ones
3	13
4̶	3̶
1	6
2	7

So, 43 – 16 = __27__.

HOME ACTIVITY Ask your child to use paper clips or other small objects to find 25 – 16. Have your child explain how he or she regrouped.

Subtract. Draw place-value blocks to show your work. Regroup if needed.

1.

Tens	Ones
5	0
1	3

Tens	Ones

2.

Tens	Ones
7	6
2	8

Tens	Ones

3. Jamal has 54 marbles. Lucas has 70 marbles. How many more marbles does Lucas have than Jamal?

_____ more marbles

4. Latoya has 95 pennies. She gives 62 pennies to her cousin. How many pennies does Latoya have now?

_____ pennies

5. Higher Order Thinking Fill in the missing numbers to make the subtraction problem true.

6. Assessment To find 36 − 17, how can you regroup 36?

(A) 2 tens and 6 ones

(B) 2 tens and 16 ones

(C) 3 tens and 16 ones

(D) 4 tens and 16 ones

Lesson 6-5
Subtract 2-Digit Numbers

Solve & Share

How is subtracting 23 from 71 like subtracting 3 from 71?
How is it different from subtracting 3 from 71? Explain.
Find both differences. Use blocks if you need to.

I can ...
use place value to subtract 2-digit numbers.

 Content Standard 2.CA.1
Process Standards PS.2, PS.3, PS.4, PS.5, PS.6

Tens	Ones
7	1
	3
−	

Tens	Ones
7	1
2	3
−	

Find 43 − 18.
Show and write the subtraction.

Tens	Ones
‖‖‖‖	⋮

Tens	Ones
☐	☐
4	3
− 1	8

You can use a frame to write the subtraction.

There are not enough ones to subtract.
Regroup 1 ten as 10 ones.

Tens	Ones
‖‖‖⟮‖⟯	⦂⦂⦂⦂⦂

Tens	Ones
3	13
4̶	3̶
− 1	8

Write 4 tens and 3 ones as 3 tens and 13 ones.

Subtract: 13 ones − 8 ones = 5 ones
3 tens − 1 ten = 2 tens

Tens	Ones
‖✕	• ✕ ✕ ...

Tens	Ones
3	13
4̶	3̶
− 1	8
2	5

So, 43 − 18 = 25.

Do You Understand?

Show Me! Why can you regroup 1 ten as 10 ones when there are not enough ones to subtract?

⭐ **Guided Practice** ⭐ Write each subtraction problem. Find the difference. Use drawings if you need to.

1. 34 − 15

Tens	Ones
2	14
3̶	4̶
− 1	5
1	9

2. 52 − 31

Tens	Ones
☐	☐
−	

3. 67 − 48

Tens	Ones
☐	☐
−	

Sometimes you need to regroup. Sometimes you don't.

© Pearson Education, Inc. 2

Independent Practice

Write each subtraction problem. Find the difference.

4. 52 – 36

Tens	Ones
☐	☐

_____

5. 94 – 54

Tens	Ones
☐	☐

_____

6. 41 – 25

Tens	Ones
☐	☐

_____

7. 33 – 28

Tens	Ones
☐	☐

_____

8. 65 – 42

Tens	Ones
☐	☐

_____

9. 70 – 48

Tens	Ones
☐	☐

_____

10. 96 – 37

Tens	Ones
☐	☐

_____

11. 87 – 45

Tens	Ones
☐	☐

_____

Solve. Draw a model to help.

12. Higher Order Thinking Tia's basketball team scored 61 points. They won by 23 points. How many points did the other team score?

_____ points

13. **Model** Don has 72 marbles. Josie has 56 marbles. How many more marbles does Don have than Josie?

_____ more marbles

Tens	Ones

−

Can you use a drawing or objects to show the problem?

---

14. **Higher Order Thinking** Write a subtraction story using two two-digit numbers. Then solve the problem in your story.

_____

_____

_____

Tens	Ones

−

_____

_____

15. **☐ Assessment** Eric can fit 90 cards in a scrapbook. He already has 46 cards in the scrapbook.

How many more cards will fit?

Ⓐ 44

Ⓑ 45

Ⓒ 46

Ⓓ 54

Name _____

Help   Tools   Games

Another Look! Remember the steps for subtracting.

Step 1
Think: Are there enough ones to subtract?

Step 2
Regroup if you need to.

Step 3
Subtract the ones.
Subtract the tens.

HOME ACTIVITY Have your child use paper and pencil to solve 65 − 37. Have your child explain the steps he or she takes to subtract.

Write the problems in the frames. Find each difference.

38 − 13

Tens	Ones
3	8
− 1	3
2	5

54 − 17

Tens	Ones
4	14
5̶	4̶
− 1	7
3	7

Be sure to cross out if you regroup.

You can use drawings to help.

Write each problem in a frame. Find the difference.

1. 37 − 14

Tens	Ones
−	

2. 64 − 18

Tens	Ones
−	

3. 45 − 26

Tens	Ones
−	

4. 73 − 25

Tens	Ones
−	

Be Precise Decide which one item each child will buy.
Subtract to find how much money is left.

Stickers 14¢
Craft sticks 36¢
Paint set 42¢
Crayons 58¢

5. Bonnie has 47¢.
She buys the

_____.

Bonnie has _____¢ left.

Tens	Ones
☐	☐

−

6. Ricky has 59¢.
He buys the

_____.

Ricky has _____¢ left.

Tens	Ones
☐	☐

−

7. Lani has 63 grapes. She
gives 36 grapes to Carla.
How many grapes does
Lani have left?

_____ grapes

Tens	Ones

−

8. Write a number to make this
a subtraction problem with
regrouping. Then find the
difference.

Tens	Ones
☐	☐

−   2   3

9. **Higher Order Thinking**
Use each number below.

| 1 | 2 | 4 | 5 |

Write the subtraction
problem that has the
greatest difference. Then solve.

Tens	Ones
☐	☐
☐	☐

−

10. **Assessment** Norma has 48 buttons.
Grace has 14 buttons. Connie has
29 buttons. How many fewer buttons
does Connie have than Norma?

34   29   19   15
Ⓐ   Ⓑ   Ⓒ   Ⓓ

© Pearson Education, Inc. 2

Solve & Share

Find 52 − 24.
Use the bar diagram and subtraction frame
to help you show and solve the problem.
How can you use addition to check your answer?

Solve

Lesson 6-6

Use Addition to Check Subtraction

I can ...
add to check my subtraction.

Content Standard 2.CA.1
Process Standards PS.1,
PS.2, PS.3, PS.4

Remember that addition and subtraction are related.
So, you can add to check subtraction.

Find 24 − 9.

The sum of the parts equals the whole.

$$\begin{array}{r} \overset{\scriptstyle 1\;14}{2\!\!\!/4} \\ -\;9 \\ \hline 15 \end{array} \quad\longrightarrow\quad \begin{array}{r} \overset{1}{1}5 \\ +\;9 \\ \hline 24 \end{array}$$

24	
9	15

Find 52 − 17.

Add to check your subtraction.

The two parts equal the whole!

$$\begin{array}{r} \overset{\scriptstyle 4\;12}{5\!\!\!/2} \\ -\;17 \\ \hline 35 \end{array} \quad\longrightarrow\quad \begin{array}{r} \overset{1}{3}5 \\ +\;17 \\ \hline 52 \end{array}$$

52	
17	35

Do You Understand?

Show Me! Why can you use addition to check
63 − 19 = 44?

☆ **Guided Practice** ☆ Subtract. Check your answer by adding. Write the missing part.

1.

$$\begin{array}{r} \overset{\scriptstyle 2\;12}{3\!\!\!/2} \\ -\;13 \\ \hline 19 \end{array} \qquad \begin{array}{r} \overset{1}{1}9 \\ +\;13 \\ \hline 32 \end{array}$$

32	
13	19

2.

$$\begin{array}{r} 78 \\ -\;49 \\ \hline \end{array} \qquad \begin{array}{r} 29 \\ +\;49 \\ \hline \end{array}$$

78	
49	

You can show the parts in any order.

Topic 6 | Lesson 6

Independent Practice Subtract. Check your answer by adding. Write the missing part.

3.
$$52$$
$$-\ 27$$

52

27 |

4.
$$80$$
$$-\ 14$$

80

14 |

5.
$$54$$
$$-\ 19$$

54

19 |

6.
$$75$$
$$-\ 62$$

75

62 |

7.
$$83$$
$$-\ 29$$

83

29 |

8.
$$48$$
$$-\ 21$$

48

21 |

9. **Higher Order Thinking** Maria uses 35 + 24 to check her answer to a subtraction problem. Write two subtraction problems Maria could have solved.

10. Math and Science 62 students are doing science experiments. 48 students have cups of water. The rest have ice cubes. How many students have ice cubes?

_____ students

11. Make Sense 37 students make clay pots. 16 students use brown clay. The rest use green clay. How many students use green clay?

_____ students

12. Higher Order Thinking Write a subtraction story about 65 − 41. Solve the story. Check your answer by adding.

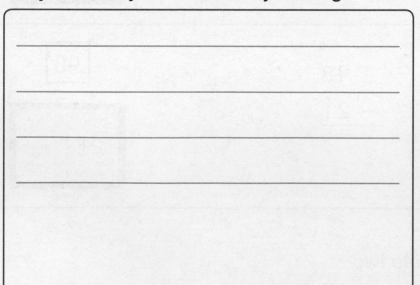

13. Assessment Bill has 17 more craft sticks than Roger. Bill has 45 craft sticks. How many craft sticks does Roger have? Which shows the solution and how to check it?

Ⓐ 15 sticks; $30 + 15 = 45$

Ⓑ 28 sticks; $28 + 17 = 45$

Ⓒ 45 sticks; $28 + 17 = 45$

Ⓓ 62 sticks; $45 + 17 = 62$

© Pearson Education, Inc. 2

Help   Tools   Games

Another Look!

You can think of subtraction as starting with the whole. Then you take away one part. The other part is left.

```
   37   Whole
 - 12   Part
   25   Part
```

```
   25   Part
 + 12   Part
   37   Whole
```

Tens	Ones

Tens	Ones

and   and

To check your work, add to put the parts back together. Your answer should be the whole.

If no regrouping is needed, then add or subtract the tens and the ones.

HOME ACTIVITY Ask your child to find 65 − 32. Then have him or her use addition to show you how to check the subtraction.

Subtract. Check your answer by adding.

1.
```
   86
 -  9    +
```

2.
```
   54
 - 19    +
```

3.
```
   63
 - 37    +
```

4. Mei Ling has 71 marbles.
Then she loses 25 marbles.
How many marbles does Mei Ling have left?

Subtract   Check

_____ marbles

$$- \underline{\hspace{1cm}} \quad + \underline{\hspace{1cm}}$$

Think about how addition and subtraction are related.

5. Denise has 51 beads.
Then she uses 32 beads to make a bracelet.
How many of her beads does Denise have left to use?

Subtract   Check

_____ beads

$$- \underline{\hspace{1cm}} \quad + \underline{\hspace{1cm}}$$

6. **Number Sense** Write the number that makes each equation true.

$63 - 20 = 20 + \underline{\hspace{1cm}}$

$58 - 40 = 18 + \underline{\hspace{1cm}}$

$75 - 30 = 15 + \underline{\hspace{1cm}}$

$89 - 46 = 30 + \underline{\hspace{1cm}}$

In an equation, each side of the equals sign shows the same value.

7. **Assessment** Lana subtracts to find $52 - 39$. Which addition equation could Lana use to check her answer?

Ⓐ $13 + 26 = 39$

Ⓑ $39 + 52 = 91$

Ⓒ $13 + 39 = 52$

Ⓓ $52 + 13 = 65$

© Pearson Education, Inc. 2

Name _____

Solve & Share

Find 82 − 56. Use any strategy you have learned or your own strategy. Show your work. Explain why your strategy works.

I can ...

subtract 2-digit numbers and decide when to regroup and when not to regroup.

Content Standard 2.CA.1
Process Standards PS.1, PS.2, PS.6, PS.7

Find 72 − 24.

One way is to break apart numbers.

72 − 24 = ?

20   4

2   2

72 − 20 = 52

52 − 2 = 50

50 − 2 = 48

So, 72 − 24 = 48.

Another way is to line up the numbers by place value.

$$\begin{array}{r} 6\ 12 \\ \not7\ \not2 \\ -\ 2\ 4 \\ \hline 4\ 8 \end{array}$$

I get the same difference either way!

So, 72 − 24 = 48.

You can check your subtraction with addition.

My work checks. My subtraction is correct.

$$\begin{array}{r} 1 \\ 2\ 4 \\ +\ 4\ 8 \\ \hline 7\ 2 \end{array}$$

Do You Understand?

Show Me! Could you solve 72 − 24 in another way? Explain.

☆ **Guided Practice** ☆ Use any strategy to subtract. Show your work. Check your work with addition.

1. 67 − 39 = _____

67 − 40 = 27

27 + 1 = 28

Check:

$$\begin{array}{r} 1 \\ 2\ 8 \\ +\ 3\ 9 \\ \hline 6\ 7 \end{array}$$

2. 78 − 42 = _____

Name _____

Independent ☆ Practice

Use any strategy to subtract. Show your work.
Check your work with addition.

3. 73 − 34 = _____

4. 78 − 25 = _____

5. 83 − 46 = _____

6. 36 − 27 = _____

7. 98 − 51 = _____

8. 45 − 34 = _____

9. 86 − 29 = _____

10. 71 − 38 = _____

11. 85 − 23 = _____

Algebra Find the missing number.

Look for a pattern.
Use mental math.

12. 34 − 8 = 35 − ☐

13. 27 − 9 = 28 − ☐

14. The hardware store has 32 hammers in stock. The store sells 16 hammers on Saturday. How many hammers are left?

_____ hammers

15. A barber does 15 haircuts on Monday. He does 28 haircuts on Friday. How many more haircuts does he do on Friday than on Monday?

_____ more haircuts

16. **A-Z Vocabulary** Complete each sentence. Use two of the words below.

addend   equation   difference   sum

$93 - 53 = 40$ is an _____.

40 is called the _____ of 93 and 53.

17. **Higher Order Thinking**
Fill in the missing digits.

$$
\begin{array}{cc}
\square & \square \\
- \ 2 & 3 \\
\hline
2 & 9 \\
\end{array}
$$

18. **Assessment** Circle the problem that you will use regrouping to solve. Then find both differences. Show your work.

$56 - 38$ $74 - 52$

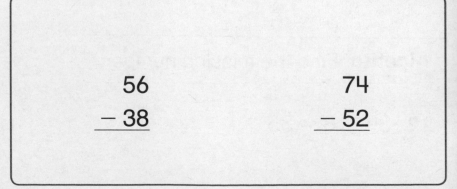

$$
\begin{array}{r}
56 \\
- 38 \\
\hline
\end{array}
\qquad
\begin{array}{r}
74 \\
- 52 \\
\hline
\end{array}
$$

Topic 6 | Lesson 7

Name _____

Another Look! Find $82 - 37$.

$$\begin{array}{r} 7\;12 \\ \not{8}\not{2} \\ -\;37 \\ \hline 45 \end{array}$$

Check

You can use addition to check your subtraction.

$$\begin{array}{r} 37 \\ +\;45 \\ \hline 82 \end{array}$$

Or you can break apart the numbers to check your work.

$82 - 37 = ?$

30   7

2   5

$82 - 30 = 52$
$52 - 2 = 50$
$50 - 5 = 45$

So, $82 - 37 = 45$.

I can subtract in different ways. I will line up the numbers by place value!

There is more than one way to check your subtraction.

HOME ACTIVITY Write $78 - 29$ on a sheet of paper. Have your child use pencil and paper to solve the problem. Then ask your child to explain how he or she found the difference.

Use any strategy to subtract. Show your work. Check your work.

1. $56 - 37 = $ _____

2. $46 - 18 = $ _____

3. $75 - 22 = $ _____

Make Sense Make a plan. Solve each problem.
Show your work.
Then check your work.

4. 45 basketballs are in a closet.
38 basketballs are full of air.
The rest need air.
How many basketballs need air?

_____ basketballs

5. Sue buys a box of 60 craft sticks.
She uses 37 craft sticks for her project.
How many craft sticks are left?

_____ craft sticks

6. **Higher Order Thinking** 36 berries are in a bowl. James eats 21 of the berries. Then he puts 14 more berries in the bowl. How many fewer berries are in the bowl now?

Is there a shortcut you can use?

_____ fewer berries

7. **Assessment** Circle the problem that you will use regrouping to solve. Then find both differences. Show your work.

83 − 45 = _____

65 − 33 = _____

© Pearson Education, Inc. 2

Topic 6 | Lesson 7

Solve & Share

Trevor made 20 apple muffins for the bake sale. Ryan made 15 banana muffins. They sold 23 muffins in all. How many muffins are left?

Solve any way you choose. Then write two equations to show your work.

I can ...
use models and equations to solve word problems.

Content Standard 2.CA.2
Process Standards PS.1, PS.2, PS.4, PS.7

_____ muffins

Some students are in the gym. 13 students leave. Now there are 15 students in the gym.

How many students were in the gym at the start?

What is happening in the story?

You can write an equation. First, think about what you need to find.

How many students were in the gym at the start?

You can use a ? for the unknown.

$? - 13 = 15$

You can also use a bar diagram to show the parts and the whole.

?

13	15

You can add to solve the problem.

$$\begin{array}{r} 1\ 3 \\ +\ 1\ 5 \\ \hline 2\ 8 \end{array}$$

So, 28 students were in the gym at the start.

Do You Understand?

Show Me! How does the bar diagram show what happens in the story problem?

1. Some key chains are in a bag. Aki takes out 17 key chains. 14 key chains are left in the bag. How many key chains were in the bag at the start?

?

17	14

   $$\begin{array}{r} \ 7 \\ +\ \ 4 \\ \hline 3\ 1 \end{array}$$

   _____ key chains

2. Some leaves are in a pile. 26 leaves blow away. 22 leaves are left. How many leaves were in the pile at the start?

?

26	22

   _____ leaves

Name _____

Independent Practice

Use a bar diagram to solve each problem. Show your work.

3. Some balls are in the closet. Mr. Thomas takes out 15 balls for class. Now there are 56 balls in the closet. How many balls were in the closet in the beginning?

_____ balls

4. Corey buys a box of 96 paper clips from the store. He uses 34 paper clips. How many paper clips does Corey have left?

_____ paper clips

5. A.J. counts 44 acorns in his yard. He picks up 27 acorns. Then 16 more acorns fall from the tree. How many acorns are in the yard now? Show your work.

Think about what to find first. Then use that answer to solve the problem.

Step 1

_____ ◯ _____ = _____

Step 2

_____ ◯ _____ = _____

 _____ acorns

Problem Solving

Make Sense Make a plan. Solve each problem. Show your work. Then check your work.

6. 27 people are at a picnic. 14 people eat hamburgers. The rest eat hot dogs. How many people eat hot dogs?

_____ people eat hot dogs

7. Some pumpkins are in a patch. 41 pumpkins are picked. Now there are 33 pumpkins in the patch. How many pumpkins were in the patch at the start?

_____ pumpkins

8. Higher Order Thinking Lauren has a stamp collection. She gives Kristen 12 stamps and Ethan 15 stamps. Lauren has 22 stamps left. How many stamps did she have at the start?

Step 1

_____ ◯ _____ = _____

Step 2

_____ ◯ _____ = _____

_____ stamps

9. ⓘ **Assessment** Lance buys 48 eggs. He uses 24 of them for baking. Then he buys 12 more eggs. How many eggs does Lance have now?

Which set of equations can you use to solve this problem?

Ⓐ $48 + 24 = 72$
$72 - 12 = 60$

Ⓒ $48 + 24 = 72$
$72 + 12 = 84$

Ⓑ $48 - 24 = 24$
$24 + 12 = 36$

Ⓓ $48 - 24 = 24$
$24 - 12 = 12$

© Pearson Education, Inc. 2

Topic 6 | Lesson 8

Help Tools Games

Another Look! 52 cars are parked in the lot.
18 cars leave. Then 10 more cars leave.
How many cars are in the lot now?

Use the answer from Step 1 to solve Step 2.

Step 1: Subtract to find how many cars are still in the lot after 18 cars leave.

Step 2: Then subtract to find how many cars are still in the lot after 10 more cars leave.

HOME ACTIVITY Have your child solve this problem: Some birds are sitting on the roof. Then thunder scares away 12 birds. Now there are 32 birds sitting on the roof. How many birds were sitting on the roof at the start?

Use the answer from Step 1 to solve Step 2.

1. 73 people are on the train. At a train stop 24 people get off and 19 people get on. How many people are on the train now?

Step 1

Step 2

_____ people

2. Rosa's book has 88 pages in all. She reads some pages on Monday. She has 59 pages left to read. How many pages did she read on Monday?

_____ pages

3. Jackie runs 19 laps on Monday. She runs 12 laps on Tuesday. How many laps did she run on both days?

_____ laps

4. **Higher Order Thinking** Zak has a bag of cherries. He gives away 18 cherries to Tim and 18 cherries to Janet. Now he has 25 cherries. How many cherries did Zak have at the start?

Step 1

_____ ◯ _____ = _____

Step 2

_____ ◯ _____ = _____

_____ cherries

5. **◑Assessment** There are 68 runners in a marathon. 28 runners finish the race. Then 22 more runners finish the race. How many runners have **NOT** finished the race?

Which pair of equations can you use to solve this problem?

Ⓐ $68 + 28 = 96$;
$96 - 22 = 74$

Ⓑ $68 + 28 = 96$;
$28 + 22 = 50$

Ⓒ $68 - 28 = 40$;
$40 - 22 = 18$

Ⓓ $68 - 28 = 40$;
$40 + 22 = 66$

Name _____

Solve & Share

Farmer Davis has 52 chickens.
He sells 15 chickens at the market.
How many chickens does Farmer Davis have now?

Use the bar diagram and equation to help you solve.
Be ready to explain how the numbers in the problem
are related.

I can ...
reason about word problems,
and use bar diagrams and
equations to solve them.

Process Standards PS.2
Also PS.1, PS.4, PS.5, PS.6
Content Standard 2.CA.2

Thinking Habits

How are the
numbers in the
problem related?

How can I show
a word problem
using pictures or
numbers?

_____ ◯ _____ ◯ _____ chickens

45 beads are in a jar. Jenny uses some beads to make a necklace.
Now 17 beads are in the jar.

How many beads does Jenny use to make the necklace?

How can I use reasoning to solve the problem?

45 beads − beads in = 17 beads
necklace   left

I can think about how the numbers are related. 45 − ? = 17 A bar diagram can show this.

I know the whole. So, I can subtract the part I know to find the missing part.

45

? | 17

$$3\ 15$$
$$\cancel{4}\ \cancel{5}$$
$$-\ 1\ 7$$
$$\overline{2\ 8}$$

45 − 17 = 28 beads

My bar diagram and equation show how the numbers relate.

Do You Understand?

Show Me! Why can you subtract 45 − 17 to solve 45 − ? = 17?

★ **Guided Practice** ★ Reason about the numbers in each problem. Complete the bar diagram and write an equation to solve. Show your work.

1. Wendy has 38 cents to spend on a snack. She buys an apple that costs 22 cents. How many cents does Wendy have left?

38 ⊖ 22 ⊜ _____ cents

38

22 | ?

2. Joe has 46 crayons. Tamila has 18 more crayons than Joe. How many crayons does Tamila have?

_____ ◯ _____ ◯ _____ crayons

© Pearson Education, Inc. 2

Tools   Assessment

Independent Practice   Reason about how the numbers in each problem relate. Complete the bar diagram and write an equation to solve. Show your work.

3. **Math and Science** Andy's class wants to test samples of river water. They want to test 47 water samples. So far, they tested 34 samples. How many more samples do they need to test?

_____ ◯ _____ ◯ _____ more samples

4. 93 dimes are in a box. Grant uses some to buy a game. Now, 66 dimes are in the box. How many dimes did Grant use to buy the game?

_____ ◯ _____ ◯ _____ dimes

5. Maria paints 62 squares for a mural. Oscar paints 38 squares. How many more squares does Maria paint than Oscar?

_____ ◯ _____ ◯ _____ more squares

Planting Trees

The second and third-grade students planted these trees in Wing Park. The second-grade students planted 26 of the spruce trees. How many spruce trees did the third-grade students plant?

38 Oak   **44 Spruce**

6. **Make Sense** What information can you get from the pictures?

_____

_____

_____

_____

7. **Model** Complete the bar diagram. Decide how the numbers in the problem relate. Then write an equation that shows how to solve the problem.

8. **Reasoning** How many spruce trees did the third-grade students plant? Explain how you solved the problem.

_____ spruce trees

© Pearson Education, Inc. 2

Name _____

Another Look! Robin collects 36 acorns.
Trisha collects 19 more acorns than Robin.
How many acorns does Trisha collect?

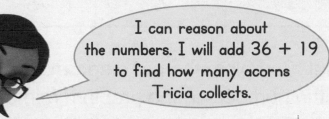

I can reason about the numbers. I will add 36 + 19 to find how many acorns Tricia collects.

This bar diagram shows comparison. The diagram and the equation show how the numbers and the unknown in the problem relate.

HOME ACTIVITY Ask your child to find 76 − 42 by drawing a bar diagram and writing an equation. Then ask your child to explain what the numbers and symbols mean.

?	
36	19

$$\begin{array}{r} 36 \\ + 19 \\ \hline 55 \end{array}$$

$\underline{36} \bigoplus \underline{19} \bigodot \underline{55}$ acorns

Reason about how the numbers in the problem relate. Complete the bar diagram and write an equation to solve. Show your work.

1. The Tigers scored 53 points in a basketball game.
   The Lions scored 12 fewer points than the Tigers.
   How many points did the Lions score?

   _____ ◯ _____ ◯ _____ points

Vacation Pictures

Adam, Tessa, and Nicki take pictures on their vacation. How many fewer pictures did Adam take than Nicki?

Use the information in the table to solve.

Number of Pictures Taken

Adam	Tessa	Nicki
19	92	78

2. **Make Sense** Will you use each number in the table to solve the problem? Explain.

_____

_____

_____

3. **Model** Complete the bar diagram. Decide how the numbers in the problem relate. Then write an equation that shows how to solve the problem.

____ ◯ ____ ◯ ____

4. **Reasoning** How many fewer pictures did Adam take than Nicki? Explain how you solved the problem.

_____ fewer pictures

Point & Tally

Name _____

Find a partner. Get paper and a pencil. Each partner chooses a different color: light blue or dark blue.

Partner 1 and Partner 2 each point to a black number at the same time. Both partners add those numbers.

If the answer is on your color, you get a tally mark. Work until one partner gets seven tally marks.

I can ...
add within 100.

Partner 1							Partner 2
49	34	76	74	61	63	89	40
60	58	80	93	78	95	100	25
36	85	74	69	50	98	65	14
55	45	87	60	84	89	49	38
20							29

Tally Marks for Partner 1

Tally Marks for Partner 2

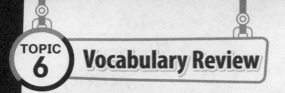

A-Z Glossary

Word List
- bar diagram
- difference
- equation
- ones
- regroup
- tens

Understand Vocabulary

Write *always*, *sometimes*, or *never*.

1. A bar diagram shows subtraction. _____

2. An 8 in the ones place of a number equals 80. _____

3. A 5 in the tens place of a number equals 50. _____

Draw a line from each term to its example.

4. equation

5. regroup

6. difference

The answer to $75 - 23$

$72 + 25 = 97$

Use Vocabulary in Writing

7. Explain how you can make a model to show and help you solve the problem. Use terms from the Word List.

Molly has 64 marbles.
Leslie has 29 marbles.
How many fewer marbles does Leslie have?

Name _____

Set A _____

You can regroup 1 ten as 10 ones when you subtract. Find 46 − 8.

Tens	Ones

46 − 8 = _38_

Did you need to regroup?

Yes   No

Subtract. You can use place-value blocks to help. Regroup if you need to.

1. 61 − 3 = _____

Did you need to regroup?

Yes   No

2. 57 − 5 = _____

Did you need to regroup?

Yes   No

Set B _____

You can draw place-value blocks to help you regroup. Find 72 − 6.

Tens	Ones
6	12
⁷	²
−	6
6	6

72 − 6 = _66_

Subtract. Draw place-value blocks. Regroup if you need to.

3.

Tens	Ones
☐	☐
2	7
−	9

Tens	Ones

Find 53 − 6. Regroup if you need to.

Tens	Ones
4 13	
5	3
−	6
4	7

Subtract. Use drawings if needed.

4.

Tens	Ones
3	8
−	9

5.

Tens	Ones
6	1
−	4

You can draw place-value blocks to help you regroup when subtracting two-digit numbers.

Find 43 − 15.

You can regroup 1 ten as 10 ones.

Tens	Ones
3 13	
4	3
− 1	5
2	8

43 − 15 = 28

Subtract. Draw place-value blocks. Regroup if you need to.

6.

Tens	Ones
7	2
− 3	6

Tens	Ones

© Pearson Education, Inc. 2

Set E

You can write subtraction problems in a frame. Find 52 − 33. Draw pictures if needed.

Tens	Ones

Tens	Ones
4	12
.5.	.2.
− 3	3
1	9

Write each subtraction problem in the frame. Find the difference.

7. 84 − 47

Tens	Ones
☐	☐
−	

8. 62 − 36

Tens	Ones
☐	☐
−	

Set F

You can check subtraction by adding. The sum of the parts equals the whole.

```
  4 8        32
− 1 6      + 1 6
  3 2        4 8
```

48	
16	32

Subtract. Check your answer by adding.

9.
```
  6 7
− 4 8
```

10.
```
  4 9
− 2 7
```

11.
```
  9 5
− 4 3
```

12.
```
  7 0
− 3 6
```

Thinking Habits

Reasoning

What do the numbers and symbols in the problem mean?

How are the numbers in the problem related?

How can I show a word problem using pictures or numbers?

Complete the bar diagram and write an equation to show the problem. Then solve. Show your work.

13. 94 bricks are needed to build a wall.
Lindy has 65 bricks.
How many more bricks does she need?

_____ bricks

14. Explain why making a bar diagram can help you solve the problem above.

_____

_____

_____

_____

_____

_____

_____

1. Would you regroup to find each difference? Choose Yes or No.

$45 - 8 = ?$ ○ Yes   ○ No

$51 - 9 = ?$ ○ Yes   ○ No

$77 - 6 = ?$ ○ Yes   ○ No

$83 - 4 = ?$ ○ Yes   ○ No

2. Sam has 74 books. He puts 28 books on a shelf. How many books are **NOT** on the shelf? Show your work.

Tens	Ones
☐	☐
−	

_____ books are **NOT** on the shelf.

3. Ryan has 46 marbles. John has 4 fewer marbles than Ryan. John gives 9 marbles to his friend. How many marbles does John have now?

Ⓐ 23

Ⓑ 33

Ⓒ 35

Ⓓ 42

4. A ship has 68 round windows. The ship also has 16 square windows. 7 of the windows are broken. How many windows are **NOT** broken?

Ⓐ 45

Ⓑ 61

Ⓒ 77

Ⓓ 91

5. Choose all of the problems that you will solve by regrouping.

☐ 45 − 0 = ?

☐ 68 − 49 = ?

☐ 84 − 37 = ?

☐ 99 − 33 = ?

6. Ben wants to find 54 − 18.
How can he regroup 54?

Ⓐ 4 tens and 4 ones

Ⓑ 4 tens and 14 ones

Ⓒ 5 tens and 4 ones

Ⓓ 6 tens and 14 ones

7. Jason has 86 photos in his computer.
He deletes 61 photos.
How many photos are left?

Use the frame to help you.

Ⓐ 5   Ⓑ 15   Ⓒ 25   Ⓓ 35

8. Claire has 53 beads.
Grace has 26 beads.
Bella has 39 beads.
How many fewer beads does
Bella have than Claire?

Show your work.

Tens	Ones

_____ fewer beads

9. Circle the problem that you will use regrouping to solve.
Then explain how you know.

$$54 - 23 \qquad 82 - 44$$

10. A book has 72 pages.
Dan reads 38 pages on Monday.
He reads 26 pages on Tuesday.
How many pages does Dan have left to read?

Which pair of equations can you use to solve the problem?

Ⓐ $38 + 26 = 64$
   $72 - 64 = 8$

Ⓒ $72 + 26 = 98$
   $98 - 38 = 60$

Ⓑ $72 - 38 = 34$
   $34 + 26 = 60$

Ⓓ $72 - 26 = 46$
   $46 + 38 = 84$

---

11. Part A

Subtract. Write the missing part in the bar diagram.

$$\begin{array}{r} 24 \\ -\ 16 \\ \hline \end{array}$$

Part B

Which addition equation can you use to check your answer?

Ⓐ $24 - 8 = 16$

Ⓑ $8 + 8 = 16$

Ⓒ $16 + 8 = 24$

Ⓓ $16 + 24 = 40$

12. Peter collects 54 stamps. He gives 29 stamps to Ruth. How many stamps does Peter have now? Show the problem in the bar diagram with a ? for the unknown number. Then write an equation to solve the problem.

_____ ◯ _____ = _____ stamps

13. Match each number from the cards to a missing number in the problem. Write the missing numbers.

4   5   13

Tens	Ones
4	☐
5	3
−	8

14. Find 72 − 38. Use any strategy to solve. Then explain why your strategy works.

_____

_____

_____

_____

© Pearson Education, Inc. 2

Name _____

Stamp Collection

Mary collects stamps.
The table shows the number of different kinds of stamps that she has.

Number of Stamps	
Flags	8
Butterflies	34
Birds	27
Flowers	61

1. How many more stamps with butterflies does Mary have than stamps with flags? Show your work and draw pictures.

_____ more stamps with butterflies

2. How many fewer stamps with birds does Mary have than stamps with flowers?
Use subtraction to solve.
Then use addition to check your work.

_____ fewer stamps with birds

3. Can you add in a different order to check your work in Item 2? Explain.

_____

_____

_____

_____

4. Luke also collects stamps.
He has 57 stamps.
His friend gives him 25 more stamps.

Then Luke gives away some stamps.
Now Luke has 44 stamps.
How many stamps did Luke give away?

Part A

How many stamps does Luke have
after his friend gives him more stamps?

_____ ◯ _____ = _____

_____ stamps

Part B

How many stamps did Luke give away?

_____ ◯ _____ = _____

_____ stamps

5. Mary puts 54 of her stamps in a book.
The book holds 96 stamps.
How many more stamps can Mary put in
the book?

Part A

Complete the bar diagram to model the problem.

Explain how the bar diagram helps you
understand the problem.

_____

_____

_____

_____

Part B

Write an equation to solve the problem.

_____ ◯ _____ = _____

_____ more stamps

© Pearson Education, Inc. 2

Topic 6 | Performance Assessment

More Solving Problems Involving Addition and Subtraction

Essential Question: How can you solve word problems that use adding or subtracting?

Digital Resources

Solve Learn Glossary

Tools Assessment Help Games

This row of trees can help slow down the wind!

This is only one of the ways to help protect land from wind or water.

Wow! Let's do this project and learn more.

Math and Science Project: Solving Problems

Find Out Find and share books that tell about ways to protect land from damage that wind or water can cause. Compare the different ways to protect the land.

Journal: Make a Book Show what you learn in a book. In your book, also:

- Show ways to solve problems caused by wind or water.

- Show ways to solve problems using addition or subtraction.

Name _____

Review What You Know

1. Write the subtraction problem below as an **equation**.

$$\begin{array}{r} 75 \\ -30 \\ \hline 45 \end{array}$$

2. Complete the **bar diagram** to model $77 + 22 = ?$

3. Circle the two addends below that are **compatible numbers**.

$$18 + 6 + 4 = ?$$

Adding to Check Subtraction

4. Use addition to check if the subtraction equation is correct.

$$51 - 22 = 29$$

Is it correct? _____

Subtracting to Check Addition

5. Use subtraction to check if the addition is correct.

$$37 + 26 = 53$$

Is it correct? _____

Number Story

6. Jim and Maria are counting birds. Jim counts 17 birds. Maria counts 33 birds. How many more birds does Maria count than Jim?

_____ more birds

Name _____

Solve & Share

Jenn has some red cubes and 11 blue cubes. She has 24 red and blue cubes in all.

She says the problem can be shown with the equation below.

$$? + 11 = 24$$

Draw what the ? represents.
Explain your answer.

I can …
model problems using equations with unknowns in any position.

Content Standard 2.CA.2
Process Standards PS.2, PS.4, PS.5, PS.8

Robert has 27 toy robots. He buys some more. Now he has 58 robots. How many robots did Robert buy?

58 is the whole. 27 is one part.

You can show the problem with an equation.

$$27 + ? = 58$$

The ? shows the addend you don't know.

$$58$$

27 | ?

You can solve the problem by adding on from 27 until you get to 58.

$$27 + 10 = 37$$
$$37 + 10 = 47$$
$$47 + 10 = 57$$
$$57 + 1 = 58$$
$$10 + 10 + 10 + 1 = 31$$
So, $27 + 31 = 58$.

Robert bought 31 robots.

You can subtract to solve the problem.

$$\begin{array}{r} 58 \\ -\ 27 \\ \hline 31 \end{array}$$

You can check by adding.
$$31 + 27 = 58$$

Robert bought 31 robots.

Do You Understand?

Show Me! Could you show Robert's robot problem with the equation below? Explain.

$$58 = 27 + ?$$

✫ Guided Practice ✫ Write an equation with a ? for the unknown to model the problem. Then solve. Show your work.

1. Mary has some game tickets. She gives 14 tickets away and now has 17 tickets left. How many tickets did she have at first?

   Equation: $? - 14 = 17$ _____ tickets

   _____

2. Tamara has $25. She earns $34 more by working. How much money does she have now?

   Equation: _____ $ _____

© Pearson Education, Inc. 2
Topic 7 | Lesson 1

Independent Practice Write an equation with a ? for the unknown to model the problem. Then solve. Show your work.

3. Erin has 32 books on her bookshelf. She gives some to friends and now has 19 books left. How many books did she give away?

Equation: _____

_____ books

4. A store sells 38 men's bikes and 47 women's bikes. How many bikes did the store sell in all?

Equation: _____

_____ bikes

5. Math and Science A field has 25 trees in it. 14 trees are new and the rest are old. How many trees are old? Write two different equations that represent the problem. Then solve.

Equation: _____

Equation: _____

_____ old trees

6. Number Sense Harry buys 22 fish. He has a round fish bowl and a rectangular fish tank. How could he place the fish in the bowl and tank?

Equation: _____

_____ fish in the bowl _____ fish in the tank

7. **Model** Rodney collects 17 leaves and Sheila collects 23 leaves. How many more leaves does Sheila collect than Rodney?

Equation: _____

_____ more leaves

8. **Model** Jun swims 18 laps and Mara swims 25 laps. How many fewer laps did Jun swim than Mara?

Equation: _____

_____ fewer laps

9. **Higher Order Thinking** Jim has 44 roses. 14 are white and the rest are red. How many are red? Write two different equations to model the problem. Then solve.

Equation: _____

Equation: _____

_____ red roses

10. **⓪ Assessment** Some wolves howl in the woods. 12 wolves join them. Now 30 wolves howl. How many wolves howled at first?

Write an equation to model the problem. Use a ? for the unknown. Then solve.

Name _____

Another Look! Jamal has some green apples and 17 red apples. He has 29 apples in all. How many green apples does he have?

You can show word problems with drawings.

You can write an equation with a ? or another symbol for the part you don't know.

12 + 17 = 29, so Jamal has 12 green apples.

29

| ? | 17 |

$? + 17 = 29$

Add mentally.
$17 + 10 = 27$
$27 + 2 = 29$

HOME ACTIVITY Ask your child to write an equation for each of 2 different problems you make up. Then have him or her show you how to solve the problems.

Write an equation with a ? for the unknown to model the problem. Then solve. Show your work.

1. Jill bikes 15 miles in the morning and 17 miles in the afternoon. How many miles does she bike in all?

Equation: _____

_____ miles

2. Maria makes 21 thank you cards. She mails 13 of the cards. How many cards does she have left?

Equation: _____

_____ cards

Write an equation with a ? for the unknown to model the problem. Then solve. Show your work.

3. **Model** Latisha eats 12 grapes with lunch and then eats some more with dinner. She eats 26 grapes in all. How many grapes does she eat with dinner?

Equation: _____

_____ grapes

4. **Model** Jack read 24 pages of a book and John read 19 pages of a book. How many more pages did Jack read than John?

Equation: _____

_____ more pages

5. **Higher Order Thinking** A train has 43 cars. 15 cars are red and the rest are blue. How many blue cars does the train have? Write two different equations that represent the problem. Then solve.

Equation: _____

Equation: _____

_____ blue cars

6. **Assessment** 63 boys enter a marathon. 48 boys finish the race and some boys do not. How many boys do **NOT** finish the race?

Write an equation to model the problem. Use a ? for the unknown. Then solve.

© Pearson Education, Inc. 2

Solve & Share

Aiden has 27 fewer crayons this week than last week. Last week he had 56 crayons. How many crayons does Aiden have this week? Show your work.

Lesson 7-2
Mixed Practice: Solve Addition and Subtraction Problems

I can …
use drawings and equations to make sense of the words in problems.

Content Standard 2.CA.2
Process Standards PS.1, PS.2, PS.3, PS.4

_____ crayons

Sally has 28 fewer blocks than Nigel.
Sally has 26 blocks.
How many blocks does Nigel have?

Let's think about who has fewer blocks and who has more blocks.

A bar diagram can help you think about the problem.

Nigel's blocks

?

26   28

Sally's blocks   28 blocks fewer

26 + 28 = ?

Sally has 28 fewer blocks than Nigel. That means Nigel has more blocks than Sally. You need to add!

Tens	Ones
1	
2	6
+ 2	8
5	4

Nigel has 54 blocks.

Do You Understand?

Show Me! How are these statements alike and different? Cal has 12 fewer blocks than Mia. Mia has 12 more blocks than Cal.

Guided Practice Solve the problem any way you choose. Use drawings and equations to help.

1. Lakota has 11 fewer magnets than Jeffrey. Lakota has 25 magnets. How many magnets does Jeffrey have?

?

25   11

25
+ 11

_____ magnets

© Pearson Education, Inc. 2

Topic 7 | Lesson 2

Name _____

Tools   Assessment

Independent Practice Solve each problem any way you choose. Use drawings and equations to help. Show your work.

2. There are 28 more students than adults at the school fair. There are 96 students at the school fair. How many adults are at the school fair?

_____ adults

3. Ellie the elephant has some peanuts. She eats 49 peanuts. Now Ellie the elephant has 31 peanuts. How many peanuts did she have before?

_____ peanuts

4. The blue team scores 16 fewer points than the green team. The blue team scores 41 points. How many points did the green team score?

_____ points

5. Higher Order Thinking Sean studies 16 fewer vocabulary words than Chris. Chris studies 10 fewer vocabulary words than Tia. Tia studies 34 words. How many words does Sean study? Explain your answer.

_____

_____

_____

6. **Reasoning** Kevin practices kicks for soccer. He kicks 13 times at recess. He kicks 14 times after school. Then he kicks 16 times before bed. How many practice kicks did Kevin take in all?

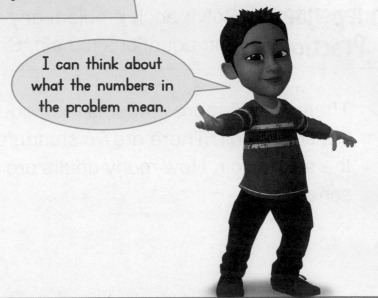

I can think about what the numbers in the problem mean.

_____ kicks

7. **Higher Order Thinking** There are 48 red tacks and blue tacks in a bag. There are fewer red tacks than blue tacks. There are at least 26 blue tacks but no more than 30 blue tacks. How many of each color could be in the bag?

Complete the chart to solve the problem.

Red Tacks	Blue Tacks	Total
22	26	48
21		48
	28	48
19		48
	30	48

8. **Assessment** Jim has 14 fewer baseball cards than Sara. Sara has 27 cards. How many baseball cards does Jim have?

Draw a line to show where each number and the unknown could be in the equation. Then solve.

| 27 | ? | 14 |

_____ – _____ = _____

_____ cards

Name _____

Another Look! A bar diagram can help you solve word problems.

Bridget has 15 fewer crackers than Jessica. Bridget has 20 crackers. How many crackers does Jessica have?

Jessica's crackers

?

| 20 | 15 |

Bridget's crackers   15 crackers fewer

Jessica has __35__ crackers.

$$\begin{array}{r} 20 \\ + 15 \\ \hline 35 \end{array}$$

Bridget has 15 fewer, which means Jessica has 15 more. Add to find the number of crackers Jessica has.

HOME ACTIVITY Tell your child Max has 10 fewer shells than Becca. Max has 20 shells. How many shells does Becca have? Then have your child write the equation. 20 + 10 = 30.

Solve each problem any way you choose. Use drawings and equations to help. Show your work.

1. Ann puts 37 photos in one book and 24 photos in another book. How many photos does she use in all?

_____ photos

2. Jorge's puzzle has 20 fewer pieces than Rosi's puzzle. Jorge's puzzle has 80 pieces. How many pieces does Rosi's puzzle have?

_____ pieces

Solve each problem any way you choose. Use drawings and equations to help. Show your work.

3. **Reasoning** Lucy makes 37 get well cards and some thank you cards. She makes 60 cards in all. How many thank you cards does Lucy make?

Think about what the numbers in the problem mean.

_____ thank you cards

4. **Higher Order Thinking** Jeff finds some bugs. He finds 10 fewer grasshoppers than crickets. He finds 5 fewer crickets than ladybugs. If Jeff finds 5 grasshoppers, how many ladybugs does Jeff find? How many crickets does he find? Write two equations to solve the problem.

_____ crickets   _____ ladybugs

5. **Assessment** Sandy has 17 fewer hockey cards than Al. Al has 55 hockey cards. How many hockey cards does Sandy have?

Draw a line to show where each number and unknown could be in the equation. Then solve.

| 17 | | ? | | 55 |

_____ + _____ = _____

_____ cards

© Pearson Education, Inc. 2

Name _____

Solve & Share

Erin has 17 more books than Isabella. Erin has 44 books. How many books does Isabella have?

Solve any way you choose. Show your work.

I can …
use drawings and equations to make sense of the words in problems.

Content Standard 2.CA.2
Process Standards PS.1, PS.2, PS.4, PS.8

_____ books

Julie has 18 more pictures than Landon.
Julie has 37 pictures. How many pictures does Landon have?

Julie's pictures

$$37$$

?	18

Landon's pictures   18 pictures more

The diagram helps you show what you know.

Landon has 18 fewer pictures than Julie. You can subtract to find the answer.

$$37 - 18 = ?$$

$$\begin{array}{r} 2\,17 \\ \cancel{3}\cancel{7} \\ -\ 18 \\ \hline 19 \end{array}$$

Add to check your answer.

$$\begin{array}{r} 1 \\ 19 \\ +\ 18 \\ \hline 37 \end{array}$$

So, Landon has 19 pictures.

You can solve word problems using models, drawings, or mental math.

Do You Understand?

Show Me! Compare the two statements:
Sam has 18 more markers than Zoey.
Zoey has 18 fewer markers than Sam.

☆ Guided ☆ Practice

Solve the problem any way you choose. Use drawings and equations to help.

1. The second grade has 19 more students than the first grade. The second grade has 68 students. How many students does the first grade have?

?	19

$$\begin{array}{r} 5\,18 \\ \cancel{6}\cancel{8} \\ -\ 19 \\ \hline \end{array}$$

_____ students

Independent Practice

Solve each problem any way you choose. Use drawings and equations to help. Show your work.

---

2. There are 11 more adults than children at a craft fair. There are 54 adults at the craft fair. How many children are at the craft fair?

_____ children

3. Caleb is 17 years old. His sister is 12 years younger. How old is Caleb's sister?

_____ years old

---

4. Dylan and his friends had some blueberries. They ate 39 blueberries. They have 21 blueberries left. How many blueberries did Dylan and his friends have at first?

_____ blueberries

5. Math and Science Addison made a dam with 18 more rocks than James. Addison's dam had 42 rocks. How many rocks did James's dam have? Explain your answer.

_____

_____

_____

_____

_____

---

6. **Reasoning** Connor has 39 sheets of green paper and some sheets of yellow paper. He has 78 sheets of paper in all. How many yellow sheets of paper does Connor have?

I can think about how the numbers in the problem are related.

_____ yellow sheets

7. **Higher Order Thinking** There are 58 red pens and blue pens in a bag. There are more red pens than blue pens. There are at least 36 red pens but no more than 40 red pens. How many of each color could be in the bag?

Complete the chart to solve the problem.

Red Pens	Blue Pens	Total
36	22	58
37		58
	20	58
39		58
	18	58

8. **Assessment** Andrew has 63 more beanbags than Evan. Andrew has 92 beanbags. How many beanbags does Evan have?

Explain how you will solve the problem. Then solve.

_____ bean bags

© Pearson Education, Inc. 2

Name _____

Another Look!

Derek has some sheets of blue paper. He has 34 sheets of red paper. He has a total of 67 sheets of paper. How many sheets of blue paper does Derek have?

You know one of the parts and the whole.

$? + 34 = 67$

Subtract $67 - 34$ to find the missing part.

$67 - 30 = 37$ $37 - 4 = 33$

So, Derek has 33 sheets of blue paper.

67
?	34

Don't forget to check that your answer makes sense!

HOME ACTIVITY Have your child solve the following problem: *Luke sold 27 more raffle tickets than Roger. Luke sold 53 tickets. How many tickets did Roger sell?* Ask your child to explain his or her solution.

Solve each problem any way you choose. Use drawings and equations to help. Show your work.

1. Joshua used 23 more craft sticks on his project than Candice. Joshua used 41 craft sticks. How many craft sticks did Candice use?

   _____ craft sticks

2. Gavin painted 14 pictures last week. He painted some more pictures this week. He painted 25 pictures in all. How many pictures did Gavin paint this week?

   _____ pictures

3. **Reasoning** Daniel tosses a number cube 19 fewer times than Jayden. Daniel tosses a number cube 38 times. How many times does Jayden toss a number cube?

I can represent a word problem with the correct numbers and symbols.

_____ times

4. **Higher Order Thinking** Wyatt has 34 blocks. Stella has 36 blocks. They give 14 blocks to Henry. Now how many blocks do Wyatt and Stella have together?

Complete the steps to solve the problem.

Step 1

_____ ◯ _____ = _____

Step 2

_____ ◯ _____ = _____

_____ blocks

5. **Assessment** Oliver runs 23 fewer laps than Nate. Nate runs 61 laps. How many laps does Oliver run?

Explain how you will solve the problem. Then solve.

_____ laps

© Pearson Education, Inc. 2

Name _____

Solve & Share

3 bees land on some flowers.
10 more bees join them. Then 4 bees fly away.
How many bees are left?

Solve the problem any way you choose.
Write equations to show how you solved each part
of the problem.

I can ...
model and solve two-step
problems using equations.

Content Standard 2.CA.2
Process Standards PS.1,
PS.2, PS.4, PS.6

_____ ◯ _____ = _____   _____ ◯ _____ = _____

Bop picked 18 flowers and then 5 more.

He gave 10 flowers to Buzz. How many flowers does Bop have now?

Look for the hidden question that you need to answer first, before you can solve the problem.

I need to find how many flowers Bop picked in all, before I can solve the problem.

$18 + 5 = ?$

$\underline{18} + \underline{5} = \underline{23}$

Bop picked 23 flowers. Then he gave 10 flowers to Buzz.

$23 - 10 = ?$

$\underline{23} - \underline{10} = \underline{13}$

Now Bop has 13 flowers.

I added 2 ones to make the next ten and then added the 3 leftover ones to find $18 + 5 = 23$. Then I subtracted 10 from 23 to get 13.

Do You Understand?

Show Me! Tom bought 15 pencils and then 7 more. He gave 10 pencils to Nyla. If you want to find how many pencils Tom has left, why do you need to solve the first part of the problem before the second part?

Guided Practice Solve any way you choose. Show your work. Write equations to solve both parts of the problem.

1. Carmen found 14 shells on Monday and 15 more shells on Tuesday. She found 6 more shells on Wednesday. How many shells did she have then?

$\underline{14} \oplus \underline{15} = \underline{29}$

$\underline{29} \oplus \underline{6} = \underline{}$

$\begin{array}{r} {}^{1}14 \\ +15 \\ \hline 29 \end{array}$ $\begin{array}{r} 29 \\ +6 \\ \hline \end{array}$

_____ shells

Independent Practice   Solve any way you choose. Show your work.
Write equations to solve both parts of the problem.

2. There are 6 red birds and
   17 brown birds in a tree.
   If 8 more brown birds come,
   how birds will there be in all?

_____ ◯ _____ = _____

_____ ◯ _____ = _____

_____ birds

3. Erika saw 16 frogs on a lily
   pad and 8 frogs in the mud.
   If 7 of the frogs hop away,
   how many frogs will be left?

_____ ◯ _____ = _____

_____ ◯ _____ = _____

_____ frogs

> Think: How can
> I break apart the problem
> into steps? What is the
> hidden problem that I need
> to solve first?

4. **Higher Order Thinking** Kevin
   has 15 photos in his scrapbook.
   He adds 21 photos. Then
   Kevin takes out some photos.
   Now he has 28 photos in the
   scrapbook. How many photos
   did Kevin take out?

_____ ◯ _____ = _____

_____ ◯ _____ = _____

_____ photos

5. **Model** There are 35 test questions. Kareem answers 10 of the questions. Then he answers 12 more questions. How many more questions does Kareem still need to answer?

_____ more questions

---

6. **A-Z Vocabulary** Circle the equations that have a **sum**. Underline the equations that have a **difference**.

$$33 - 18 = 15 \qquad 79 + 16 = 95$$

$$46 + 34 = 80 \qquad 52 - 52 = 0$$

7. **Algebra** Find the missing numbers.

$$35 + \blacksquare = 100 \qquad \blacksquare = \text{\_\_\_\_}$$

$$100 - \blacktriangle = 18 \qquad \blacktriangle = \text{\_\_\_\_}$$

---

8. **Higher Order Thinking** There are 25 friends at a party. Another 20 friends arrive. Then some friends leave the party. Only 7 friends stay. How many friends leave the party?

Write two equations to solve the problem.

_____

_____ friends leave the party.

9. **Assessment** Bill caught 22 fish and threw 6 fish back. He caught 8 more fish. How many fish does Bill have now?

Which equations can be used to solve the problem?

Ⓐ $22 + 6 = 28$ and $28 - 8 = 20$

Ⓑ $22 - 6 = 16$ and $8 - 6 = 2$

Ⓒ $22 - 6 = 16$ and $16 + 8 = 24$

Ⓓ $22 + 6 = 28$ and $28 + 8 = 36$

Name _____

Another Look! You can solve problems in different ways.

Jenna had 13 red markers and 15 blue markers. Then she lost 12 markers. How many markers does Jenna have left?

Step 1
Add to find out how many markers Jenna had in all.

Step 2
Subtract the number of markers Jenna lost.

$$13 \atop +\,15$$
28

$$28 \atop -\,12$$
16

I broke apart the problem into two parts. I wrote the numbers like this. Then I used place value to solve each part.

$\underline{13} \,(+)\, \underline{15} = \underline{28}$ $\underline{28} \,(-)\, \underline{12} = \underline{16}$ $\underline{16}$ markers

HOME ACTIVITY Make up story problems that take two questions, or steps, to solve. Ask your child to solve both parts of each problem.

Solve any way you choose. Show your work. Write equations to solve both parts of the problem.

1. There were 15 red apples and 6 green apples in a bowl. Eric ate 2 of the apples. How many apples are in the bowl now?

Step 1 _____ ◯ _____ = _____

Step 2 _____ ◯ _____ = _____

_____ apples

2. Be Precise Three students use the table to record how many jumping jacks they did each day. Complete the table and the sentences.

Hank did _____ jumping jacks on Friday.

Emma did _____ jumping jacks on Thursday.

Tana did _____ jumping jacks on Wednesday.

Jumping Jacks				
	Wednesday	Thursday	Friday	**Total**
Emma	30	_____	15	88
Hank	33	32	_____	85
Tana	_____	35	25	100

3. Higher Order Thinking Kendra drew 26 stars. She erased 12 stars. Then Kendra drew some more stars. Now there are 29 stars. How many more stars did Kendra draw? Write an equation for each part. Then solve.

4. Assessment Ken needs to buy 100 nails. He buys 25 nails at one store and 36 nails at another store. How many more nails does Ken need to buy?

Ⓐ 75

Ⓑ 64

Ⓒ 61

Ⓓ 39

It helps to break apart the problem into steps.

© Pearson Education, Inc. 2

Lesson 7-5

Continue to Solve Two-Step Problems

Solve & Share

You have 26 library books. You return some books. Then you take out 15 more books. Now you have 27 books. How many books did you return?

Solve any way you choose. Show your work.

I can ...
use different ways to solve two-step problems.

Content Standard 2.CA.2
Process Standards PS.1, PS.3, PS.4, PS.6

Mia sees 15 yellow birds and 16 red birds. Some birds fly away and now Mia sees 14 birds. How many birds flew away?

I need to solve the first step of the problem in order to solve the second step.

Mia sees __31__ birds in all.

There are 14 birds left after __17__ fly away.

The bar diagrams helped me see the parts and the whole in each step of the problem.

?
15	16

```
    1      5
    1      6
⊕ _____
    3      1
```

31
?	14

```
    2     11
    3      1
⊖ _____
    1      7
```

Do You Understand?

Show Me! Why do you need two steps to solve the problem above?

1. There are some boys painting and 9 girls painting. In all, 17 children are painting. Then some more boys come to paint. Now there are 15 boys painting. How many more boys come to paint?

Step 1

$$\underline{8} + \underline{9} = \underline{17}$$

some boys   girls   children in all

Step 2

$$\underline{} + \underline{} = \underline{}$$

some boys   more boys   boys in all

_____ more boys come to paint.

Tools   Assessment

Independent Practice Solve each problem any way you choose. Show your work.

2. Jake has 16 toy cars. Lidia has 5 fewer toy cars than Jake. How many toy cars do they have in all?

They have _____ cars in all.

3. Sandy has 12 balloons. Tom has 11 more balloons than Sandy. Some of Tom's balloons popped and now he has 14 balloons. How many balloons popped?

_____ balloons popped.

4. 25 wolves howl together in the woods. 14 wolves join them. Then 22 wolves run away. How many wolves are left?

_____ wolves are left.

5. **Higher Order Thinking** Explain how you solved Item 4.

_____

_____

_____

_____

6. **Make Sense** Tim bakes 24 more muffins than Gina. Gina bakes 13 muffins. Lea bakes 16 fewer muffins than Tim.

How many muffins does Lea bake?

I can check that my work and answer make sense.

_____ muffins

7. **Higher Order Thinking** Write a two-step math story using the numbers 36, 65, and 16. Then solve the problem. Write equations to show each step.

_____

_____

_____

_____

8. **Assessment** There are 44 marbles in a jar. Some are red and 23 are blue. Julie adds 13 red marbles to the jar. Now how many red marbles are in the jar?

Which equations show a way to solve the problem?

Ⓐ $44 - 23 = 21$
$21 + 13 = 34$

Ⓑ $44 - 23 = 21$
$21 - 13 = 8$

Ⓒ $23 + 21 = 44$
$44 - 13 = 31$

Ⓓ $23 + 44 = 67$
$67 + 13 = 80$

Name _____

Help   Tools   Games

Homework
& Practice 7-5
Continue to
Solve Two-Step
Problems

Another Look! Use the answer from Step 1 to solve Step 2.

Tomas has 14 toy cars. Jonah has 6 more toy cars than Tomas.
How many toy cars do they have in all?

Step 1: Add to find out how many toy cars Jonah has in all.

$$\underline{14} + \underline{6} = \underline{20}$$

Step 2: Add to find the number of toy cars they have in all.

$$\underline{20} + \underline{14} = \underline{34}$$

They have 34
toy cars in all.

HOME ACTIVITY Ask your child to solve two-step problems. Use small objects found at home as props.

Use the answer from Step 1 to solve Step 2.

1. Dani picked some red flowers and 9 pink flowers for a total of
21 flowers. Then Dani gave Will 5 red flowers. How many red
flowers does Dani have left?

Step 1: Subtract to find how many red flowers Dani picked.

$$\underline{} - \underline{} = \underline{}$$

Step 2: Subtract to find how many red flowers Dani has left.

$$\underline{} - \underline{} = \underline{}$$

$$\underline{} \text{ red flowers}$$

Mr. and Mrs. Morley picked their crops. Use the data in the chart to solve each problem.

Fruit and Vegetables Picked				
Apples	Peaches	Pumpkins	Corn	Squash
?	23	47	25	17

2. **Make Sense** Mr. Morley takes the apples and peaches to his fruit stand. He takes 58 pieces of fruit in all. He sells 13 apples. How many apples are at the fruit stand now?

_____ apples

3. **Higher Order Thinking** Write and solve a two-step problem about the data in the chart above.

_____

_____

_____

_____

_____

4. **A-Z Vocabulary** Complete the **bar diagram**. Use two possible **addends** with a **sum** of 25. Then complete the equation.

_____ + _____ = 25

5. **Assessment** There are 21 students at the school picnic. Then 42 more students join them. Later, 30 students leave.

How many students are still at the picnic?

21	33	63	93
Ⓐ	Ⓑ	Ⓒ	Ⓓ

© Pearson Education, Inc. 2

Solve

Solve & Share

Write a number story for this equation.

$$20 = ? + ?$$

Then complete the equation to match your story.

I can …
use reasoning to write and solve number stories.

Process Standards PS.2
Also PS.1, PS.3, PS.4, PS.7
Content Standard 2.CA.2

Thinking Habits

How are the numbers in the problem related?

How can I use a word problem to show what the equation means?

$$20 = \underline{\hspace{1cm}} + \underline{\hspace{1cm}}$$

Write a number story for 68 − 33. Then write an equation to match your story.

How can I show what numbers and symbols mean?

I think about what 68, 33 and the − sign mean in the problem. I can use that to write a story.

Subtraction stories can be about separating or about comparing. This story is about separating.

Harry finds 68 acorns. He gives 33 acorns to Joyce. How many acorns does Harry have left?

$68 − 33 = ?$

Subtract to answer the question in the problem.

68 − 33 = 35
So, Harry has 35 acorns left.

$$\begin{array}{r} 68 \\ -33 \\ \hline 35 \end{array}$$

Do You Understand?

Show Me! Write a number story about comparing for $68 − 33 = ?$.

☆Guided Practice☆

Complete the number story. Then complete the equation to match the story. Draw a picture to help, if needed.

1. $47 − 18 = \underline{\hspace{1cm}}$

   Blake collects __47__ cans.

   He recycles __18__ cans.

   How many cans does Blake have now?

   _____ cans

© Pearson Education, Inc. 2

Tools Assessment

Independent Practice Write a number story to show the problem.
Complete the equation to match your story.

2. 22 − 17 = _____

_____

_____

_____

_____

3. 84 − 62 = _____

_____

_____

_____

_____

4. 28 + 12 = _____

_____

_____

_____

5. 39 + 47 = _____

_____

_____

_____

_____

Problem Solving

Toy Car Collection

The picture at the right shows a toy car collection. Use the picture to write and solve number story problems.

6. **Reasoning** Write an addition story about the toy car collection.

_____

_____

_____

_____

7. **Reasoning** Write a subtraction comparison story about the collection.

_____

_____

_____

_____

8. **Model** Write an equation for each number story that you wrote in Item 6 and Item 7. Then solve any way you choose. Show your work.

© Pearson Education, Inc. 2

Name _____

Homework & Practice 7-6
Reasoning

Another Look! You can write a number story about each problem. Then complete the equation to match the story.

22 − 15 = ?

There are __22__ red buttons.

There are __15__ blue buttons.
How many more red buttons are there than blue buttons?

22 − 15 = __7__

So, there are __7__ more red buttons.

36 − 17 = ?

__36__ grapes are on the table.

__17__ are red and the rest are green.
How many grapes are green?

36 − 17 = __19__

So, __19__ grapes are green.

HOME ACTIVITY Write problems such as 41 − 28 = ? and 55 + 37 = ?. Ask your child to write or say a number story about the problem. Have your child complete the equation to match the story.

Write a number story to show the problem. Complete the equation to match your story.

1. 31 − 8 = _____

_____

_____

_____

_____

2. 23 + 37 = _____

_____

_____

_____

_____

Bakery Muffins
The picture at the right shows information about muffins at Herb's Bakery. Use the picture to write and solve number story problems.

33 Berry   18 Bran   29 Apple

3. **Reasoning** Write an addition story about the muffins at the bakery.

_____

_____

_____

4. **Reasoning** Write a subtraction story about the muffins at the bakery.

_____

_____

_____

5. **Model** Write an equation for each number story that you wrote in Item 3 and Item 4. Then solve any way you choose. Show your work.

Name _____

Find a Match

Find a partner. Point to a clue. Read the clue.

Look below the clues to find a match. Write the clue letter in the box next to the match.

Find a match for every clue.

I can …
add and subtract within 20.

Clues

A Is equal to $5 + 4$

B Is equal to $8 + 7$

C Is equal to $20 - 10$

D Is equal to $12 - 7$

E Is equal to $9 + 3$

F Is equal to $13 - 9$

G Is equal to $11 - 8$

H Is equal to $7 + 6$

I Is equal to $2 + 4$

J Is equal to $5 + 6$

K Is equal to $14 - 7$

L Is equal to $10 + 6$

☐ $10 - 7$	☐ $19 - 9$	☐ $8 + 8$	☐ $12 - 8$
☐ $18 - 9$	☐ $13 - 8$	☐ $13 - 7$	☐ $8 + 3$
☐ $4 + 9$	☐ $15 - 8$	☐ $9 + 6$	☐ $6 + 6$

A-Z
Glossary

Word List
- bar diagram
- compatible numbers
- difference
- equation
- open number line
- regroup
- sum

Understand Vocabulary

Write T for *true* or F for *false*.

1. _____ An equation is a model you can use to help solve a problem.

2. _____ 43 is the difference in the equation $43 - 16 = 27$.

3. _____ Addition and subtraction can be shown using a bar diagram.

4. _____ An equation is a model you can use to represent a problem.

5. _____ A sum is the answer to a subtraction problem.

Draw a line from each term to its example.

6. regroup

7. sum   The answer to $18 + 45$

8. open number line   15 ones = 1 ten and 5 ones

Use Vocabulary in Writing

9. Explain how you can count on to find $58 + 23$. Use at least one term from the Word List.

© Pearson Education, Inc. 2

Name _____

Set A

You can model problems.

A store has some rings. Then 34 rings are sold. Now the store has 47 rings. How many rings did the store have at first?

$? - 34 = 47$

1
47
+ 34
‾‾‾‾
81 rings

Reteaching

Write an equation with a ? for the unknown to represent the problem. Then solve using the bar diagram.

1. A store has 52 juice boxes. Then some juice boxes are sold. Now the store has 35 juice boxes. How many juice boxes were sold?

   Equation: _____

   _____ juice boxes

Set B

Trent has 29 more toy cars than Bill. Trent has 72 toy cars. How many toy cars does Bill have?

6 12
7̶2̶
− 29
‾‾‾‾
43

This means Bill has 29 fewer toy cars than Trent. Subtract to solve. Bill has 43 toy cars.

Solve the problem any way you choose. Show your work.

2. A game has 19 more red cards than blue cards. The game has 43 red cards. How many blue cards does the game have?

   _____ blue cards

Lacie buys 28 peaches. She gives 12 to Ted. Then she buys 15 more. How many peaches does Lacie have now?

$28 - 12 = \underline{16}$ $16 + 15 = \underline{31}$

$\underline{31}$ peaches

Use the answer from the first step to solve the second step. Use the bar diagrams to help.

3. Craig scores 27 points. Next he scores 33 points. Then he loses 14 points. How many points does Craig have now?

$27 + 33 = \underline{\hphantom{xxx}}$ $\underline{\hphantom{xx}} - \underline{\hphantom{xx}} = \underline{\hphantom{xx}}$

$\underline{\hphantom{xxx}}$ points

Thinking Habits

Reasoning

How are the numbers in the problem related?

How can I use a word problem to show what the equation means?

Write a number story for the problem. Complete the equation to match your story.

4. $28 + 35 = \underline{\hphantom{xxx}}$

_____

_____

_____

_____

Name _____

1. Jodi has 28 apples. She buys some more.
Now Jodi has 43 apples.
How many apples did she buy?

Use the bar diagram to help you
write an equation. Then use
the open number line to solve.

_____ ⃝ _____ = _____

_____ apples

2. Alayna draws 18 more stars
than Pearl. Alayna draws
37 stars. How many stars
does Pearl draw?

Can you use the equation to solve the
problem? Choose Yes or No.

$37 - 18 = ?$ ⃝ Yes ⃝ No

$18 + 37 = ?$ ⃝ Yes ⃝ No

$18 + ? = 37$ ⃝ Yes ⃝ No

$? + 18 = 37$ ⃝ Yes ⃝ No

3. Emily has 17 fewer ribbons than Piper.
Piper has 48 ribbons.
How many ribbons does Emily have?

Solve any way you choose.
Show your work.

_____ ribbons

4. Write a number story for $72 - 36 = ?$.
Then solve the story problem.

$72 - 36 =$ _____

5. Joy needs 99 coats for children in need.
She gets 54 coats from her school.
She gets 22 coats from friends.
How many more coats does Joy need?

Write equations to solve.
Then write the answer.

_____ ◯ _____ = _____

_____ ◯ _____ = _____

Joy needs _____ more coats.

6. Shane has 27 more cards than Tom.
Shane has 62 cards.
How many cards does Tom have?

Explain how you will solve the problem.
Then solve.

Tom has _____ cards.

---

7. Grace found 36 shells.
She threw 8 shells back into the sea.
Then she found 9 more shells.
How many shells does Grace have now?

Which pair of equations shows a way to solve the problem?

Ⓐ $36 - 8 = 28$
$28 - 9 = 19$

Ⓑ $36 - 8 = 28$
$28 + 9 = 37$

Ⓒ $36 + 9 = 45$
$45 + 8 = 53$

Ⓓ $36 + 8 = 44$
$44 + 9 = 53$

Name _____

School Fair

Meadow School is having a school fair. The table shows the number of tickets Ms. Davis's class has sold.

Number of Tickets Sold	
Monday	42
Tuesday	17
Wednesday	21

1. How many fewer tickets did Ms. Davis's class sell on Wednesday than on Monday?
Complete the bar diagram to model the problem. Then solve.

_____ fewer tickets

2. Ms. Davis says the class can have a party if they sell 95 tickets.

Part A

Write an equation to show how many tickets the class has sold.

Then solve the equation. Show your work.

_____ tickets sold

Part B

How many more tickets does the class have to sell to have a party? Explain.

_____ tickets

3. The table shows the number of tickets Mr. Rios's class has sold.

How many more tickets did his class sell on Monday and Tuesday than on Wednesday?

Number of Tickets Sold	
Monday	24
Tuesday	18
Wednesday	28

Write two equations to solve both parts of the problem.

_____ ◯ _____ = _____

_____ ◯ _____ = _____

_____ more tickets

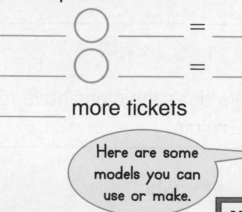

Here are some models you can use or make.

Models
arrays
bar diagrams
drawings
equations
open number lines
place-value blocks

4. Part A

Write a number story about selling tickets for the school fair. Use numbers that you can add or subtract.

_____

_____

_____

_____

Part B

Write an equation to match your story. Then solve any way you choose. Show your work.

TOPIC 8 Work with Time and Money

Essential Question: How can you solve problems about counting money or telling time to the nearest 5 minutes?

Digital Resources

Solve | Learn | Glossary

Tools | Assessment | Help | Games

Different materials are used to make money!

How would you describe different types of money?

Wow! Let's do this project and learn more.

Math and Science Project: Money Matters

Find Out Collect examples of different types of coins and dollar bills. Describe how different coins and bills look and feel. Sort the money by size, color, and whether or not you can bend it.

Journal: Make a Book Show what you find out in a book. In your book, also:

• Tell how different types of coins are alike. Tell how they are different.

• Show as many different ways as you can to make 25¢.

Name _____

Review What You Know

A-Z Vocabulary

1. Draw the hands to show **8 o'clock**.

2. Circle the number of minutes in one **hour**.

30 minutes

50 minutes

60 minutes

3. Write the time below to the **half hour**.

_____ o'clock

Doubles Facts

4. Write each sum.

$$
\begin{array}{r} 7 \\ +7 \\ \hline \end{array}
\qquad
\begin{array}{r} 9 \\ +9 \\ \hline \end{array}
\qquad
\begin{array}{r} 10 \\ +10 \\ \hline \end{array}
$$

Doubles facts are fun.

Array

5. Use mental math. How many squares are in the array?

_____ squares

Math Story

6. Some pennies are in a cup. Jan takes out 22 of the pennies. Now, 14 pennies are left in the cup. How many pennies were in the cup at the start?

_____ pennies

My Word Cards

Study the words on the front of the card.
Complete the activity on the back.

A-Z
Glossary

dime

nickel

penny

quarter

half-dollar

cents (¢)

I cent
or I¢

10 cents
or 10¢

My Word Cards

Use what you know to complete the sentences.
Extend learning by writing your own sentence using each word.

A _____

is 1 cent or 1¢.

A _____

is 5 cents or 5¢.

A _____

is 10 cents or 10¢.

The value of a coin is measured in

_____.

The symbol for cents is

_____.

A _____

is 50 cents or 50¢.

A _____

is 25 cents or 25¢.

My Word Cards

Study the words on the front of the card.
Complete the activity on the back.

A-Z
Glossary

greatest value

The quarter has the greatest value.

least value

The dime has the least value.

dollar

$1 or 100¢

dollar sign

$37

↑
dollar sign

dollar bills

tally mark

Ways to Show 30¢			
Quarter	Dime	Nickel	Total
I		I	30¢
	III		30¢
	II	II	30¢
I		IIII	30¢
		⊬ℍ I	30¢

Use what you know to complete the sentences.
Extend learning by writing your own sentence using each word.

One _____

equals 100¢.

The coin that has the

_____

_____

is the coin that is worth the least.

The coin that has the

_____

_____

is the coin that is worth the most.

Use a _____

_____

to keep track of each piece of information in an organized list.

_____

can have different dollar values, such as $1, $5, $10, or $20.

A _____

_____

is a symbol used to show dollar money values.

My Word Cards

Study the words on the front of the card.
Complete the activity on the back.

A-Z
Glossary

quarter past

It is quarter past 4.

half past

It is half past 9.

quarter to

It is quarter to 4.

a.m.

breakfast time

p.m.

dinner time

A _____

_____

is 15 minutes before the hour.

30 minutes past the hour is

_____

_____.

A _____

_____

is 15 minutes after the hour.

Clock time from noon to midnight can be shown as

_____.

Clock time from midnight to noon can be shown as

_____.

Solve & Share

Kelsey had 10 cents in her piggybank.
She finds 5 cents more and puts it in her bank.
Then Kelsey's mother gives her 20 cents to put in her bank.

How many cents does Kelsey have in her bank now?

I can ...
solve problems with coins.

Content Standards 2.M.7,
2.NS.1
Process Standards PS.1,
PS.2, PS.3, PS.5

_____ cents

dime 10¢

  nickel 5¢

 penny 1¢

  quarter 25¢

half-dollar
50¢

Micah has the coins shown below.
How many cents does Micah have?
Count on to find the total value.

Micah has 91 cents.
The cent sign is ¢.

50¢   75¢   85¢   90¢   91¢

Do You Understand?

Show Me! How many quarters have the same value as a half-dollar?

How many dimes have the same value as a half-dollar?

How many cents would Micah have if he didn't have the half-dollar?

☆ Guided Practice   Count on to find each total value.

1. Li has these coins. How many cents does Li have?

25¢   50¢   _____   _____   _____   **Total**

2. Manny has these coins. How many cents does Manny have?

_____   _____   _____   _____   **Total**

Name _____

Tools   Assessment

Independent Practice ⭐ Count on to find each total value.

3. Jan has these coins. How many cents does Jan have?

    ➡️

_____ _____ _____ _____

Total

---

4. Tim has these coins. How many cents does Tim have?

     ➡️

_____ _____ _____ _____ _____

Total

---

5. Manny has these coins. How many cents does Manny have?

     ➡️

_____ _____ _____ _____ _____

Total

---

6. Algebra Stacey had 92¢ this morning. She lost a coin.
Write the name of the coin Stacey lost.

   [_____]   ➡️ 92¢

Total

Topic 8 | Lesson 1   four hundred forty-five **445**

7. **Explain** Tori has 2 quarters, I dime, and I nickel. How many cents does Tori have? Show how you found your answer.

8. **Higher Order Thinking** Write a story about what coins you could use to buy an orange for 60¢.

9. Ⓓ**Assessment** Lucas has these coins.

He is buying a gift for his brother. If he had one more nickel, which item would he have exactly enough money to buy?

41¢   51¢   76¢   84¢

Ⓐ   Ⓑ   Ⓒ   Ⓓ

10. Ⓓ**Assessment** Jamie has 90¢. Which coins could she have? Choose all that apply.

☐

☐

☐

☐

Name _____

Another Look! You can count on to find the total value of a group of coins.

Luanne has one quarter and two nickels. How many cents does Luanne have?

Tim has one half-dollar and two dimes. How many cents does Tim have?

HOME ACTIVITY Show your child 5 coins. Ask your child to find the total value and write that amount with a cent symbol.

Start with 25¢. Count on by fives.

Start with 50¢. Count on by tens.

Think: 25¢   5¢ more   5¢ more

Think: 50¢   10¢ more   10¢ more

25¢   30¢   35¢   50¢   60¢   70¢

Count on to find each total value.

1. Sarah has these coins. How many cents does Sarah have?

       →   _____ Total

25¢   _____   _____   _____   _____

2. Marc has these coins. How many cents does Marc have?

       →   _____ Total

3. Higher Order Thinking Find the coins needed to buy each toy. Use the fewest coins possible. Write how many of each coin to use.

Count on as you use each coin.

67¢				
82¢				
46¢				

---

4. **Assessment** Will has 37¢. Which coins could he have? Choose all that apply.

☐ quarter, dime, penny, penny

☐ quarter, penny, penny

☐ dime, dime, dime, penny, penny

☐ quarter, nickel, penny, penny

---

5. **Assessment** Jamal has these coins.

He needs 85¢ to buy a toy car.
How many more cents does Jamal need?
Draw the coin or coins he needs.

© Pearson Education, Inc. 2

Solve & Share

Choose 5 coins. Which coin has the least value? Which coin has the greatest value? What is the total value of money you have?

I can ...
solve problems with coins.

Content Standards 2.M.7, 2.NS.1
Process Standards PS.3, PS.4, PS.5, PS.6

_____ greatest _____ ¢

_____ least _____ ¢

Total: _____ ¢

Seline has these coins.

How many cents does Seline have?

Start with the coin of **greatest value**.

Count on to the coin of **least value**.

So, Seline has 90¢.

50¢   75¢   85¢   90¢

Do You Understand?

Show Me! Why is it a good idea to put 1 nickel, 1 penny, and 1 quarter in a different order to find the total?

☆ **Guided Practice** ☆

Draw the coins from the greatest to the least value. Count on to find each total. You can use coins.

1.

60¢ Total

25¢   50¢   55¢   60¢

2.

_____ Total

_____ _____ _____ _____

Total

© Pearson Education, Inc. 2

Topic 8 | Lesson 2

Name _____

Independent Practice ☆ Count on to find each total value.

3. Eboo has these coins. How many cents does Eboo have?

It helps to put the coins in order from greatest value to least value.

____ ____ ____ ____   The total is _____.

4. Hanna has these coins. How many cents does Hanna have?

____ ____ ____ ____   The total is _____.

5. Mary has 3 dimes and 2 nickels. How many cents does she have?

_____

6. Danny has 4 nickels, 1 quarter, 2 dimes, and 3 pennies. How many cents does he have?

_____

7. **Number Sense** What 4 coins have a total value of 20¢? Draw the coins. Label the value of each coin.

8. Math and Science Greg's science class wants to sort these coins by their color. What is the total value of the silver coins?

_____ ¢

9. Model Draw the fewest number of coins to show 80¢.

10. Higher Order Thinking Write a story about finding 75¢. Draw the coins.

11. 🅸**Assessment** Lydia has 3 coins. The total value is 40¢. She has 1 quarter and 1 nickel. Which shows her third coin?

40¢

Ⓐ

Ⓒ

Ⓑ

Ⓓ

Name _____

Help   Tools   Games

Homework & Practice 8-2

Continue to Solve Problems with Coins

Another Look! To count coins, start with the coin that has the greatest value. Count on from the greatest to the least value.

Find the total value of the coins Seth has.
Draw an X on the coin with the greatest value.

Think: 50¢   60¢   70¢   75¢

Start with 50¢.   50¢   60¢   70¢   75¢

HOME ACTIVITY Have your child take 4 coins from a cup of mixed coins and count on to find the value. Ask your child to record the value with a cent symbol.

Find each total value. Draw an X on the coin with the greatest value.

1.

Start with _____.

_____   _____   _____   _____

2.

Start with _____.

_____   _____   _____   _____

Topic 8 | Lesson 2   Digital Resources at PearsonRealize.com   four hundred fifty-three **453**

3. Megan had 50¢. She lost 1 nickel.
Circle the 5 coins that show how much she has left.

4. Yoshi had 55¢. He gave his sister a dime.
Circle the 3 coins that show how much he has left.

5. Kayla had 60¢. She gave her brother 4 pennies.
Circle the 3 coins that show how much she has left.

6. **A-Z** **Vocabulary** Circle the **nickel**. Put a square around the **half-dollar**. What is the total value of all the money?

_____ ¢

7. **Assessment** Karen has 85¢. She has a half-dollar and a dime. Which other coin does Karen have?

Ⓐ   Ⓒ

Ⓑ   Ⓓ

Name _____

Solve & Share

What is one way you can show 100¢ with coins? Use coins to model. Draw and label the coins you use.

I can ...
solve problems with dollar bills and coins that model 100 cents.

Content Standards 2.M.7, 2.NS.1
Process Standards PS.2, PS.4, PS.6, PS.7

100¢

This is **1 dollar**.
The **dollar sign** is **$**.

$1 bill
$1 = 100¢

Here are some other **dollar bills**.

$5 bill

$10 bill

$20 bill

Maria had these dollar bills. What is the total value?

$20 $30 $40 $45 $50 $51

20 + 10 + 10 + 5 + 5 + 1

Count on from the greatest bill to the least bill. Maria has $51.

Do You Understand?

Show Me! How is counting dollar bills like counting coins? How is it different?

☆ **Guided Practice**   Solve each problem.

1. Mr. Park has these dollar bills. Count on to find the total value.

_____

2. Ms. Lenz has these dollar bills. Count on to find the total value.

_____

Remember to count from the greatest bill to the least bill.

Topic 8 | **Lesson 3**

Name _____

Independent Practice ✩ Solve each problem.

3. Mr. Higgins has these dollar bills.
Count on to find the total value.

_____

4. Ms. Nguen has these dollar bills.
Count on to find the total value.

_____

5. Mr. Abreu has these dollar bills.
Count on to find the total value.

_____

6. Ms. Wills has these dollar bills.
Count on to find the total value.

_____

7. Number Sense Mr. Anson has $26 in his wallet.
What is the least number of bills he can have?
Draw the bills.

_____ bills

8. Model Diana buys shoes on sale for $28. Draw dollar bills that she could use to pay for the shoes.

9. Mrs. Baker has two $10 bills and three $5 bills in her purse. Does she have enough money to buy a dress that costs $33? Explain.

10. Higher Order Thinking Roger buys a baseball bat that costs $27. He pays the clerk with two $20 bills. What bills can the clerk give him back as change?

11. **Assessment** The dollar bills below show the total cost of tickets for a soccer game.

How much do the tickets cost?

$5	$31	$40	$41
Ⓐ	Ⓑ	Ⓒ	Ⓓ

© Pearson Education, Inc. 2

Name _____

Help   Tools   Games

Another Look! What is the total value of the dollar bills shown below?

Count on from greatest bill to least bill to find the total value of dollar bills.

HOME ACTIVITY Have your child make different groups of dollar bills that total $37.

$20 $30 $40 $45 $46

20 + 10 + 10 + 5 + 1

Solve each problem.

1. Ms. Lopez has these dollar bills. Count on to find the total value.

_____

2. Ms. Lenz has these dollar bills. Count on to find the total value.

_____

3. Jack buys a bicycle on sale for $59. Draw dollar bills that he could use to pay for the bike.

4. **Look for Patterns** Marvin counts six $5 bills. Write each value that he counts. What pattern do you see in the ones digits of the values he counts?

_____

_____

_____

_____

5. **Higher Order Thinking** Maria has two $20 bills, three $5 bills, and four $1 bills. What other bill or bills does she need to buy a present that costs $69?

6. **Assessment** The dollar bills below show the money that Sam has saved.

How much money has Sam saved?

$52	$43	$42	$5
Ⓐ	Ⓑ	Ⓒ	Ⓓ

© Pearson Education, Inc. 2

Solve & Share

Timmy takes money out of his piggy bank.
He takes out two $10 bills, three $5 bills, and 6 $1 bills.
How much money does Timmy take out?

Draw a picture to show your work.

$ _____

Lesson 8-4
Continue to Solve Problems with Dollar Bills

I can ...
solve problems with dollar bills.

Content Standards 2.M.7, 2.CA.2
Process Standards PS.1, PS.2, PS.4, PS.6

Chloe has a $20 bill and a $1 bill. Her sister Violet has $6 less than Chloe. Do they have enough money to buy a $35 scarf for their mother?

$35

You can show how much money Chloe has with a $20 bill and a $1 bill.

$20 + $1 = $21

$20

$1

You can find how much money Violet has by subtracting $21 − $6.

$21 − $6 = $15

$10

$5

Add to find if Chloe and Violet have enough money to buy the scarf.

$21 + $15 = $36

Violet could have a $10 bill and a $5 bill.

$36 is enough to buy a $35 scarf.

Do You Understand?

Show Me! How can you keep track of the amounts of money in the word problem?

☆ Guided Practice ☆

Solve each problem any way you choose. Show your work.

1. Sam had some money in his wallet. He went to the carnival and spent $12. Now Sam has $5. How much was in his wallet before the carnival?

$ _?_ − $_12_ = $_5_

$_12_ + $_5_ = $_17_

$_17_

2. Morgan has $7. Her grandmother gives her a $10 bill and a $5 bill. How much money does Morgan have now?

$____

© Pearson Education, Inc. 2

Name _____

Independent Practice ✮ Solve each problem any way you choose. Show your work.

3. Mia has two dollars. Ethan gives her two $5 bills. Noah gives her one $10 bill. How much money does Mia have in all?

$_____

4. A sweater costs $38. Charlie has one $20 bill, one $10 bill, and two $1 bills. How much more money does he need to buy the sweater?

$_____

5. Eli has $64 dollars. One of the bills is a $20 bill. What are the other bills Eli could have?

Draw a picture to show one solution.

6. Higher Order Thinking Jen bought three $5 raffle tickets and eight $1 raffle tickets. How much did Jen spend on raffle tickets?

Jen spent $_____ on raffle tickets.

Explain how you solved the problem.

7. **Make Sense** Lily has two $10 bills, three $5 bills, and one $1 bill. She gives Grace $11. How much money does Lily have left?

8. **Make Sense** Isaac wants to buy a backpack for $20. He has two $5 bills and nine $1 bills. How much more money does he need to buy the backpack?

How much is two $10 bills?

$_____

$_____

9. **Higher Order Thinking** Henry has two $10 bills, two $5 bills, and three $1 bills. Mr. Harper has one $100 bill. Henry says he has more money because he has seven bills and Mr. Harper only has one bill. Is Henry correct? Explain.

10. ⓘ **Assessment** Olivia has one $20 bill, three $5 bills, and nine $1 bills. How much more money does Olivia need to buy a coat that costs $49? Explain.

What bills can you use to show how much money Olivia needs?

Name _____

Help Tools Games

Another Look! Kim has $4 in her bank.
She needs $20 to buy the gift she picked out for her mom.
How much more money does Kim need?

$20 − $4 = $ _16_

Kim needs $16 more.

Add to check your work.
$4 + $16 = $20
So, the answer makes sense.

HOME ACTIVITY Have your child use coins and bills to show various amounts in different ways.

$10 + $5 + $1 = $16

Solve each problem any way you choose. Show your work.

1. Mrs. Brown had $16 dollars in her wallet. After shopping at the store, she now has $8. How much money did Mrs. Brown spend at the store?

2. Evelyn has $7. Liz gives her one $5 bill and two $1 bills. How much money does Evelyn have now?

$_____

$_____

3. **Be Precise** Aiden has three $20 bills and two $10 bills. He wants to save a total of $95. How much more money does he need? What bills could they be?

_____

_____

4. Carter has one $20 bill, one $10 bill, four $5 bills and two $1 bills. Aubrey has two $10 bills, five $5 bills, and seven $1 bills. Who has more money? Explain.

_____

_____

_____

5. **Higher Order Thinking** Mark has $24. His brother has $8 more than Mark has. How much do they have in all?

Step I

$_____ ◯ $_____ = $_____

Step 2

$_____ ◯ $_____ = $_____

Mark and his brother have $_____ in all.

6. ◯**Assessment** Emma has two $10 bills, three $5 bills, and two $1 bills. How much more money does she need to buy a game that costs $45? Explain.

_____

_____

_____

What bills can you use to show how much more money Emma needs?

_____

Name _____

Solve & Share

Suppose you want to buy a pencil that costs 35¢. How many different ways can you use nickels, dimes, or quarters to make 35¢? Show each way. Tell how you know.

Quarter	Dime	Nickel	Total Amount
			35¢
			35¢
			35¢
			35¢
			35¢
			35¢

I can ...
reason about values of coins and dollar bills, and find different ways to make the same total value.

Process Standards PS.2 Also PS.1, PS.3, PS.4, PS.8 Content Standards 2.M.7, 2.CA.2

Thinking Habits

What do the numbers and symbols in the problem mean?

How do the values of the coins relate to the total?

I have some quarters, dimes, and nickels. I want to buy a banana.

30¢

How many ways can I make 30¢?

How can I reason about the different ways to make a total?

A table can show the coins. I can use **tally marks** to record the number of coins.

Ways to Show 30¢			
Quarter	Dime	Nickel	Total
I		I	30¢
	III		30¢

$$25¢ + 5¢ = 30¢$$
$$10¢ + 10¢ + 10¢ = 30¢$$

Tally marks make it easy to show the different ways.

Ways to Show 30¢			
Quarter	Dime	Nickel	Total
I		I	30¢
	III		30¢
	II	II	30¢
	I	IIII	30¢
		THH I	30¢

I can write an equation to show and check each way.

I can make 30¢ in 5 different ways.

Do You Understand?

Show Me! Use the chart above. Write equations to show the ways to make 30¢ using dimes and nickels.

Guided Practice Use reasoning. Complete the table.

1. Tony wants to buy a pencil.

55¢

He has half-dollars, quarters, and nickels. Find all the ways he can make 55¢.

How do the tally marks relate to money values?

Half-Dollar	Quarter	Nickel	Total
I		I	55¢

Tools   Assessment

Independent Practice ✰ Use reasoning. Complete each table.

2. Sue needs $12 to buy a book. She has $1 bills, $5 bills, and $10 bills. Find 3 more ways Sue can make $12.

$10 Bill	$5 Bill	$1 Bill	Total
I		II	$12

3. Raul wants to buy a bookmark for 14¢. He has dimes, nickels, and pennies. Find all of the ways he can make 14¢.

Dime	Nickel	Penny	Total
	II	IIII	14¢

You can write equations to check your work.

Number Sense What is the least number of bills or coins that you could use to make each amount? You can use the tables above to help.

4. $12

Number of bills: _____
Bills I would use:

_____

5. 14¢

Number of coins: _____
Coins I would use:

_____

6. Write an equation to show the total value of 2 nickels and 4 pennies.

_____

Problem Solving

Carnival Game Money

Don wants to use these coins to play as many carnival games as he can. Each game costs 40¢.

How can Don spend the coins that are shown at the right?

7. **Use Models** Choose from the coins shown. Show one way Don can spend 40¢ on one game. Write an equation.

_____

_____

8. **Make Sense** You used some of the coins for one of the ways. How will you know which coins are left to spend?

_____

_____

9. **Reasoning** Show how Dan can spend the coins to play games. Use tally marks in the table.

Which coin is left over?

Quarter	Dime	Nickel	Penny	Total

© Pearson Education, Inc. 2

Name _____

Another Look! Show three ways to make 25¢.
Two ways are shown in the table.

Use coins to help you find a
third way. Show I dime.
Make I tally mark.
How many nickels do you
need to add 15¢?

_3_

Make 3 tally marks.

HOME ACTIVITY Ask
your child to use quarters,
nickels, and dimes to show
all the ways to make 70¢
with those coins.

Ways to Show 25¢

Quarter	Dime	Nickel	Total
I			25¢
	II	I	25¢
	I	III	25¢

Use reasoning to solve each problem.

1. Show three ways to make $20.
   Use tally marks to record the bills.

Ways to Show $20

$20 Bill	$10 Bill	$5 Bill	Total

2. What is the least number of coins you
   could use to make 45¢?
   Make a table, if needed.

   Number of coins: _____

   Coins I would use: _____

   _____

Least Number of Bills

The Williams family wants to buy these toys. They have $20 bills, $10 bills, $5 bills, and $1 bills. They want to use the least number of bills to pay for each item.

Which bills will they use to pay for each item?

3. **Explain** Marci thinks the family should use three $5 bills and three $1 bills to buy the doll. Does Marci's way use the least number of bills? Explain.

_____

_____

_____

4. **Generalize** How can you find the least number of bills to use to pay for any of the 3 items?

_____

_____

_____

_____

5. **Reasoning** Complete the Williams's shopping card. Record the least number of bills they could use to pay for each item. Use tally marks.

Item	$20 Bill	$10 Bill	$5 Bill	$1 Bill
Doll				
Basketball				
Bicycle				

Solve

Solve & Share

An airplane is due to arrive at 3:15.
How can you show this time on the clock below? Explain.

I can ...
tell time to the nearest 5 minutes.

Content Standard 2.M.5
Process Standards PS.2, PS.5, PS.6, PS.8

Both clocks show 8:05.

minute hand

8:05

The minute hand moves from number to number in 5 minutes.

To tell time to five minutes, count by 5s. Both clocks show 8:35.

8:35

I can start at 8:00 and count by 5s to tell the time.

There are 60 minutes in 1 hour.

hour hand

9:00

The minutes start over again each hour.

Do You Understand?

Show Me! The time is 9:35. What time will it be in 5 minutes?

In 15 minutes?

In 25 minutes?

☆ Guided Practice ☆

Complete the clocks so both clocks show the same time.

1.

6:45

2.

3:25

3.

:

4.

5:40

© Pearson Education, Inc. 2

Tools Assessment

Independent Practice

Complete the clocks so both clocks show the same time.

5.

6.
2:25

7.

8.
4:40

9.

10.

11. Number Sense Complete the pattern.

7:00   7:05   7:10   :

12. **Reasoning** One of the clocks is running a little slow. The other clock is running a little fast. Estimate the correct time.

_____

13. **Number Sense** Look at the time on the first clock.
What time will it be in 5 minutes?
Write that time on the second clock.

14. **Higher Order Thinking** Draw a clock that shows your favorite time of the day. Explain why it is your favorite time.

_____

_____

_____

15. **�❶ Assessment** The minute hand is pointing to the 7. Which number will it be pointing to 10 minutes later?

Ⓐ 5

Ⓑ between 7 and 8

Ⓒ 8

Ⓓ 9

Another Look! You can use two kinds of clocks to tell time.

The minute hand moves from mark to mark in 1 minute.

There are 5 moves between each number. So, the minute hand moves from number to number in 5 minutes.

There are 30 minutes in a half hour and 60 minutes in an hour.

The hour hand moves from number to number every 60 minutes.

> **HOME ACTIVITY** Draw three clock faces showing 3:20, 10:50, and 7:05. Have your child tell you the time each clock shows.

Count by 5s. Write the time.

1.

2.

3. **Generalize** The time is shown on the clock below.

Draw the time on the clock in the box at the right. Then complete each sentence.

The minute hand is pointing to the _____.

The hour hand is between _____ and _____.

Higher Order Thinking Each riddle is about a different clock. Solve the riddle and write the time.

4. My hour hand is between the 3 and the 4. My minute hand is pointing to the 7.

What time do I show? _____

5. My hour hand is between the 5 and the 6. My minute hand is pointing to the 4.

What time do I show? _____

6. My hour hand is between the 11 and the 12. My minute hand is pointing to the 3.

What time do I show? _____

7. My hour hand is between the 1 and the 2. My minute hand is pointing to the 9.

What time do I show? _____

8. **Assessment** The clock shows the time that Sharon starts to walk to the library. The walk takes 10 minutes. At what time does Sharon get to the library?

5:00 5:10 5:20 5:30
Ⓐ   Ⓑ   Ⓒ   Ⓓ

Name _____

Solve & Share

Both of these clocks show the same time.
How many different ways can you say this time?
Write each way.

6:45

I can …
say the time in different ways.

Content Standard 2.M.5
Process Standards PS.3,
PS.4, PS.6, PS.8

Look at the times. Count by 5s to tell the time.
What are other ways to name the same times?

Times after the half hour are often read as times before the next hour.

1:15

1:30

1:50

3:30

3:45

3:50

15 minutes after 1, **quarter past** 1

30 minutes after 1, **half past** 1

50 minutes after 1

30 minutes before 4

15 minutes before 4, **quarter to** 4

10 minutes before 4

Do You Understand?

Show Me! Write two ways to say 5:30.

☆ Guided Practice ☆

Complete so both clocks show the same time. Then circle another way to say the time.

1.

half past 2

30 minutes before 2

2.

quarter to 7

quarter past 6

© Pearson Education, Inc. 2

Topic 8 | Lesson 7

Independent Practice

Complete so both clocks show the same time. Then write the time before or after the hour.

3.

4:45

_____ minutes before 5

4.

12:15

quarter past _____

5.

:

25 minutes after _____

Higher Order Thinking Look at the clock to solve each problem.

6. What time will it be in 30 minutes? Write this time in two different ways.

_____

_____

7. What time will it be in 50 minutes? Write this time in two different ways.

_____

_____

8. **A-Z Vocabulary** Miguel is meeting a friend at **half past** 4.
Complete both clocks to show this time.

9. **Generalize** A train left the station at 6:55. What are two other ways to say this time?

_____

_____

10. **Higher Order Thinking** Draw a clock with hands that show 11:45.
Then write two ways to say the time.

_____

_____

11. **Assessment** James gets home at 6:00. He starts his homework at quarter past 6. At what time does James start his homework?

Ⓐ

Ⓒ

Ⓑ

Ⓓ

Name _____

Another Look! Here are different ways to say time before and after the hour.

6:15

15 minutes after 6 or quarter past 6

6:30

30 minutes after 6 or half past 6

6:45

45 minutes after 6 or quarter to 7

2:40

20 minutes before 3 or 40 minutes after 2

HOME ACTIVITY Draw several clock faces. Have your child draw the time for 7:15, 2:30, and 5:45. Then have your child say the time using the terms *quarter past, half past,* and *quarter to.*

Count by 5s to tell the time. Write the time on the line below the clock. Then write the missing numbers.

I.

__30__ minutes after _____

or half past _____

_____

2.

_____ minutes after _____ or

_____ minutes before _____

_____

3. **Explain** The time is 6:10. Is the hour hand closer to 6 or 7? Explain your reasoning.

Write the time. Then answer each question.

4. Nancy arrives at 10 minutes before 8.

School starts at

Is Nancy early or late for school?

_____

_____

5. Sean arrives at quarter to 7.

Dinner starts at

Is Sean early or late for dinner?

_____

_____

6. **⬤Assessment** Joyce wakes up at 10 minutes after 7. It takes her 40 minutes to get ready and walk to school. What time does Joyce get to school?

Ⓐ

Ⓑ

Ⓒ

Ⓓ

© Pearson Education, Inc. 2

Solve & Share

Look at the clock and tell what time Ethan wakes up for school. Write the time on the digital clock and circle morning or evening.

I can ...
tell time and use reasoning to state if the event is happening in the a.m. or p.m.

Content Standard 2.M.5
Process Standards PS.2, PS.6, PS.8

Ethan wakes up at:

Circle

morning

evening

You can use the terms **a.m.** and **p.m.** to tell about time.

Use a.m. for morning times. I wake up at 8 a.m.

Use p.m. for afternoon or evening times. I go to bed at 8 p.m.

I eat breakfast at:

8:20

(a.m.)   p.m.

I eat lunch at school at:

11:45

(a.m.)   p.m.

I eat dinner with my family at:

6:30

a.m.   (p.m.)

Do You Understand?

Show Me! What might you be doing at 6:15 a.m.? At 6:15 p.m.?

☆ Guided ☆ Practice

Complete the clocks so both clocks show the same time. Then circle a.m. or p.m. to tell when you would do each activity.

1. Ride the bus to school

8:45

(a.m.)   p.m.

2. Do your homework

4:30

a.m.   p.m.

Name _____

Independent Practice

Complete the clocks so both clocks show the same time.
Circle a.m. or p.m. to tell when you would do each activity.

3. Take the bus home from school

a.m.   p.m.

4. Walk the dog before breakfast

a.m.   p.m.

5. Read a book before bedtime

a.m.   p.m.

6. Take swimming lessons on Saturday morning

10:15

a.m.   p.m.

7. Watch a movie on Friday night

7:20

a.m.   p.m.

8. Go to a party on Saturday afternoon

2:00

a.m.   p.m.

9. Higher Order Thinking Jen and Maria have dance lessons at the time shown on the clock.
Write the time two different ways. Is it a.m. or p.m.? Explain.

_____

_____

10. Be Precise Draw hands on the clock to show what time your school begins each day. Then write the time. Include a.m. or p.m.

11. Math and Science Stargazing is looking at the stars. The best time to stargaze is on a clear moonless night.

Gina went outside to stargaze at 9:00. Is this 9:00 a.m. or 9:00 p.m.? Explain.

_____

_____

12. Higher Order Thinking Grace starts her homework at 4:15.
She finishes her homework 45 minutes later. Draw the hands on the clocks to show both times. Write both times on the digital clocks.

Circle a.m. or p.m. below to tell when Grace does her homework.

a.m.   p.m.

13. ⓘ Assessment Circle a.m. or p.m. to tell when you would do each activity.

Brush your teeth before bedtime   a.m.   p.m.   Walk the dog before dinner   a.m.   p.m.

Go to soccer practice after school   a.m.   p.m.   Watch the sunrise   a.m.   p.m.

Name _____

Another Look! Circle a.m. or p.m. to tell when each activity takes place.

Mom goes swimming in the morning.	I go to soccer practice after school.	Dad goes for a walk after dinner in the evening.

 9:15   4:00   6:45

(a.m.)   p.m.   a.m.   (p.m.)   a.m.   (p.m.)

a.m. means before noon. p.m. means after noon.

HOME ACTIVITY Write three things that you do at different times of the day. Have your child tell you whether you do these things in the a.m. or the p.m.

Complete the clocks so both clocks show the same time. Circle a.m. or p.m. to tell when each activity takes place.

I. Eat a snack in the morning

  10:15

(a.m.)   p.m.

2. Brush your teeth after lunch

  :

a.m.   p.m.

3. **A-Z** **Vocabulary** Write an example of an event that could happen in the **a.m.** Write an example of an event that could happen in the **p.m.**

_____

_____

_____

_____

4. **Higher Order Thinking** Guess what time it is. Right now, it is p.m.

In 10 minutes it will be a.m. What time is it now? Explain.

_____

_____

Write the time in the clock.

5. **Assessment** Alexis wakes up in the morning at the time shown on the clock. What time does Alexis wake up?

Ⓐ 7:15 a.m.

Ⓑ 8:15 a.m.

Ⓒ 7:15 p.m.

Ⓓ 8:15 p.m.

6. **Assessment** Circle a.m. or p.m. to tell when you would do each activity.

Watch the sunset	a.m.	p.m.
Eat breakfast	a.m.	p.m.
Walk home from school	a.m.	p.m.
Take the bus to school	a.m.	p.m.

Name _____

Find a Match

Find a partner. Point to a clue. Read the clue.

Look below the clues to find a match. Write the clue letter in the box next to the match.

Find a match for every clue.

I can ...
add and subtract within 20.

Clues

A Is equal to 12 − 5	**E** Is equal to 3 + 3	**I** Is equal to 17 − 8
B Is equal to 9 + 2	**F** Is equal to 15 − 7	**J** Is equal to 6 + 9
C Is equal to 12 − 10	**G** Is equal to 8 + 6	**K** Is equal to 8 − 5
D Is equal to 8 + 9	**H** Is equal to 12 − 8	**L** Is equal to 9 + 9

☐ 8 − 0	☐ 10 + 8	☐ 10 + 5	☐ 9 + 8
☐ 10 − 6	☐ 4 + 7	☐ 7 − 4	☐ 3 + 4
☐ 8 − 6	☐ 9 + 5	☐ 14 − 8	☐ 12 − 3

A-Z
Glossary

Word List
- a.m.
- cents (¢)
- dime
- dollar
- dollar bills
- dollar sign
- greatest value
- half-dollar
- half past
- least value
- nickel
- penny
- p.m.
- quarter
- quarter past
- quarter to
- tally mark

Understand Vocabulary

1. Circle the name of the coin with the *greatest value*.

quarter   nickel   dime

2. Circle the name of the coin with the *least value*.

half-dollar   penny   quarter

3. Cross out the time that is **NOT** quarter past 5 or quarter to 5.

4:45   5:15   5:25

4. Cross out the time that is **NOT** half past 8 or quarter past 8.

8:30   8:45   8:15

When does each event happen? Write a possible time.
Use a.m. or p.m.

5. school ends

_____

6. eat breakfast

_____

7. sunrise

_____

Use Vocabulary in Writing

8. Explain how you can show ways to make 1 dollar (100¢) using coins. Use terms from the Word List. Give examples.

Set A _____

When you count coins, start with the coin of greatest value.

Randi has the coins shown below. Count on to find the total value.

quarter (25¢)   dime (10¢)   nickel (5¢)

25¢   35¢   40¢

Randi has 40¢.

Another Example

Duanc has the coins below. How much money does Duane have?

25¢   50¢   60¢   70¢

Duane has 70¢.

Solve each problem.
Count on to find the total value.

1. These coins are in a jar. How many cents are in the jar?

Draw the coins in order.

Count on. _____ _____ _____

There is _____ in the jar.

2. The coins shown below are in a box. How much money is in the box?

There is _____ in the box.

Dollar bills are paper money and can have different dollar values.

$1 bill
$1 = 100¢

$5 bill

$10 bill

$20 bill

Matt has $56. Two of his bills are $20 bills. What other bills could Matt have? You can count on to get to $56.

$20, $40, $50, $55, $56
       +$10 +$5 +$1

The other bills Matt could have are a $10 bill, a $5 bill, and a $1 bill.

Solve each problem.

3. Mr. Park has these dollar bills. Count on to find the total value.

Remember to count from the greatest bill to the least bill.

_____

4. A cookbook costs $36. Mrs. Beeson has a $10 bill and a $5 bill. How much more money does Mrs. Beeson need to buy the cookbook?

$_____

© Pearson Education, Inc. 2

Set C

Thinking Habits

Reasoning

What do the numbers and symbols in the problem mean?

How do the values of the coins relate to the total?

Use reasoning. Finish the table.

5. Mitch has dimes, nickels, and pennies. Find ways he can make 11¢. Show a tally mark for each coin you use.

Dime	Nickel	Penny	Total
I		I	II¢

Did you find all the different ways?

Set D

It takes 5 minutes for the minute hand to move from one number to the next. Count on by 5s.

Read the time.
Write the same time on the digital clock.

6.

You can say the number of minutes before the hour or after the hour.

10 minutes before 5

(10 minutes after 5)

(10 minutes before 5)

10 minutes after 5

Circle the time each clock shows.

7.

5 minutes before 3

5 minutes after 3

8.

15 minutes before 10

15 minutes after 10

Use a.m. from midnight to noon.
Use p.m. from noon to midnight.

Circle a.m. or p.m. to tell when you would do each activity.

Walking the
dog before bed

a.m. (p.m.)

Eating a morning
snack

(a.m.) p.m.

9. Afternoon recess

a.m. p.m.

10. Feeding fish after breakfast

a.m. p.m.

© Pearson Education, Inc. 2

Name _____

1. Chen has these coins.
How much money does Chen have?

Count on to find the total.

_____ cents

2. Ellen has 4 coins.
The total value is 46¢.
She has 1 quarter, 1 dime,
and 1 penny.
Which shows her fourth coin?

Ⓐ   Ⓑ   Ⓒ   Ⓓ

3. Nancy has 31¢.
Which coins could she have?
Choose all that apply.

☐

☐

☐

☐

4. George has quarters, dimes, and nickels.
Show all the ways he can make 25¢. Use
tally marks.

Circle the way that uses the least number
of coins.

Ways to Show 25¢			
Quarter	Dime	Nickel	Total

5. Mr. Zink has the dollar bills shown below.

How many dollars does Mr. Zink have?

$36 $31 $26 $5

Ⓐ   Ⓑ   Ⓒ   Ⓓ

6. Claire has two $20 bills, two $5 bills, and three $1 bills. How much more money does Claire need to buy a bike that costs $89? Explain.

What bills can you use to show how much money Claire needs?

7. Kay has saved $30.
Show three different ways to make $30.
Use tally marks in the table at the right.

Circle the way that uses the least number of bills.

Ways to Show $30			
$20 Bill	$10 Bill	$5 Bill	Total

© Pearson Education, Inc. 2

Topic 8 | Assessment

Name _____

8. Sandy wakes up in the morning at the time shown on the clock.

What time does Sandy wake up?

Ⓐ 5:10 a.m

Ⓒ 5:10 p.m.

Ⓑ 6:10 a.m.

Ⓓ 6:10 p.m.

9. Sara's baseball game starts at the time shown on the clock.

Is this the time her game starts? Choose Yes or No.

45 minutes after 4   ◯ Yes   ◯ No

15 minutes before 5   ◯ Yes   ◯ No

quarter to 4   ◯ Yes   ◯ No

quarter to 5   ◯ Yes   ◯ No

---

10. The clock shows the time that Holly leaves for school.
It takes 15 minutes to walk to school.
At what time will Holly arrive at school?
Choose all that apply.

☐ half past 7

☐ quarter past 8

☐ 30 minutes after 8

☐ half past 8

11. The first clock shows the time the sun rises.
Write the same time on the second clock.
Then circle a.m. or p.m.

a.m.   p.m.

12. Look at the time on the first clock.
What time will it be in 10 minutes?
Write that time on the second clock.

13. Circle a.m. or p.m. to tell when you would do each activity.

Watch the sunset at 7:40.   a.m.   p.m.

Take a music lesson after school.   a.m.   p.m.

Brush your teeth before school.   a.m.   p.m.

Eat breakfast at 6:45.   a.m.   p.m.

14. Draw lines to match the time on each clock in the first row to the same time shown in the second row.

© Pearson Education, Inc. 2

Name _____

The Toy Store

Terry's family owns a toy store.
These are some of the things
that they sell.

$14
$21
$1
38¢

1. Lorna paid for a box of crayons
with 6 coins.
Ken paid for a box of crayons
with 7 coins.
Draw the coins that each of them used.

Lorna's 6 coins	Ken's 7 coins

2. Kim goes to the toy store
with these coins.

Part A

What is the total value of the coins Kim
has? Explain how you know.

_____

_____

_____

Part B

How much more money does Kim need to
buy the book? Explain.

3. Kay's father buys a toy train at the toy store for $50.

Part A

Show five different ways that he could have paid $50. Use tally marks to complete the table.

Ways to Show $50			
$20 Bill	$10 Bill	$5 Bill	Total
			$50
			$50
			$50
			$50
			$50

Part B

Which way uses the least number of bills to make $50? Explain.

4. Ted walks to the toy store in the afternoon.

Part A

He starts walking at the time shown on the digital clock. Draw hands on the second clock to show the same time.

Is the time on the clocks above 3:35 a.m. or 3:35 p.m.? Explain how you know.

_____

_____

Part B

Ted gets to the store 10 minutes later. Write this time in two different ways.

© Pearson Education, Inc. 2

Glossary

A

add

When you add, you join groups together.

$$3 + 4 = 7$$

addend

numbers that are added

$$2 + 5 = 7$$

↑ ↑

addends

after

424 comes after 423.

| 420 | 421 | 422 | 423 | 424 | 425 | 426 | 427 | 428 | 429 |

a.m.

clock time from midnight until noon

angle

the corner shape formed by two sides that meet

array

a group of objects set in equal rows and columns that forms a rectangle

B

bar diagram

a model for addition and subtraction that shows the parts and the whole

bar graph

A bar graph uses bars to show data.

before

421 comes before 422.

break apart

You can break apart a number into its place value parts.

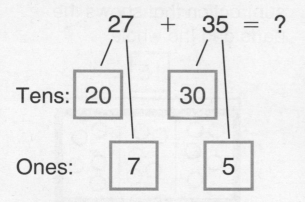

$$27 + 35 = ?$$

Tens: 20   30

Ones: 7   5

C

cents

The value of a coin is measured in cents (¢).

1 cent (¢)   10 cents (¢)

centimeter (cm)

a metric unit of length that is part of 1 meter

CENTIMETERS

coins

money that is made out of metal and that can have different values

1¢   5¢   10¢   25¢   50¢

column

objects in an array or data in a table that are shown up and down

← column

1	2	3	4	5
11	12	13	14	15
21	22	23	24	25
31	32	33	34	35

compare

When you compare numbers, you find out if a number is greater than, less than, or equal to another number.

$$147 \, > \, 143$$

147 is greater than 143.

compatible numbers

numbers that are easy to add or subtract using mental math

$$8 + 2$$
$$20 + 7$$
$$53 + 10$$

compensation

a mental math strategy you can use to add or subtract

$$38 + 24 = ?$$
$$+2 \quad -2$$

You add 2 to 38 to make 40. Then subtract 2 from 24 to get 22. 40 + 22 = 62. So, 38 + 24 = 62.

cone

a solid figure with a circle shaped base and a curved surface that meets at a point

cube

a solid figure with six faces that are matching squares

cylinder

a solid figure with two matching circle shaped bases

 D

data

information you collect and can be shown in a table or graph

Favorite Fruit	
Apple	7
Peach	4
Orange	5

decrease

to become lesser in value

$$600 \longrightarrow 550$$

600 decreased by 50 is 550.

denominator

the number below the fraction bar in a fraction, which shows the total number of equal parts

$\frac{3}{4}$ ⟵ denominator

difference

the answer in a subtraction equation or problem

$$14 - 6 = 8$$

↑
difference

digits

 43

Numbers are made up of 1 or more digits. 43 has 2 digits.

dime

10 cents or 10¢

division

an operation that tells how many equal groups there are or how many are in each group

$$12 \div 3 = 4$$

divided by

what you say to read a division symbol

$$18 \div 3 = 6$$

↙ divided by

dollar

One dollar equals 100¢.

dollar bills

paper money that can have different dollar values, such as $1, $5, $10, or $20

dollar sign

a symbol used to show that a number represents money

$37

↑
dollar sign

doubles

addition facts that have two addends that are the same

$$4 + 4 = 8$$

↑   ↑
addend   addend

edge

a line formed where two faces of a solid figure meet

edge

eighths

When a whole is separated into 8 equal shares, the parts are called eighths.

equal groups

groups that have the same number of items or objects

2   2   2

equal shares

parts of a whole that are the same size

All 4 shares are equal.

equals (=)

has the same value

$$36 = 36$$

36 is equal to 36.

equation

a math sentence that uses an equal sign (=) to show that the value on the left is equal to the value on the right

$$3 + ? = 7$$
$$14 - 6 = 8$$

estimate

When you estimate, you make a good guess.

This table is about 3 feet long.

even

a number that can be shown as a pair of cubes.

8 is even.

expanded form

a way of writing a number that shows the place value of each digit

$$400 + 60 + 3 = 463$$

face

a flat surface of a solid figure that does not roll

faces

fact family

a group of related addition and subtraction facts

$$2 + 4 = 6$$
$$4 + 2 = 6$$
$$6 - 2 = 4$$
$$6 - 4 = 2$$

factors

numbers that are multiplied together to give a product

$$7 \times 3 = 21$$

factors

flat surface

flat surfaces that are **NOT** faces

foot (ft)

a standard unit of length equal to 12 inches

fourths

When a whole is divided into 4 equal shares, the shares are called fourths.

fraction

a number, such as $\frac{1}{2}$ or $\frac{3}{4}$, that names part of a whole or part of a set

$\frac{1}{2}$ $\frac{3}{4}$

G

greater than (>)

has greater value

$$5 > 1$$

5 is greater than 1.

greatest

the number in a group with the largest value

35   47   58   61
greatest

greatest value

The coin that has the greatest value is the coin that is worth the most.

The quarter has the greatest value.

H

half-dollar

50 cents or 50¢

half past

30 minutes past the hour

It is half past 9.

halves (half)

When a whole is divided into 2 equal shares, the shares are called halves.

height

how tall an object is from bottom to top

heptagon

a polygon that has 7 sides

hexagon

a polygon that has 6 sides

hour

An hour is 60 minutes.

hundred

10 tens make 1 hundred.

inch (in.)

a standard unit of length that is part of 1 foot

INCHES

---

increase

to become greater in value

$$550 \longrightarrow 600$$

550 increased by 50 is 600.

---

least

the number in a group with the smallest value

35 47 58 61

least

---

least value

The coin that has the least value is the coin that is worth the least.

The dime has the least value.

---

length

the distance from one end to the other end of an object

---

less than (<)

has less value

$$2 < 6$$

2 is less than 6.

---

line plot

A line plot uses dots above a number line to show data.

Lengths of Shells

Number of Inches

Start at 23. Count on 2 tens. 33, 43

mental math

math you do in your head

$$23 + 20 = 43$$

---

meter (m)

a metric unit of length equal to 100 centimeters

A long step is about a meter.

---

minute

a standard length of time

There are 60 minutes in 1 hour.

multiplication

an operation that gives the total number when you join equal groups

$$3 \times 2 = 6$$

To multiply 3×2 means to add 2 three times.

$$2 + 2 + 2 = 6$$

near doubles

addition facts that have two addends that are close

$$4 + 5 = 9$$
$\uparrow$ $\uparrow$
addend   addend

nearest centimeter

The whole number centimeter mark closest to the measure is the nearest centimeter.

about 2 cm long

CENTIMETERS

halfway mark

nearest inch

The whole number inch mark closest to the measure is the nearest inch.

about 2 inches long

INCHES

halfway mark

next ten

the first ten greater than a number

30 is the next ten after 27.

nickel

5 cents or 5¢

nonagon

a polygon that has 9 sides

number line

a line that shows numbers in order from left to right

1 2 3 4 5 6 7 8 9 10

numerator

the number above the fraction bar in a fraction, which shows how many equal parts are described

$\dfrac{3}{4}$ ←—— numerator

octagon

a polygon that has 8 sides

odd

a number that can **NOT** be shown as pairs of cubes

9 is odd.

ones

digits that shows how many ones are in a number

$54 + 14 = 68$

open number line

An open number line is a tool that can help you add or subtract. It can begin at any number.

$26 + 20 = 46$

order

to place numbers from least to greatest or from greatest to least

27 72 107 117 171

least ↱   greatest ↱

parallelogram

a quadrilateral that has 4 sides and opposite sides parallel

part

a piece of a whole or of a number

2 and 3 are parts of 5.

partial sum

When you add numbers, the sum of one of the place values is called a partial sum.

	Tens	Ones	
	5	7	
+	2	8	
	7	0	← partial sum
+	1	5	← partial sum
	8	5	← sum

penny

I cent or I¢

pentagon

a polygon that has 5 sides

picture graph

a graph that uses pictures to show data

Favorite Ball Games	
Baseball	
Soccer	
Tennis	

Each = 1 student

place-value chart

a chart matches each digit of a number with its place

Hundreds	Tens	Ones
3	4	8

plane shape

a flat shape

circle   rectangle   square   triangle

p.m.

clock time from noon until midnight

polygon

a closed plane shape with 3 or more sides

product

the answer to a multiplication problem

$$4 \times 2 = 8$$

↑
product

pyramid

a solid figure with a base that is a polygon and faces that are triangles that meet in a point

Q

quadrilateral

a polygon that has 4 sides

quarter

25 cents or 25¢

quarter past

15 minutes after the hour

 4:15

It is quarter past 4.

quarter to

15 minutes before the hour

 3:45

It is quarter to 4.

rectangular prism

a solid figure with bases and faces that are rectangles

regroup

to name a number or part in a different way

Tens	Ones

10 ones can be regrouped as 1 ten. 1 ten can be regrouped as 10 ones.

related

Addition facts and subtraction facts are related if they have the same numbers.

$$2 + 3 = 5$$
$$5 - 2 = 3$$

repeated addition

adding the same number repeatedly

$$3 + 3 + 3 + 3 = 12$$

right angle

an angle that forms a square corner

row

objects in an array or data in a table that are shown across

1	2	3	4	5
11	12	13	14	15
21	22	23	24	25
31	32	33	34	35

← row

S

separate

to subtract or to take apart into two or more parts

$$5 - 2 = 3$$

side

a line segment that makes one part of a plane shape

side

solid figure

a shape that has length, width, and height

These are all solid figures.

sphere

a solid figure that looks like a ball

standard form

a way to write a number using only digits

436

subtract

When you subtract, you find out how many are left or which group has more.

$$5 - 3 = 2$$

sum

the answer to an addition equation or problem

$$3 + 4 = 7$$

$$
\begin{array}{r}
4 \\
+\ 3 \\
\hline
\text{sum} \longrightarrow 7
\end{array}
$$

symbol

a picture or character that stands for something

The symbol will be ⚭.
Each ⚭ represents
1 student.

tally mark

a symbol used to keep track of each piece of information in an organized list

Ways to Show 30¢			
Quarter	Dime	Nickel	Total
I		I	30¢
	III		30¢
	II	II	30¢
	I	IIII	30¢
		IIII I	30¢

tens

the digit that shows how many groups of ten are in a number

238

thirds

When a whole is divided into 3 equal shares, the shares are called thirds.

thousand

10 hundreds make 1 thousand.

times

another word for multiply

times

$$7 \times 3 = 21$$

trapezoid

a polygon with 4 sides and one pair of sides are parallel

triangular prism

a solid figure that has two triangle shaped bases and three faces that have rectangle shapes.

U

unequal

Unequal parts are parts that are not equal.

5 unequal parts

unit

You can use different units to measure.

about 12 inches
about 1 foot

unit fraction

a fraction that reperesents one equal part of a whole or a set

$\frac{1}{2}$ $\frac{1}{4}$ $\frac{1}{8}$

unknown

a symbol that stands for a number in an equation

$$34 + ? = 67$$

↑
unknown

V

vertices (vertex)

corner points where 2 sides of a polygon meet or where edges of a solid figure meet

vertex

W

whole

a single unit that can be divided into parts

The two halves make one whole circle.

width

the distance across an object

word form

a way to write a number using only words

The word form for 23 is twenty-three.

Y

yard (yd)

a standard unit of length equal to 3 feet

A baseball bat is about a yard long.

Photographs

Every effort has been made to secure permission and provide appropriate credit for photographic material. The publisher deeply regrets any omission and pledges to correct errors called to its attention in subsequent editions.

Unless otherwise acknowledged, all photographs are the property of Pearson Education, Inc.

Photo locators denoted as follows: Top (T), Center (C), Bottom (B), Left (L), Right (R), Background (Bkgd)

F13C Pearson Education;**F13CL** Pearson Education;**F13CR** Pearson Education;**F13L** Pearson Education;**F13R** Pearson Education;**001BL** Lori Martin/Shutterstock;**001BR** An Nguyen/Shutterstock;**001C** Africa Studio/Fotolia;**001L** Africa Studio/Fotolia;**001R** karandaev/Fotolia;**077BL** michaklootwijk/Fotolia;**077BR** Jitka Volfova/Shutterstock;**077L** Charles Brutlag/Shutterstock;**077R** Erni/Fotolia;**119L** FiCo74/Fotolia;**119R** Antonio Scarpi/Fotolia;**189** Beboy/Shutterstock;**253** Deborah Benbrook/Fotolia;**321** GlebStock/Shutterstock;**389** Paylessimages/Fotolia;**435** Ambient Ideas/Shutterstock;**456** Pearson Education;**494C** Pearson Education;**494** Pearson Education;**494B** Pearson Education;**494T** Pearson Education;**503** Es0lex/Fotolia;**504B** Pearson Education;**504BL** Pearson Education;**504BR** Pearson Education;**504C** Pearson Education;**504CL** Pearson Education;**504CR** Pearson Education;**504T** Pearson Education;**504TC** Pearson Education;**504TL** Pearson Education;**583** kalafoto/Fotolia;**635** Klagyivik Viktor/Shutterstock;**675** Nagel Photography/Shutterstock;**678** Optionm/Shutterstock;**687** Ant Clausen/Fotolia;**759** Bonita R. Cheshier/Shutterstock;**788** Lledó/Fotolia;**790** Ivan Kruk/Fotolia;**799L** Karichs/Fotolia;**799R** Ivonne Wierink/Fotolia;**845B** Pearson Education;**845BC** Pearson Education;**845CT** Pearson Education;**845T** Pearson Education;**851** Yurakr/Shutterstock;**868** StudioSmart/Shutterstock;**932** Pearson Education;**934** Pearson Education;**G2L** Pearson Education;**G2R** Pearson Education;**G3L** Pearson Education;**G3R** Pearson Education;**G4B** Pearson Education;**G4C** Pearson Education;**G4CB** Pearson Education;**G4CT** Pearson Education;**G4T** Pearson Education;**G6BL** Pearson Education;**G6BR** Pearson Education;**G6TC** Pearson Education;**G6TL** Pearson Education;**G6TR** Pearson Education;**G7C** Pearson Education;**G7L** Pearson Education;**G7R** Pearson Education;**G8L** Pearson Education;**G8R** Pearson Education;**G9L** Pearson Education;**G9R** Pearson Education;**G10L** Pearson Education;**G10R** United State Mint.

Grade 2 Lessons Exclusively for Indiana

Volume 1

IN 1 Checking Addition To 100 With Estimation IN3
(Use after Lesson 4-8.) 2.CA.2, PS.1, PS.2, PS.6, PS.8

Topic 4 Assessment Items for Indiana Lesson 1 .... IN9

IN 2 Time Intervals IN11
(Use after Lesson 8-8.) 2.M.5, PS.1, PS.5, PS.6, PS.7

IN 3 Time Relationships IN17
(Use after Lesson 8-8.) 2.M.6, PS.2, PS.3, PS.6, PS.8

Topic 8 Assessment Items for Indiana Lessons 2 and 3 .... IN23

You will use these lessons throughout the year.

Volume 2

IN 4 Ordinal Numbers to 30 .... IN27
(Use before Lesson 9-1.) 2.NS.4, PS.2, PS.3, PS.4, PS.6

IN 5 Skip Counting by 2s, 5s, 10s. 100s to 1000 .... IN33
(Use after Lesson 9-7.) 2.NS.1, PS.2, PS.3, PS.7

Topic 9 Assessment Items for Indiana Lessons 4 and 5 .... IN39

IN 6 Number Patterns with Addition and Subtraction to 1000 .. IN41
(Use after Lesson 11-6.) 2.CA.7, PS.2, PS.3, PS.7, PS.8

Topic 11 Assessment Items for Indiana Lesson 6 .... IN47

IN 7 Capacity IN49
(Use after Lesson 12-9.) 2.M.4, PS.2, PS.5, PS.6

Topic 12 Assessment Items for Indiana Lesson 7 .... IN55

IN 8 Right Rectangular Prisms IN57
(Use after Lesson 15-4.) 2.G.1, 2.G.2, PS.3, PS.4, PS.5, PS.6

IN 9 Composing and Decomposing 2D Shapes IN63
(Use after Lesson 15-4.) 2.G.3, PS.1, PS.3, PS.4, PS.5

IN 10 Composing and Decomposing 3D Shapes IN69
(Use after Lesson 15-4.) 2.G.3, PS.1, PS.3, PS.4, PS.5

Topic 15 Assessment Items for Indiana Lessons 8,
9, and 10 .... IN75

Name _____

Solve & Share

The school band has 21 boys and 31 girls. Sara says there are about 50 students in the band. Do you agree? Show your work and explain.

I can ...
add 2-digit numbers and use estimation to check whether my answer is reasonable.

Content Standard 2.CA.2
Process Standards PS.1, PS.2, PS.6, PS.8

Mia has 32 baseball cards and 45 football cards. How many sports cards does she have in all?

An estimate can help you check whether your answer is reasonable.

Estimate by rounding each addend to the nearest ten. Round to the greater ten when you are exactly halfway.

halfway   halfway

30 32   40   45   50

Estimate: 30 + 50 = 80

Now solve by adding. Mia has 77 sports cards.

The answer is reasonable because 77 is close to 80.

$$\begin{array}{r} 3\ 2 \\ +\ 4\ 5 \\ \hline 7\ 7 \end{array}$$

Do You Understand?

Show Me! Henry found 39 + 22. His sum was 51. Estimate to decide if his answer is reasonable. Why or why not?

☆ **Guided Practice** ☆   Estimate by rounding to the nearest ten. Use the number line to help. Show your estimate with an equation. Then solve.

20   30   40   50

1. Josh drove 42 miles on Monday and 29 miles on Tuesday. How many miles did he drive in all?

Estimate: _____

$$\begin{array}{r} 4\ 2 \\ +\ 2\ 9 \\ \hline 7\ 1 \end{array}$$

2. Enza read 21 books in July and 32 books in August. How many books did she read in all?

Estimate: _____

$$\begin{array}{r} 2\ 1 \\ +\ 3\ 2 \\ \hline \end{array}$$

Tools Assessment

Independent Practice Estimate by rounding to the nearest ten. Use the number line to help. Show your estimate with an equation. Then solve.

30   40   50   60

3. Jackson earned $59 cutting lawns and $33 babysitting. How much did he earn in all?

```
   5   9
+  3   3
_____
```

Estimate: _____

4. There are 28 boys and 28 girls in the chorus at Vivian's school. How many students are in the chorus in all?

```
   2   8
+  2   8
_____
```

Estimate: _____

5. For her recycling project, Alisha collected 58 aluminum cans and 32 plastic bottles. How many items did she collect in all?

```
   5   8
+  3   2
_____
```

Estimate: _____

6. At the book fair, Armando bought a puzzle book for $32 and a mystery book for $41. How much did he spend in all at the book fair?

```
   3   2
+  4   1
_____
```

Estimate: _____

7. **Higher Order Thinking** Dane added $28 + 19$. His sum was 47. He rounded each addend to the nearest ten and said that the estimated sum was 40. Is his estimate correct? Why or why not?

8. **Reasoning** Mrs. Kline graded 31 math worksheets on Friday and 28 spelling papers on Saturday. How many papers did she grade in all? Estimate and then solve.

Estimate: _____ papers

Actual: _____ papers

9. **Reasoning** While bird watching, Tristan saw 39 cardinals and 32 robins. How many birds did he see in all? Estimate and then solve.

Estimate: _____ birds

Actual: _____ birds

10. **Higher Order Thinking** Charlotte estimated she spent 40 minutes on homework. She spent 12 minutes on reading and some minutes on science.

How many minutes could she have spent on science? Provide a possible answer and explain.

_____

_____

_____

11. **Assessment** Rayva has 48 stickers. Julia has 41 stickers. Which equation is the best to estimate about how many stickers they have in all?

Ⓐ $40 + 40 = 80$

Ⓑ $50 + 50 = 100$

Ⓒ $50 + 41 = 91$

Ⓓ $50 + 40 = 90$

Name _____

Help   Tools   Games

Another Look! You can use an estimate to check if your answer is reasonable.

While shopping, Jenna spent $22 on a purse and $39 on shoes. How much did she spend in all?

Estimate by rounding each addend to the nearest ten.

Step 1

22 rounds to 20.
39 rounds to 40.

Show your estimate as an equation.

Estimate:

$$20 + 40 = 60$$

Step 2

Add the ones. Regroup ones if needed. Add the tens.

```
  1
  2 | 2
+ 3 | 9
----|----
  6 | 1
```

Jenna spent $61.

The answer is reasonable because 61 is close to 60.

HOME ACTIVITY Write 78 + 21 on a sheet of paper. Have your child find an estimate. Once finished, have your child find the sum and then use the estimate to check whether their sum is reasonable. Repeat with other problems.

Estimate by rounding to the nearest ten. Show your estimate as an equation. Then solve.

1. Sasha used 49 white balloons and 49 blue balloons to decorate for the school dance. How many balloons were used in all?

   Estimate: _____

2. There are 28 girls and 31 boys in Grade 2 at Hoover Elementary School. How many students are in Grade 2 in all?

   Estimate: _____

Estimate by rounding to the nearest ten. Show your estimate as an equation. Then solve.

3. **Reasoning** Mr. Harper has 28 science students and 33 math students. How many students does he have in all?

Estimate: _____

Actual: _____ students

4. **Reasoning** Shelby counted 42 cars and 57 vans in the parade. How many vehicles did she count in all?

Estimate: _____

Actual: _____ students

5. **Higher Order Thinking** Becky adds the number of stickers she collected. She has 26 butterfly stickers, 13 heart stickers, and 39 animal stickers. The sum is 78.

When Becky used estimation to check whether her answer is reasonable, she got 80. Is her estimation close? Why or why not?

_____

_____

_____

6. **Ⓘ Assessment** Jasper has 18 science fiction books and 24 mystery books. Which equation is the best to estimate about how many books he has in all?

Ⓐ $18 + 24 = 42$

Ⓑ $10 + 20 = 30$

Ⓒ $20 + 20 = 40$

Ⓓ $20 + 30 = 50$

Name _____

Solve each problem.

1. While at the nature center, Eric counted 18 squirrels and 28 birds. How many animals did he count in all?

Estimate: _____ animals

Actual: _____ animals

2. Mr. Cortez has 19 boys and 19 girls in his science class. How many students does he have in all?

Estimate: _____ students

Actual: _____ students

3. Diego drove 43 miles on Thursday and 38 miles on Friday. Which equation would you use to estimate about how many miles he drove in all?

Ⓐ $40 + 40 = 80$

Ⓑ $40 + 30 = 70$

Ⓒ $40 + 20 = 60$

Ⓓ $43 + 38 = 81$

4. Hannah added 48 and 29. Her sum was 67. Is she correct? Estimate to decide if her answer is reasonable. Then find the sum.

_____

_____

Name _____

Solve & Share

Avery spent 2 hours at soccer practice. Practice ended at 6:00 p.m. At what time did soccer practice start? Explain your answer. Use the clocks to help.

I can ...
solve problems involving addition and subtraction of time intervals on the hour or half hour.

Content Standard 2.M.5
Process Standards PS.1, PS.5, PS.6, PS.7

Start

End

_____

- - - - - - - - - - - - -

_____

Casey went to the park at 2:30 p.m. He needs to be home in 30 minutes. At what time should Casey be home?

You can use a clock to add a time interval of 30 minutes!

Start at 2:30 and count by 5s to find the time in 30 minutes.

Remember that 30 minutes is a half hour.

When you add 30 minutes to 2:30 p.m., the time will be 3:00 p.m.

Casey should be home at 3:00 p.m.

Do You Understand?

Show Me! Kendra has an art class at 11:30 a.m. The class lasts 30 minutes. Kendra thinks her class will end at 12:00 a.m. Is she correct? Explain your answer.

☆ Guided Practice Use the clocks to solve.

1. Matt's trumpet lesson is 60 minutes long. His lesson starts at 5:30 p.m. At what time does his lesson end?

2. Serena went on a nature hike for 3 hours. When she returned from her hike, it was 8:00 p.m. At what time did she start hiking?

Topic 8 | Indiana Lesson 2

Name _____

Independent Practice ☆   Solve each problem.

3. Tara wants to leave for school 30 minutes before it starts. She says school starts at 8:00 a.m. At what time does Tara want to leave for school?

_____

4. Max worked for 6 hours on Saturday. He ended work at 3:00 p.m. At what time did he start working?

_____

5. Sarah goes fishing. The clock on the left shows when she starts. The clock on the right shows when she stops. How long did Sarah fish?

_____ hours

6. **Higher Order Thinking** Wyatt's baseball game began at 4:30 p.m. The game lasted for 1 hour and 30 minutes. At what time did the game end? Explain how you solved the problem.

_____

_____

_____

_____

7. **Make Sense** Mallory's dance practice ended at 5:00 p.m. Practice started at 3:00 p.m. How long was dance practice?

_____

8. **Make Sense** Mrs. Ramirez's flight left the airport at 8:30 a.m. If the flight is 5 hours long, at what time will the flight be over?

_____

9. **Higher Order Thinking** Harry ends his homework at 5:00 p.m. He did homework for 1 hour and 30 minutes. At what time did Harry start his homework? Explain how you solved the problem.

_____

_____

_____

10. **Ⓓ Assessment** Ricky drove to visit his cousins who live 3 hours away. He started driving at 1:00 p.m. At what time did he arrive?

Ⓐ 4:00 p.m.

Ⓑ 3:00 p.m.

Ⓒ 11:00 a.m.

Ⓓ 10:00 a.m.

Name _____

Another Look! Zoe practices her flute for 30 minutes each day. Today, she ended at 3:30 p.m. At what time did she start?

Step 1: Zoe finishes practice at 3:30 p.m.

Step 2: Count back by 5s to find the time 30 minutes before 3:30 p.m.

Step 3: Zoe starts to practice at 3:00 p.m.

HOME ACTIVITY Have your child keep track of when you begin and end events at home, such as dinner. Then ask him or her how long each event lasted.

Use the clock to solve each problem.

1. Rob's baby brother naps for 3 hours. His nap started at 11:00 a.m. At what time will his nap end?

_____

2. Leah read for 30 minutes last night. The clock shows the time she finished reading. At what time did Leah start reading?

_____

Solve each problem. Use or draw clocks to help.

3. **Make Sense** Carly's birthday party starts at 12:30 p.m. and ends at 3:30 p.m. How long does Carly's party last?

_____

4. **Make Sense** Every night Carlos sleeps for 9 hours. He wakes up for school at 7:00 a.m. At what time does Carlos go to bed?

_____

5. **Higher Order Thinking** Oscar starts his art project at 5:00 p.m. It took him 2 hours and 30 minutes to finish it. At what time did Oscar finish? Explain how you solved the problem.

_____

_____

_____

6. **Assessment** The school day begins at 8:00 a.m. and ends at 3:00 p.m. How long is the school day?

Ⓐ 7 hours

Ⓑ 8 hours

Ⓒ 6 hours

Ⓓ 11 hours

Name _____

Solve & Share

Jesse spent 2 weeks at camp this summer. Tyrell went to camp for 10 days. Who spent more time at camp? Explain. Use the chart to help.

I can ...
describe relationships of time.

Content Standard 2.M.6
Process Standards PS.2, PS.3, PS.6, PS.8

Units of Time	
1 minute	60 seconds
1 hour	60 minutes
1 day	24 hours
1 week	7 days
1 year	52 weeks
1 year	12 months
1 year	365 days

Time can be expressed using different units that are related to each other.

Units of Time	
I minute	60 seconds
I hour	60 minutes
I day	24 hours
I week	7 days
I year	52 weeks
I year	12 months
I year	365 days

So, 2 weeks would be 14 days.

Marta wants to spend as much time as possible playing her favorite sport. Would she rather spend 18 months or 2 years playing her favorite sport?

First find the number of months in 2 years.

To find the number of months in 2 years, add $12 + 12$.

$$\begin{array}{r} 1\;2 \\ +\;1\;2 \\ \hline 2\;4 \end{array}$$

24 > 18. I'd rather spend 2 years playing my favorite sport!

Do You Understand?

Show Me! Gilbert was invited to spend 2 days at his cousin's house. He thinks he will be there for 72 hours. Is he correct? Why or why not?

☆ Guided ☆ Practice

Use the chart to help you solve each problem. Show your work.

1. The Mendez family plans a trip for 2 weeks. How many days will their trip last?

_____ days

2. Would you rather spend 50 hours or 2 days doing something you don't like?

_____ days

Independent Practice

Use time relationships to solve each problem. Show your work.

3. Mallory has lived in her new house for 5 years. How many months is that?

_____ months

4. Jesse's class took an outdoor education trip for 3 days. How many hours is that?

_____ hours

5. Steve likes playing at the beach as long as possible. Would he rather play at the beach for 2 hours or 100 minutes?

_____

_____

6. Higher Order Thinking Elliott spent 2 hours at the school fair. How many minutes did he spend at the fair? Solve without using an equation. Explain your method.

_____

_____

_____

7. **Generalize** Aisha spends 4 days dog sitting. How many hours does she spend dog sitting?

_____ hours

8. **Generalize** Big Lake's summer camp is 30 days Round Lake's summer camp is 6 weeks. Which summer camp is longer?

_____

_____

_____

9. **Higher Order Thinking** Which is longer, 52 months or 4 years? By how many months longer?

_____

_____

10. **Assessment** Mark the times that are greater than 50 days. Choose all that apply.

☐ 6 weeks

☐ 7 weeks

☐ 8 weeks

☐ 9 weeks

Name _____

Homework & Practice IN 3
Time Relationships

Another Look! Time can be expressed using different units that are related to each other.

Parker's little sister is 4 years old. What is her age in months?

Units of Time
1 minute = 60 seconds
1 hour = 60 minutes
1 day = 24 hours
1 week = 7 days
1 year = 52 weeks
1 year = 12 months
1 year = 365 days

Step 1:

There are 12 months in 1 year.

To find her age in months, add

$12 + 12 + 12 + 12.$

Step 2:
Start by adding the ones. Add in any order. Regroup if needed. Then add the tens.

```
  1 | 2
  1 | 2
  1 | 2
+ 1 | 2
-------
  4 | 8
```

She is 48 months old.

HOME ACTIVITY Have your child review the units of time. Ask him or her several questions such as, "Would you rather do chores for 1 hour or 25 minutes?", "Would you rather go on a vacation for 14 days or 1 week?" Have him or her explain why.

Use time relationships to solve. Show your work.

1. Students jog in place for 2 minutes during gym class. How many seconds are in 2 minutes?

_____ seconds

2. Otto checks out books from the library for 3 weeks. In how many days are the books due?

_____ days

3. **Generalize** Maxwell has 5 weeks of vacation from his job every year. How many vacation days does Maxwell have every year?

_____ days

4. **Generalize** Ezra likes to visit her grandma. Do you think she would rather spend 50 hours or 3 days visiting her grandma?

_____

_____

_____

5. **Higher Order Thinking** Lukas's baby brother is 4 weeks old. Lukas told his class that his brother is 28 days old. Is he correct? Explain your answer.

_____

_____

6. **Assessment** Mark the times that are less than 1 year. Choose all that apply.

☐ 350 days

☐ 54 weeks

☐ 14 months

☐ 10 months

Name _____

Solve each problem.

1. How many months are in one year?

   Ⓐ 6 months

   Ⓑ 12 months

   Ⓒ 24 months

   Ⓓ 52 months

2. The clocks show the start and stop times of art class. How long is art class? Choose all that apply.

   ☐ 60 minutes   ☐ one hour

   ☐ 30 minutes   ☐ half hour

3. The class trip to the zoo is in 3 weeks. How many days until the class trip?

   _____ days

4. The movie was 2 hours. It ended at 12:00 p.m. When did it start?

   _____

5. Maddie is 4 years old. Brooke is 60 months old. Who is older? How do you know? Explain your answer.

   _____

   _____